GOOD TIME GIRLS

of NEVADA and UTAH

A Red-Light History of the American West

Jan MacKell Collins

TWODOT®

GUILFORD, CONNECTICUT
HELENA, MONTANA

A · TWODOT® · BOOK

An imprint of Globe Pequot, the trade division of
The Rowman & Littlefield Publishing Group, Inc.
4501 Forbes Blvd., Ste. 200
Lanham, MD 20706
www.rowman.com

Distributed by NATIONAL BOOK NETWORK

British Library Cataloguing in Publication Information available

Library of Congress Cataloging in Publication Data
Names: Collins, Jan MacKell, 1962– author.
Title: Good time girls of Nevada and Utah : a red-light history of the American West /
   Jan MacKell Collins.
Description: Guilford, Connecticut : TwoDot, [2022] | Includes bibliographical
   references and index. | Identifiers: LCCN 2021052819 (print) | LCCN 2021052820
   (ebook) | ISBN 9781493050987 (paperback) | ISBN 9781493050994 (epub)
Subjects: LCSH: Prostitution—Nevada—History—19th century. | Prostitution—
   Utah—History—19th century. | Prostitutes—Nevada—History—19th century. |
   Prostitutes—Utah—History—19th century. | West (U.S.)—Social conditions—
   19th century. | West (U.S.)—Economic conditions—19th century.
Classification: LCC HQ145.W47 C65 2022 (print) | LCC HQ145.W47 (ebook) |
   DDC 306.74/2097809034—dc23/eng/20211228
LC record available at https://lccn.loc.gov/2021052819
LC ebook record available at https://lccn.loc.gov/2021052820

♾️™ The paper used in this publication meets the minimum requirements of American National Standard for Information Sciences—Permanence of Paper for Printed Library Materials, ANSI/NISO Z39.48-1992.

CONTENTS

———•●•———

CONTENTS

ACKNOWLEDGMENTS

M y favorite part of living in the Pacific Northwest is all the trails that I can take when visiting family and friends who remain "back home" in places east of me. These days, a favorite route is driving south through Reno, Nevada, to Carson City, and then back over to Highway 50 via Silver City and Virginia City before veering down Highway 95 to Tonopah and Goldfield. Or, I can cut over to that loneliest stretch of road, Highway 50, through Austin, Eureka, and Ely. It's a long drive sometimes, but it's worth it to see all of the great little historic towns Nevada has to offer along the way. Many of these places remain unspoiled and untouched by the modern world, their quiet friendliness a welcome sight versus bigger, harsher cities where history seems to be getting lost more and more as time goes on.

I wouldn't be honest if I said my trips through Nevada were not nearly always fraught with a deadline to get somewhere. That would be why I often come out of the state with a box full of books, brochures, maps, and pamphlets, but rarely remember where I got them or who gave them to me. Thank goodness for my trusty camera. That being said, let me just say that I am thankful to the people of Nevada, from those at the Austin Historical Society to the virtual museum at Tonopah Station to that funny, sweet old man who waves every single time I drive through Goldfield, for keeping history alive for all of us to see. Closer to home, I am also indebted to Tish Mowe of Powers, Oregon, who kindly thought of me when she found George Williams III's great little history book, *The Red Light Ladies of Virginia City, Nevada.* Williams also wrote *Rosa May: The Search for a Mining Camp Legend*, which gives history buffs the most thorough understanding of the mysterious little lady who has become a true legend in both Virginia City, Nevada, and Bodie, California. Both books are excellent starting points to finding out more about the West's shady ladies.

I also have fond memories of my times in Utah, beginning with my family's visits to Monument Valley back in the 1960s and 70s. In those days, there was only a single stone monument commemorating Four Corners where Utah, Arizona, Colorado, and New Mexico share their common border. Utah has some truly gorgeous country, and I saw a lot of it thanks to my parents. Later, as an adult, I saw even more, lazing about on a Lake Powell houseboat for a week, admiring Glen Canyon, looking for petroglyphs outside of Moab, and being a tourist in general. But it wasn't until I was researching Utah's inglorious prostitution history that I began digging deep into the roots of the state's underbelly and really exploring the land.

Since Utah's history is heavily entrenched in Mormonism, I wasn't sure what I would find there in the way of prostitution history—or what I would be allowed to find. But as I went from place to place, through Green River, Provo, Salt Lake City, Ogden, Park City, and beyond, I was pleased at the reactions of those who aided me in my research. It was truly refreshing to find historians and librarians who not only knew about Utah's more illicit history, but willingly shared it with me. I would like to thank Ben at the Park City Museum in Park City, who was a great help. I also had much fun working with Ellen Kiever, archivist at Uintah County Library in Vernal, and would like to also thank Robin at the Special Collections section of the Provo County Library in Provo—all of whom I worked with back when I was researching historical prostitution in 2006. From there, the helpful people I encountered get a bit blurry. There was the nice officer at the semi-ghost-town-turned-ski-resort of Alta who directed me to the visitor center just before I encountered my first moose face-to-face. In Salt Lake City, I had a lot of fun trying to find the old Stockade red-light district ruins while exploring the city, but they were long gone. Ogden was particularly wonderful, largely due to the historic signage along historic 25th Street that points out the former brothels of Dora Topham, one of my favorite madams.

Here at home, my hat is again off to Professor Jay Moynahan, who has quite possibly performed more research on shady ladies across America than anyone else and who shared the story of No-Nose Maggie with me. Although I've have never met them, the stellar research of Bob McCracken and Jeffrey D. Nichols remain a boon to researchers looking for history on Utah's wanton women. There are lots of others out there that deserve a nod of thanks. These include those who follow me on social media, historians who chat with me about wild women via email, my partner of three years, Nancy Degnan, who came to me wanting history and received plenty of it for our own wonderful project, and, of course, my editors at TwoDot who are unfailing in their support of what I write. On a more personal level, my husband, Corey, deserves a huge thank you for putting up with me. He has been cooking and cleaning as much and as quietly as he can so I can work. And a special thank-you goes out to my niece, Dawn Santabanez, who has never once lost faith in me and, in turn, makes me proud of her every single day.

INTRODUCTION

———•◦•———

Prostitution in the American West

According to the United States Census Bureau, America's states comprising "the West" are identified as Alaska, Arizona, California, Colorado, Idaho, Montana, Nevada, New Mexico, Oregon, Utah, Washington, and Wyoming. I've already written about most of these places in my Good Time Girls series of books, the exceptions being Nevada and Utah. It is the latter two that I am focusing on here. During early Anglo explorations beginning in the mid-1800s, these landlocked realms of primitive civilization offered much to incoming pioneer settlers, including the ladies of the evening who traipsed back and forth across their borders in search of fortune. Nevada and Utah are similar too in that each state offers everything from desert plains to high plateaus to forests and peaks towering over thirteen thousand feet in altitude.

Their geographies aside, Nevada and Utah are vastly different with regards to the histories of their industries and cultures. Admitted to the union way back in 1864, Nevada was the scene of mining discoveries early on, especially the Comstock Lode which yielded America's largest silver discovery back in 1859. Utah, admitted to the union in 1896, had long been home to Mormon colonization, which focused on farming. In both places, however, good time girls could find a multitude of men looking for company. The men seeking their own wealth were diverse. Many were miners, loggers, railroad workers, soldiers, cowboys and homesteaders, while others were capitalists, mine owners, land barons, railroad tycoons and more. Most of these men came West sans their families or even a wife, and a good many of them were lonely.

It is important to understand that the role of prostitutes in the American West expanded much further than having sex with men for money. Rugged mining camps and primitive towns seldom offered much in the way of creature comforts until women began coming West. Their trunks and satchels contained elements of femininity in the way of soft and sometimes elegant dresses, but also perfumes, powders, keepsakes, and other familiar items of the fairer sex. They hung curtains in their windows and pictures on their walls, and brought along the tools of the feminist trade in the way of sewing machines, irons, spinning wheels and china plates. The presence of women gave some sense of order and civilization to the West, and even the poorest of prostitutes could offer the warmth and comfort so many men yearned for. And the fancy madams setting up their more elegant parlor houses offered the male species a chance to relax in a calming yet entertaining atmosphere.

Ideally, brothels offered a way for men to temporarily forget the drudgery of their immediate outside world. Here too, wayward women could offer their input, advice, and common sense as to how their new hometowns should develop. It was important to the ladies that these places did well; the better the towns did, the more the prostitution industry prospered, and the more money they made. Lucky was the working girl whose customer professed a desire to marry her and remove her from the often gritty and downright dangerous business of prostitution. Equally lucky was the man who made a soiled dove his wife. Prostitutes were in the business of knowing what a man wanted and, besides, more than a few of them brought their domestic skills to the table as well.

If the meshing of prostitution and civilized life during the 1800s had been easy, writing about it now might seem a little less exciting. But in a day when chastity was indeed a virtue, and no proper lady was supposed to lift her skirts for any man without the sanctity of marriage, mixing brothel life with proper life was like pouring water into oil. Throw in a healthy dose of hypocritical governments who took in the fines and fees of soiled doves but failed to assist them when they were in need, newspapers who often insulted and laughed at them, and add some Utah Mormonism, and here was a civilization in true turmoil. The issue of prostitution became a virtual weapon, thrown smack dab into the midst of the ongoing fight between Mormons who believed a man could have more than one wife versus Gentiles who believed Mormons were committing a sin by doing so. Only Madam Dora Topham of Utah made any sense of it at all when she rightfully reckoned that as long as there were men willing to pay for sex, there would always be women willing to sell it. Dora was a sensible and smart woman.

Lucky Nevada has historically had it easier than Utah in its approach to the pleasure trade. The law initially treated the wild women of the camps and towns and cities as they would elsewhere in the West by fining and/or arresting them. In the years before and after the turn of 1900, however, Nevada's big players (i.e., sporting men of wealth) saw the many benefits of letting prostitution flourish. It paired nicely with the saloons, casinos, sporting events, and other types of men's entertainment. Also, the prostitution industry paid its dues in the way of taxes and licenses for selling both sex and liquor. It also kept miners, menial laborers, and other working-class males content. And it kept wealthy gamblers around a little longer and enticed them to spend a little more money. The idea caught on, to the point that by the time certain counties in Nevada legalized the skin trade, few thought to rebuke it.

No matter where they came from, where they landed, or how they lived, the shady ladies of Nevada and Utah make the history of each state more colorful than it otherwise might have been. Let's not forget that few, if any, of these women actively chose a career in the sex trade. Aside what they did for a living, each of these women had hopes and dreams and desires when they were young that likely did not include working as a prostitute. Whether they achieved such aspirations is explained here, with the caveat that each and every one of these women remains an important facet in American history and the making of the American West.

CHAPTER 1

Naughty Nevada

Driving along Nevada's remote highways today, it is common to see signs pointing the way to the legal bordellos, which have been in place since 1971. The signage varies, from the simple word "Brothel" painted on a billboard-sized piece of wood, to neon letters with the name of the place blazing against the blue Nevada sky. Long before teddies and other modern-day lingerie served as uniforms for ladies of the evening, however, prostitutes of the nineteenth century hauled their own sexy petticoats, stockings, and camisoles to what would become known as the Silver State.

Beginning in about 1844, the early pioneers who traveled the California Trail through today's Nevada only included a scant few women. Like other early trails, travelers occasionally encountered friendly Natives whose customs allowed for openly trading, gifting, and selling their wives and daughters to Anglos for sex. One unfortunate incident, however, was recorded of a white traveler who "lured an Indian girl off the road and ravished her." The girl's angry relatives caught the man and approached his wagon train with the prisoner, demanding death to the guilty party. "No voice was raised in protest" when the Natives voiced their plan for the man to be "shot, scalped, skinned, and dismembered." The violator was left to his fate as the wagon train moved on.[1]

Discovery of the Comstock Lode in 1859 paved the path for soiled doves flocking to Nevada.
Courtesy Library of Congress Prints and Photographs Division

Fifteen years later, in 1859, Nevada became notable as the site of the famed "Comstock Lode" silver discovery. The boom brought miners from every corner of the world looking for riches. News of the discovery spread to California and other places as prominent towns including Carson City, Virginia City, and Gold Hill were settled as important commercial and supply centers. Soon, soiled doves also were flocking into other camps, towns, and cities as Nevada's mining industry gained a strong foothold in the American economy. It was only natural for the prostitution industry to do well, too.

Carson City and Virginia City, founded in 1858 and 1859 respectively, were two of the earliest communities in the Comstock to sport sizable red-light districts. Others would soon follow. By 1860 the number of men in Nevada was calculated at 2,379, while women numbered only 147. More women would come during the next fifteen years, and they mostly fell into two categories: those coming west with their husbands, and those capitalizing on the number of lonely men in the Comstock. The latter especially came from the East or from the goldfields of California, and sometimes as far away as San Francisco. They coolly took advantage of the various classes of men: the lowly miners toiling for valuable minerals, the middle-class merchants supplying the miners, and the investors who purchased mines and made their riches without having to dirty their hands. At Unionville, established in 1860, some twenty newcomers arrived daily. Almost immediately there were nine saloons and a number of bordellos in the camp. The naughty ladies of Unionville initially did well, but the settlement's ample water supply and shady trees made it equally attractive to families. As fewer single men remained in town, the ladies moved on.

In 1861, Nevada Territory was officially carved from a chunk of Utah Territory. And although the first territorial census in 1862 did not list occupations for those who were documented, wayward women must certainly have been among them. In a time when most miners lived in tiny rooms, sometimes sharing their quarters with others and sleeping in shifts, men sought public places in which to spend their leisure time. More often than not, the saloons, gaming establishments, and bawdy houses were their only choices for socializing and entertainment, or even a warm fire on a cold night. Prostitutes provided a place for these men to stay, at least for a while, and their soft, scented bosoms gave comfort to those far from home with no other place to find solace in the harsh, often unforgiving conditions in which they lived.

Soon after Pioche was established around 1863, the town's seedy reputation began to build. By 1869 the town was dubbed "the wildest in the west," with numerous shootings and other violent deaths. In one instance, a bartender called Faddiman lasted only a week before a customer shot him to death and wandered next door to the barbershop of "Nigger Liz," where he slit the woman's throat. Robbery was the motive, and the sheriff was able to shoot the guilty party to death. He was buried in "Murderer's Row," a special place just for outlaws in the town cemetery. Sheriffs in Pioche were nobody to fool with; another time, an officer dug graves for two "desperados" and made them stand at the openings while he shot them to death.[2] By 1873, Pioche's population was at six thousand people, and there were a record seventy-eight saloons and thirty-four brothels.

Nevada became the thirty-sixth state in the union in 1864. A short time later, the Nevada State Legislature allowed for incorporated cities to regulate their own prostitution industry. But the new state fairly bulged at the seams as new mineral discoveries were made just south of its borders and pioneer prospectors continued pouring in. The population was not lost on the good time girls coming west. If the exact numbers of the ladies were unknown, the havoc they wreaked was not: Between 1865 and 1880, the County Hospital in Storey County alone treated 731 cases of venereal disease.

In 1867, Nevada's southern boundary was expanded into the gambling state we know today. Hundreds of camps would continue popping up across Nevada like desert wildflowers. Some blossomed into leading cities, while many more faded into the past. All of them held intrigue and the hope of making good money for the wayward women who traveled between them. Notably, prostitution was legal and condoned during these early years, allowing counties and towns to either let the industry run on its own steam, govern their red-light ladies at will, or prohibit them altogether. In some settlements, like the silver camp of Hamilton (founded in 1868), the red-light district was located "near the edge of town" and included several brothels.[3] In Winnemucca (founded in 1869), however, the Pussycat Saloon and brothel was near the heart of the original downtown. It is just a guess that the Pussycat was originally named something else. One source claims it was built in 1839, an impossible date since very few, if any, Anglo men or women were in Nevada at that time. When the original brothel was torn down circa 2008, however, the Pussycat was deemed one of Nevada's oldest bordellos.[4]

Although the town of Tybo was founded in 1870, it took two years for a brothel to make its appearance. Tybo's prostitution industry appears to have been "widely accepted"; when one of the town's soiled doves left in 1877, the *Tybo Sun* noted that there "is a void in Tybo society, that will be sadly felt by the festive coal-burner and bullwhacker. The coy and bewitching hurdy [prostitute] whose arts and blandishments so often interwove the tendrils of her heart about these stalwart sons of toil in all the fascinations of waltz and schottish [*sic*], has donned her cleanest linens and departed to new fields of conquest. Verily, the gods smile unpropitious upon the boys." Naturally the *Sun* rejoiced in May of 1878 when a new bordello opened. "Our cup of harmony is nearly full," the paper reported. "Now that we have a hurdy-house, all we need is a brass band to practice at the next door and we would be fixed." The paper was less than happy later that same month, however, when a man huffed too much benzene and "got out of hand" in one of Tybo's bordellos. "To show what kind of a hairpin he was, he began flourishing a pistol, which exploded during the interesting performance," the *Sun* wrote, but the "ball merely grazed his hand, instead of perforating a vital part." The man was thrown in jail for the night "for his idiotic practice."

The *Sun* was again in mourning in August when one of its brothels closed up and the red-light ladies moved on. "One by one the roses fall," lamented the writer. "This time it's the hurdy house that's passed in its chips. No more doth the hair of the horse torture the bowels of the cat; no more doth the 'music' that 'hath charms' disturb our slumbers, or 'soothe the savage breast' enough to make him put up his 'little one-half dollar.' The hurdies have folded their 'store close' and stolen silently away, leaving a blank silence on the evening air and a void in the lives of many. She's gone where the woodbine twineth, [sic] the proverbial spout, and the 'sound of revelry by night' is hushed. Yes, she's busted, and alas, we weep at the remembrance of 'departed' joys."

Newspapers in Belmont felt the same way. During 1874, the *Belmont Courier* commented on a female employee of the Crook Shop who was refused admittance to a "respectable party," while men who "danced with the 'hurdy-gurdy girl' suffered no diminishment in respectability." The *Courier* challenged the law under which the Crook Shop harlot was turned away, and posed a logical opinion of the matter: "If there is any difference between Tweedle Dee and Tweedle Dum, we confess our ignorance." On the opposite end of the pendulum was a pointed note that places like J. R. Seymour's "hurdy dance house," a place called the Cosmopolitan Saloon, "could be suppressed at once" with a similar law.[5]

When Nevada's second state census was conducted in 1875, there were 3,572 women living on the Comstock alone. Of those, 487 were labeled as prostitutes or some other word denoting their naughty occupation. Nine of them were madams. Not surprisingly, many of the working girls in the 1875 census were documented as Chinese, the male population of which had set up noodle joints, opium dens, laundry services, and other labor-intensive occupations. Most of the "China girls" were in their twenties, although some were as young as nineteen and as old as thirty-five. These ladies tended to be identified outright as "prostitute" in the census records, while most Anglo ladies of the evening were noted as being employed in a "bawdy house." Both types of women were subject to violence by this time, as evidenced by news articles and court documents from various parts of Nevada. Sometimes the assailant was of the same sex: In 1876, Gus Botto and Jesse Bieglow argued one night over free tickets to the opera in Eureka. The argument escalated to the point that Bieglow shot Botto to death. With Botto was a prostitute known as Hog Eyed Mary. A short time after the incident, Mary was stabbed to death by Bulldog Kate Miller.

Incidents of violence against women escalated during the 1870s, enough that a new law in 1877 decreed that "Any male person in the State who is more than eighteen years of age, who shall willingly and violently strike, beat, or torture the body of any maiden or woman who is more than sixteen years of age, shall be deemed guilty of a misdemeanor, and upon conviction in any court of competent jurisdiction, shall be sentenced to be firmly tied or lashed in a standing posture to the post or pillar described in Section I of the Act, and shall be kept in such tied and standing posture for a period not less than two hours or more than ten hours in the daytime of any day, except Sunday, and it shall be the duty of the Sheriff, Constable, or other peace officer who shall be detailed to enforce the sentence of the Court, to fasten upon the breast garments of the culprit leaving a placard bearing in large Roman characters the words, 'Woman beater' or 'Wife beater,' as the case may be."[6] The law did not apply to women who beat other women; one hapless mistress suffered injuries in 1879 when her lover's wife discovered the couple in a comfortable room at the International Hotel in Elko. The affronted spouse did nothing to her husband, but shattered a handy bottle of champagne over his companion's head.

Notably, the 1880 census for Eureka shows that "China girls" almost exclusively comprised the town's red-light district, the two exceptions being Mary Brown and Claude Leonard. But a new law in 1881 would prove unsettling to all red-light ladies, and their male companions. This time, county commissioners would now be permitted to "license, tax, regulate, prohibit, or suppress all houses of ill fame."[7] Although the law was inconvenient for brothel owners, it did little to deter houses of ill repute from operating. At Battle Mountain, whose mining history dated back to the 1860s, the Desert Club opened during the late 1800s with five rooms in which prostitutes worked. In 1885, when the Micca House opened in Paradise Valley, the structure was intended for use as a combination post office, meat market, dry goods store, and several other businesses on the bottom floor. The upper floor consisted of bedrooms (presumably for rent) and apartments. During the building's stint as a saloon and/or gambling hall, however, the upper floor was used as a brothel. And in 1902, a brothel called Mona's II opened in Elko and remained in business under that name until about 1914.

The good time girls of Nevada continued infiltrating the mining camps well after the turn of 1900. One of the last gold booms in the state occurred in 1906 at Rawhide, located in the southern portion very near the California border. News of the new gold discoveries traveled fast; within six months, Rawhide featured 125 "brokerage offices" which were buying and selling mining shares. There also were numerous barbershops, hotels, restaurants, thirty-seven saloons, and a red-light district in Stingaree Gulch that cut a quarter-mile long swath through the town—yet there were only two churches.[8] Stingaree Gulch's golden years during 1907-08 featured numerous cribs and brothels and housed between five hundred and six hundred naughty ladies.

One time in 1908, romance novelist Elinor Glyn was a guest of honor at Rawhide. The town fathers realized that her visit could put the town on the map. The writer was seeking a firsthand look at a real boomtown, and her host was Tex Rickard, himself a well-known boxing promoter. Elinor duly arrived from San Francisco in the company of two friends, Ray Baker and Sam Newhouse. But Rickard went slightly overboard as he toiled to make the trip memorable for the trio. As the group watched a poker game in progress, he arranged for the players to fake a shoot-out and two "bodies" were carried outside. Next, the group visited Stingaree Gulch, where the scarlet women had been "coached to make every effort to seduce Mrs. Glyn's friends." Elinor and her party departed Rawhide with the eyeful of a raw western town they came looking for, plus a dash extra.[9]

What Elinor Glyn did not experience was the real, gritty side of Rawhide. Soon after her visit a saloon owner from faraway Rhyolite, Jack

McDougal, sauntered into town and wandered into the Tanaan saloon in Stingaree Gulch. The Tanaan was owned by a woman named Leslie Noman, who took a liking to McDougal—until he became abusive. One day McDougal was drinking heavily at the tavern when he began arguing with Leslie. When the angry drunk threw a beer mug and hit the woman in the face, she picked up her revolver from behind the bar and shot McDougal in the gut. He died three days later, and Leslie was acquitted for acting in self-defense.

By the 1920s, a new era had dawned upon Nevada and the rest of the country. Prohibition was in effect, other states had outlawed prostitution, and reformers were very much on the rise. But the state of Nevada proved to be one tough old gal, and battles between authorities over the issue of prostitution were frequent. In 1923, Reno mayor Harry Stewart and others took umbrage at the "restricted district" on the east side of town along the Truckee River. The largest bordello was the Stockade, aka the Riverside. A tall wood fence spanned across the front of the building. Inside were "two rows of small rooms known as cribs, twenty-five on each side, with a dance hall at the far end. Up to three shifts of women per day rented the cribs, registered with the police and underwent regular medical screenings." The cribs were rented out for $2.50 for an eight-hour shift.[10]

Stewart had no sooner launched his attack against the restricted district when a new mayor, Edwin E. Roberts, was elected. Roberts put an end to Stewart's tirade by pushing through an all new amendment that let the brothels of Reno remain legal so long as they operated 250 feet or more from any public building. Finally, federal law made all brothels across the nation illegal in 1942. But the war against Reno's red-light district, whose madams and pimps maintained that Nevada's law still allowed prostitution, raged on for several more years. When Mae Cunningham's brothel was closed down in 1949, the lady challenged her right to remain open. At the time, however, the county commissioners were found to have the right to "abate brothels as 'public nuisances,'" and therefore close them—even though technically, prostitution remained legal in Nevada.

Even more committed efforts were made to close houses of prostitution throughout the state beginning in 1951. Author Alexa Albert credits Joe Conforte, who would later own the famed Mustang Ranch, with heading the movement to legalize prostitution across Nevada beginning in 1955.[11] Conforte and others fought the state for over fifteen years before finally, in 1970, Storey County passed the first official brothel licensing ordinance in the United States. Other counties, eager to increase their income, jumped on the bandwagon. The one exception was Clark County, the locale of Las Vegas, which quickly moved to keep the industry illegal in counties with a population of over 200,000. As of 2020, prostitution remained legal in the counties of Churchill, Esmerelda, Lander, Mineral, Nye, and Storey. In other counties, the industry was legalized in Elko, Carlin, Wendover, and Wells in Elko County; Winnemucca in Humboldt County; Mound House in Lyon County and Ely in White Pine County. Today the ladies happily offer services at close to two dozen brothels throughout Nevada, many of them dotting the surrounding landscapes in anything from upscale mobile homes to ranch houses.

CHAPTER 2

————— •●• —————

Coquettes of Carson City

Move over, *Bonanza*. To the chagrin of many historians, the sequined sirens of the popular television show during the 1960s and early 1970s pale in comparison to the real good time girls that ran amuck in Carson City during its early days. They were not all beautiful, not all eloquent, and not all in distress. Rather, Carson's wicked women were raw, unhindered vixens who were in the business of making as much money as they could, and quickly. Unless Little Joe's pockets were filled with gold or silver, they likely would have had little time for him let alone his brothers and father.

Carson City's beginnings date back to 1851, when Eagle Station operated along the Carson River as a trading post and rest stop for those traversing the California Trail's Carson Branch. Back in those days, this portion of Nevada was part of Utah Territory, with the government offices headquartered in faraway Salt Lake City. Tired of being controlled by "Mormon-influenced officials," settler Abraham Curry and others began working to create their own territory.[1] In 1858 Curry was able to purchase Eagle Station, and renamed the small settlement Carson City. Curry hoped to make Carson City the territorial capital, which would eventually be achieved in 1864.

The gold and silver discoveries at the nearby Comstock Lode were a boon to Carson City. The first territorial census in 1860 recorded around a thousand people in the fledgling town. Soon, Carson City was a popular "jumping off place" for thousands of prospectors heading to other nearby gold camps and as far away as the California mining camp of Bodie and even San Francisco. The number of permanent residents would soon grow to somewhere between five thousand and seven thousand people.[2] Many of these folks were no doubt prospectors who came to try their luck in hopes of striking it rich.

By 1870, the usual assortment of naughty girls had set up shop in Carson City. One house of ill repute was occupied by five women who were each documented in the census as working as a "hurdy." They ranged in age from eighteen to twenty-three years. All five ladies—Anna Helloubout, Lizzie "Hwpi" [*sic*], Eve Langstaff, Mary Schafer, and Lizzie Schimpf—were born in Prussia. Each woman had a customer with her when the census taker came by, whose information was duly recorded. Bouncer Alexander Shear also was on hand to maintain order. The five hurdies aside, thirty-six Chinese women were outright identified as prostitutes by the census. Most of them, but not all, lived in Carson City's Chinatown. Ha Sing, for instance, is documented as living (or at least being present) in a different part of town with two men from Denmark and France, respectively.

One of Carson City's earliest madams was Mary Ann Phillips. Notably, Mary Ann was already around fifty-three years old when she first appeared on record in December of 1874, but where she came from nobody could say. The mysterious femme was quite wealthy, to the extent that she was able to purchase a two-story house from Jennie Dupey at the corner of 4th and Ormsby Streets for a whopping $3,350. One source says she also kept a separate house in nearby Virginia City for raising her children. Did Mary Ann know that Carson City was planning to designate an official red-light district around her property? She must have, for

By 1870, Carson City was teeming with life—and good time girls.
Courtesy Library of Congress Prints and Photographs Division

the June 9, 1875, issue of the *Carson Appeal* announced that the ladies of the red light were "restricted to Ormsby Street between Second and Fifth Street."[3] Mary Ann's brothel was in the middle of the new district, and remained so after the city issued another ordinance prohibiting any house of ill-fame from operating anywhere except on Ormsby Street between Fourth and Fifth Streets. Furthermore, the windows of these houses were to be "closed from street gaze by blinds or curtains."[4]

The 1880 census reveals little more about Mary Ann, although her housing situation appears rather unusual. Living with her was a Black woman named Jennie Moore who, like Mary Ann, had no occupation listed but has been identified by other sources as a madam. Also in the house was a Chinese cook identified as Pon Gee, a sixty-five-year-old upholsterer named Lewis Wentworth, and twenty-seven-year-old Rosa E. White, who said she worked as a dressmaker. Nothing else is known about Mary Ann, except that she died in 1883 and was buried at Carson City's Lone Mountain Cemetery. Somebody thought to erect a tombstone for her with the word "Mother" at the top. Two years later, Mary Ann's former brothel was known as the Palace.

Mary Ann Phillips was not the only madam to appear in the 1880 census. There also was Mercedes Barega, who hailed from Ecuador. Mercedes first appeared in Carson City's *Morning Appeal* newspaper in October of 1877 when her brothel near the western corner of Ormsby and Fourth Street caught fire. The house was saved, and it was noted that the madam was insured for $1,300. But Mercedes was in trouble by January of 1878, when the *Morning Appeal* gave notice that her taxes were delinquent. The tax applied not just to her house, but also her furnishings and a piano, as well as her bank account which held $5,700. Mercedes owed a total of $423 in taxes, plus 35 percent interest. When the woman didn't pay what she owed, the property was put up for a sheriff's sale in March.

It is unclear as to whether Mercedes regained possession of her property at Ormsby and Fourth Street. She was, however, back in business by May of 1879 when a scuffle between two Spanish women broke out at her brothel. "Hair and cotton flew in great quantities," reported the *Morning Appeal*, "and the language accompanying was more emphatic than refined or classical."[5] The following month, it was revealed by the *Morning Appeal* that Mercedes kept a small boy. The child was walking along Ormsby Street when he "threw a handful of dirt at a *mahala* [a Native woman] and she in return picked up a stone and hit the little fellow in the stomach completely knocking the wind out of him. As soon as he recovered his breath he ran off, screaming as if he were followed by a hundred *mahalas*," said the paper.[6]

The boy, known only as Juan, was later identified as Mercedes's foster son. The *Morning Appeal* did not say how he came to live with the madam, but Mercedes turned out to be less than an ideal mother. In July, she was taken to court for cruelty to the boy. Per the judge's orders, she agreed to send Juan to Virginia City for schooling. He did not appear in the census in June of 1880, when Mercedes was living with three other women on Ormsby Street identified as Nettie Smith, Minnie Henderson, and Lottie Gordon. Two months later, however, the *Morning Appeal* expressed shock that little Juan had been seen walking down Ormsby with Mercedes. The writer talked of the woman's prior arrest for "brutally maltreating the little Spanish boy," who had indeed been sent to the Sisters of Mercy in Virginia City but had been transferred to the Catholic Orphan's Asylum in Carson City. Unfortunately, nothing more was reported about Juan.[7]

Mercedes could not seem to stay out of the public eye. In October, two men who had insulted a proper woman on a train and fought with her husband were arrested at Mercedes's place. Then in December, one of her male employees was arrested for stealing from her. By February of 1881, Mercedes had enough and took an ad out in the *Appeal*, giving notice that her "large frame house" at the corner of Third and Ormsby Streets, as well as eight houses on Ormsby between Third and Fourth Streets, were for sale or rent. Those interested could chat with her at No. 1 Ormsby at Third Street. She apparently sold the property within a month.[8]

Today only one brothel from Carson City's heyday survives. It is an unassuming, quaint, and simple home at 110 West 4th Street at the corner of what was then Ormsby Street but is now South Curry Street. For all of its simplicity, however, one important aspect of the house stands out: It is allegedly Nevada's oldest surviving brothel. A structure is known to have been on the property as early as 1865, but it remains unknown whether it was the existing building. Joseph Olcovich purchased the property in 1870, and still lived there when Ormsby Street was officially declared as the red-light district in 1875. Ten years later, according to the 1885 Sanborn map, the house was still a private home, although Mary Ann Phillips's Palace was directly across the street. Sometime between 1890 and 1907, 110 West 4th Street officially became identified as a brothel, aka "female boarding." Who the occupants were remains a mystery, since the 1900 census yields almost no information about Carson City's red-light ladies. Also, it is hard to say whether subsequent owners—Rodolf and Guiseppe Giandeini in 1905, William Harbin in 1906, C.H. Peters in 1907, and Harbin's widow, Helen, in 1908—purposely rented the building for use as a brothel.[9]

The 1910 census for Carson City also yields few clues, listing only nine "fallen women":

Fallen Women of Carson City, 1910

Name	Age	Birthplace	Marital Status	Residence
Vera Marx	37	New York	Married	6 4th Street
Emma Lee	27	New York	Single	6 4th Street
Ruth Lee	25	Ohio	Single	6 4th Street
Frank Preston	39	Illinois	Widow	6 4th Street
Gam Chin	36	California	Married	6th Street
Sou Toy Gee	50	China	Married	6th Street
Noddi	26	Japan	Single	6th Street
Tammer	32	Japan	Single	6th Street
Guen Lock Get	45	China	Married	Tale [sic] Street

Of these women, Vera Marx was identified as head of the household (i.e., madam) of 6 4th Street. Also, Sou Toy Gee was only eight years old when she immigrated to America from China—an indication that she may have been brought over against her will as a sex slave. But none of the women, it appears, had anything to do with the house at 110 4th Street. Adding to the confusion is that the house's address changed over time according to Sanborn maps: #8 in 1885, 1890, and 1907, and #305 by 1941. Linda White, who ran a gift shop in the house in 1998 said, "One guy used to deliver groceries here in the 30s. Everyone says the girls were really nice." But it is just a guess by historians that the house was being used as a brothel by 1942, when the government tried to officially close all houses of ill repute nationwide. Most interesting is that Carson City did not officially pass an anti-prostitution ordinance until 1980.[10]

CHAPTER 3

——•●•——

Rosa May and Erni Marks

Certain historians believe that the Rosa E. White, who lived with Mary Ann Phillips during Carson City's 1880 census, might have been the famed Rosa May who later appeared in Bodie, California. The romanticized and much-loved harlot lived and worked in both Carson City and Virginia City before making her way to Bodie. But the 1880 census records Rosa White's birthplace as Maine, and that of her parents as New Hampshire. Census records for Rosa May in 1900 and 1910 in Bodie document her birthplace as Pennsylvania and that of her parents as Ireland. Rosa's birth year also remains a mystery: In 1880, Rosa White's year of birth was recorded to be circa 1853. In 1900, Rosa May told the census taker she was born in January of 1855. And in the 1910 census, "Rosie" May was guessed to have been born in 1864.

Others maintain that Rosa May's last name really was Olaque. This is based on reports of Rosa Olaque, a Spanish girl who began appearing in Bodie courts starting in 1879. But the two women only appear to have shared the same first name. The only thing about Rosa that most of her biographies agree upon is that her parents were Irish immigrants. And despite the discrepancies and the mysteries about her, Rosa May's early life in Nevada makes for an interesting story for one reason that is a boon to historians: Rosa May managed to save a number of letters describing life in the demimonde, as well as her longtime love affair with Ernest "Erni" Marks.

Rosa May's letters indicate that she quite possibly had spent time in New York, Colorado, and Idaho before arriving in Nevada. Her first destination was Virginia City, where she lived beginning in 1873 or 1875. It was probably there that she met Ernest Marks, a German immigrant who would become an integral part of her life. It is highly likely that Marks met Rosa in the demimonde, since his letters to Rosa express his familiarity with the red-light districts of nearby Gold Hill and Virginia City. According to the 1900 census, Marks was born in 1853 in Prussia and came to America as a child. Later he would claim he became a naturalized citizen in San Joaquin County, California, circa 1866, but lost his papers proving his citizenship. He eventually settled in Gold Hill, perhaps with his family.

Shortly after Rosa moved to No. 1 Ormsby Street in Carson City in about 1878, Marks began corresponding with her from Gold Hill some fourteen miles away—a two-hour train ride. Over time, he would write eighteen known letters to Rosa. They were sent to various addresses in Carson City, depending on where the lady lived at the time. Some were mailed to post office boxes, while others were sent to her at the Ormsby Street address. In 1878, the madam of the house at No. 1 Ormsby was Jennie Moore, the same woman who was found living with Mary Ann Phillips in 1880.

Marks's first letter in Rosa's possession was dated July 7, 1878, and was written from Lake Tahoe. Interestingly, the letter addresses the recipient as both Jennie (twice) and Rosa (once)—an indication that the man was possibly a bit tipsy, since he later acknowledged that he had a drinking problem. This first letter also was rather crass, even by today's standards, and alludes to the fact that Marks might have been suffering from a venereal disease: He expressed his hope that "pop and gin and medicine" would make him "sound as a roach," and commented that "getting up at night to release the Dr. from a crooked posish [*sic*] is not what it is cracked up to be." He also assured Rosa that "I have seen one or two chances to give the Dr. a chance but he and I do not give it a thought. I suppose a great love of Jennie [*sic*] blinds us to everything else." The "Dr." was clearly what Marks called his own genitalia. He also told of encountering a woman, presumably a prostitute, who asked, "Don't you get lonesome when you have no ladies around?" Marks likely thought Rosa would appreciate it that the "Dr. did not show any symptoms of wanting any and I was very glad to see he had not forgotten his Rosa." More than likely, however, the statement merely left a bad taste in the girl's mouth.

Marks was in Gold Hill when he wrote his next letter on December 20 and thanked Rosa for her "loveing [*sic*] letter." But the note was full of mixed messages, such as when Marks expressed annoyance that "every man and woman and child knew of you and I. I get it from some quarter every day. And it makes me feel so bad sometimes that I hardly know what to do." Yet he opened his letter by saying "I miss my pet at night, no one knows except poor me and I am still going hungry and suppose I will till I see my pet." Marks also claimed he had not been seeing any other women, although he also described spending the evening with his friend Tom and a prostitute named Donnie. The threesome encountered a man named Jack, who was formerly Donnie's paramour and nearly went to blows with Tom. "If there had been a scrape I should have been into it," Marks wrote, "as I think it is time someone else has a chance to do a little fucking in this town beside the so called sports." Still, Marks seemed to care about Rosa when he learned she had been cheated by a "married man," Charles Boscowitz. "I hope you will be careful and not let yourself be bilked any more," he wrote. The letter closed with Marks telling Rosa that even if he heard a rumor "that you had a lover," he would refuse to believe it because "my Rosie loves her baby don't you darling." The letter ended with Marks sending "great love and a million kiss [*sic*]."

Marks's letter is most interesting to historians today. He knew Rosa worked as a prostitute, but presented himself as her boyfriend. He also felt that Rosa's line of work would not prevent her from reciprocating as his girlfriend. Yet it annoyed him that others knew of their relationship. And although he wrote that "I am now good and keep away from" the people he referred to as "the dizy [*sic*] girls and boys," this and other letters showed that he did indeed spend time with such people.[1] Was the relationship between Erni Marks and Rosa May typical of those between prostitutes and their customers and/or boyfriends? Given that other prostitutes across the West also pursued legitimate relationships with their clients, it is probably so.[2]

Marks continued to express concern for Rosa and tried to please her. A letter on December 27 noted that he was drinking a lot less, but was nervous because of it. He also had been to Virginia City, a mile or so from Gold Hill, where he encountered a man named Dan, who had owed Rosa money when she left for Carson City. Marks said he "came very near to telling him if he thought so much of you, he might send you some money now but I thought I had better not." In her last letter to him, Rosa had implied that "six beauties" she knew of, possibly at her place of employment with Jennie Moore, did not include herself. Marks made sure to compliment her, telling her that "Well love you are handsomer in my eyes than any one I know." He also acknowledged that Rosa was pleased with the Christmas presents he had sent to her, and promised to bring her pet bird to her if he could. "I don't know where Ormsby Street is—so you must tell me as near as you can," he wrote. It would be a long time before Marks could keep his promise. His letters kept coming, however, telling Rosa of his struggles to stop drinking and of his occasional—but allegedly chaste—visits to Virginia City's demimonde on C Street.

On January 4, 1879, Rosa received a letter of a different kind. It was from a Mrs. Carr of New York whose daughter, Mamie Nenninger, had died in Carson City. It was Rosa who responded to Mrs. Carr's inquiry about Mamie. "I thank you and the other ladies for the kind interest you have taken in my daughter and God bless you all for your kindness," Carr wrote. She also inquired as to Mamie's cause of death. "You said if you could get further information you would let me know. . . . If there is anything valuable to me as keepsakes if you could send them on I would be grateful." Notably, Mrs. Carr addressed her letter to Rosa May at 18 South D Street, the address of Cad Thompson's bordello in Virginia City. The letter must have been forwarded to Rosa at Carson City, since Marks's next letter to Rosa came to her there. His letter, penned on January 5, answered Rosa's accusations of him sleeping with other women ("Pet I did not get into some girl's box"), and her resentfulness that Marks may have been sending her "traffic," (i.e., male customers). On January 7, another letter stated that Marks's friend, Tom Reynolds, "was in your house last night but you were engaged and he left." But the man expressed no jealousy, seemed genuinely glad to hear from Rosa, and assured her he was true to her. "I have not since you have gone had anything to do with woman or single girl or married, widow or grass widow or woman of any kind," he wheedled. And although he had once again broken his promise to come see her, he did apologize and wrote Rosa a poignant poem:

> *For today there is no hard task*
> *No burden that I would not bear with grace*
> *No sacrifice I could name or ask*
> *That were granted could I see your sweet face.*

Marks did not write to Rosa again for nearly a month (depending on whether she kept all of his letters). His next letter, dated February 5, was short and light, acknowledging that Rosa had hosted "a drinking party" and talking of the weather. But the couple apparently suffered no problems, for a short time later Marks at last took the train to Carson City to see Rosa May. The visit served to make the man yearn for Rosa even more; shortly after his visit he wrote wistfully, "God forgive me Rosa, it's breaking my heart to sit here doing nothing and you in that damn town. I want to take you out of it or help you along." But Marks had no money, not even enough to return the favor when he received a valentine from Rosa.

The next letter in Rosa's collection was dated April 17, and differed in attitude. Marks offered no more than casual notes about various friends and their relationships, but said very little about his own affair with Rosa. He portrayed the same attitude in subsequent letters, plus a dash of melancholy as he weathered illnesses, money problems, and blisters on his hands from his most recent job. But the "doctor, I'm happy to let you know, is well and quite as of yore," he wrote on June 12. As much as he was suffering, Marks's libido appeared to be intact. Even after sharing such an intimate fact, however, he sometimes signed his letters "respectfully," sans the love and kisses that had formerly been the norm. When he didn't respond to her letters in a timely manner, Rosa was quick to anger. "Your very short and cross letter is at hand today," Marks wrote on July 30, and "I am very, very hurt to see you wrote good-bye." The letter ended with Marks firing off, "It makes me feel bad that you would believe that I don't think of you as I always did. You can think as you please for it is a privilege we all have and I shall do the same, I shall not quarrel."

Rosa May perhaps had her own reasons for being short with Marks. By fall, it was clear that the harlots of both Carson City and Virginia City were not making enough money to make ends meet. Rosa and the other girls at Mary Ann Phillips's house had been forced to "walk the streets in order to rustle up trade." Although business was no better in Virginia

City, Rosa apparently believed she could make more money there and left Carson City on August 12. If she took the train, Rosa would have passed through Gold Hill, but there is nothing to support the likelihood that she stopped off for a visit with Ernest Marks.

In Virginia City, Rosa went to work for Madam Cad Thompson, with whom she apparently had a previous business relationship. She also wrote to her friend and fellow prostitute, Emma Hall, in Carson City and told her she was doing well. "It must be an agreeable change to go out at night and come in the morning with a shining $20 more than you would see here in [a month]," Emma responded. Emma also mentioned several other prostitutes: Mary Ann Phillips, a woman named Lilly, Emana Boyd, and Bell Graham. Like Rosa, both Emma and Lilly had boyfriends, and both were named Charley. "My Charley sends his love to you," Emma wrote, "Also Lilly and her Charley."

The only known letter to survive that was written by Rosa herself was an August 18 letter to Leo Miller. "Friend Leo," it read, "Having arrived in town again I write to inform you of my address and if you wish to call and see me I would be pleased to have you do so I am living with Mrs. C. Thompson. Hoping to see you soon, I am as ever Yours Respectfully Rosa May No. 18 D St." Apparently the letter was never delivered to Miller, as it remained in Rosa's possession. But the letter also brings the question of how many other men Rosa sent correspondence to in order to drum up extra business. Another note, from clothing dealer Isaac Isaacs, invited Rosa to "come to my room to night if you wish come between 9 and 10. The front door will be open so walk right in to my room and I will be up as soon as I close the store." A postscript read, "You know where I live?"

As of New Year's Day, 1880, Ernest Marks and Rosa May had made up. Interestingly, Marks was now in Virginia City but Rosa had returned to Carson City. On January 1, Marks wrote that he had received two letters Rosa sent to him, wherein she had apparently felt that she might be bothering him. "Oh! No my darling, do not for a moment think your constant writing annoys me," he responded. He also told her "I have not drank a drop today," and talked of coming to visit her "tomorrow or the next day." It is the last letter from Marks in the pile found among Rosa May's keepsakes. Rosa did not remain in Carson City much longer, as evidenced as a letter she received in Virginia City from Cad Thompson that March.[3]

By June, Rosa's friends from Carson City—Emma Hall, Lilly, Emana Boyd, and Bell Graham—had also left town, or at least did not appear in the 1880 census taken on June 25. Aside from Mary Ann Phillips and her crew (prostitutes Jennie Moore and Rose E. White, cook Gee Pon, and sixty-five-year-old Lewis Wentworth), other houses of prostitution are believed to have been run by Carrie Stein and Elizabeth Goodrick with two girls apiece, and Minnie Henderson and Amy Powell with three girls apiece. The youngest two were seventeen-year-olds Millie Clinton and Ninnie Lee. The oldest were thirty-year-olds Carrie Stein and Nellie Silverton. Thirty-eight-year-old Bealgras [sic] of Mexico might have been a servant. Forty-year-old Mercedes Barega (spelled Barrigo), documented as a native of Ecuador, also remained in town. Most of the other women in the census were American born, the exceptions being Carrie Stein of Bavaria, Lottie Gordon of India, and Nellie Silverton of England. A possible freelancer was "Habele Blondenite" [sic], who was a native of France. The women occupied five different houses which intermingled with those of respectable couples, some with children. Each of their occupations was recorded as "keeping house." Nearly one thousand Chinese residents were recorded as well, but unlike earlier census records, none of them were recorded as prostitutes.

None of the possible good time girls appearing in Carson City's census, with the exception of the Rose E. White identified by others, match anything known about the elusive Rosa May. Nor does the lady appear in the 1880 census at Virginia City, which was conducted over a week before the one at Carson City. Neither, for that matter, does Ernest Marks. Both are conspicuously missing from the 1880 census in Nevada. All that is known for sure is that by March of 1884, Ernest Marks had moved to Bodie where newspapers reported he was involved in a shooting scrape. Rosa May would next surface in Bodie too, during the 1900 census, and is believed to have died in 1912.[4] In 2020, one of the houses Rosa May lived in while she was in Carson City was identified as once being located in the vicinity of the Carson Nugget Casino's parking lot. At some point in the last forty years or so, the house was moved to the nearby ghost town of Sutro, and today serves as the caretaker's home. It is the only known remaining remnant of the mysterious little lady who captured the heart of historians across the West.

CHAPTER 4

---•◦•---

Not So Virginal Virginia City

When the famed Comstock Lode was discovered during the late 1850s, Virginia City was founded nearby in 1859. The tiny camp was named for Virginia, the birthplace of one of the Comstock partners, James "Old Virginny" Fennimore, aka James Finney. Within a year the population was 2,857, of which 159 were women. It was probably at this early date that two brothels were in residence on C Street. The occupants likely did not know that for the next twenty-two years, Virginia City would be known as the "largest, richest mining town in the American West." Two hundred ninety-three million dollars in silver would be produced during this time.[1]

As of the 1860 census there were no documented prostitutes in Virginia City, although writer Ronald James surmised that "careful examination of the information concerning the documented 111 adult women suggests that probably fewer than 12 single women were working in that capacity."[2] More women were coming, for by the time Virginia City, aka the "Queen of the Comstock," was incorporated in 1861 there were three thousand souls living there.[3] Good time girls were likely already present, in small numbers, when the city incorporated. Over time the ladies were relegated, perhaps by themselves, to three separate red-light districts in close proximity of one another. The first, and largest, was along the west side of D Street in a five-block area between Washington Street and north to Mill Street. The D Street district was likely most profitable since many brothels backed right up to the saloons on C Street, and the Virginia and Truckee Railroad Depot was situated across the street. Around the district, other brothels opened and closed over time on E Street and as far east as B Street.

A second red-light district was a much bawdier area that was dubbed the "Barbary Coast" after the raucous demimonde of the same name in San Francisco. Its locale was along the west side of C Street between Silver Street and Flowery Street. Many of the brothels here doubled as saloons, with low-rent ladies in the back. These places were rated as "gin shops of the lowest class." Interspersed with houses of prostitution were other businesses, from bakeries and hotels to dance halls and saloons. Also on C Street was the city hall and police station in the early days. [4] "The Barbary Coast was notorious for fights, shootings, card cheating, and drugged drinks," noted Virginia City's newspaper, the *Territorial Enterprise*, a few years later. "Prostitutes working in saloons along the Coast were frequently ill-treated and were occasionally locked up for 'safekeeping.' Two women sometimes shared the same bed in cramped backrooms where they both slept and brought customers." [5] The third red-light district could be found in Chinatown, located near the cemetery, which came into being during the 1860s and 1870s and offered opium to the ladies and others. None of the ladies in Virginia City were required to purchase a license to operate, but they paid in other ways—namely high rents to landlords and bribe money to police, plus non-gratis visits by officers and city officials. Curiously, prostitutes of the town hung blue, not red, lanterns outside their doors. And, they were especially popular during the snowy winter months when mining came to a standstill.

Gold Hill, a satellite town south of Virginia City, sprang up in 1862. The peak population of Gold Hill ranged between five thousand and seven thousand. Although wayward women are hard to track in Gold

Hill there is at least a suggestion that some prostitutes worked, or at least lived, in the blue-collar town. Perhaps because of this, Gold Hill's naughty houses rarely made the newspapers. One brothel was described by the *Gold Hill Evening News* in 1873 as having a small reception parlor with a badly worn horsehair sofa, a spotted carpet, and three chairs. The madam was an old woman, according to the account. Also, writer Ronald James found documentation between 1876 and 1880 of "an anonymous Chinawoman [*sic*] who had cost her owner $800 [and] suicided by means of laudanum in the back of Stern's store in Gold Hill. She was one of the six Chinese women who chose death over a life of hopeless slavery."[6]

By 1863, Virginia City's population has been estimated as being between ten thousand and thirty thousand depending on the source. There were enough good time girls by then to inspire city fathers to create a new law making it illegal to operate brothels anywhere west of D Street, south of Sutton Avenue, or north of Mill Street. But the ordinance was largely ignored, either because nobody cared to enforce it, or because the city was growing so much that there were too many shady ladies to fit in the designated district. Or, perhaps, both. Either way, Virginia City's wild women were soon making the news on a regular basis. In April, the Virginia City *Evening Bulletin* reported that one prostitute, who was married, left her husband after she became pregnant and moved to a brothel in Salt Lake City, Utah. It is not recorded whether anyone felt empathy for the lady, nor what became of her.

One of the most notorious women of Virginia City was Margaret McMann, better known as Buffalo Joe. On a night in 1863, Joe "got rowdy during a night of drinking at the National Lager Beer Saloon and was tossed out. A couple of men savagely beat her outside the establishment. She then went to the Sazarac Saloon, was escorted out for being loud, and was beaten up again on the street." Buffalo Joe's drinking habits were well-known in Virginia City, as well as her "sloppy" house of ill repute. She was frequently in trouble with the law, and known to be loud, vulgar, and obnoxious on those occasions she was arrested. While celebrating New Year's in 1864, Joe became so drunk that she failed to notice that someone had robbed her of both her money and her jewelry. Another time, a drunken Joe was arrested after exposing herself in public. While in jail, she got into "a bloody fight" with another madam who also was drunk.[7]

Then there was Jessie Lester, whose business sense was clearly the opposite of Buffalo Joe's. Jessie kept a silent partner named J.A. Batchelor, or Batchellor, from whom she purchased her two-story brothel on D Street. For his investment, Batchelor received 5 percent of the money Jessie made. Jessie's place featured two parlors on the first floor. Each was decorated with chandeliers, lace curtains, Brussels carpets, chairs, and a sofa. There were five bedrooms on the second floor, including Jessie's own boudoir with a mahogany bedroom set, a marble-topped wash stand, a dresser, and lamp tables. Her bed had a spring mattress, very chic for the time, topped by a horsehair mattress. There was no kitchen, dining room, or indoor plumbing, which appeared to be the norm for dwellings in early Virginia City. By dining out, Jessie and her girls not only fed money back into the city's economy but also could drum up business.

As fine as her furnishings were, even Jessie sometimes suffered violence from her customers. In 1863, for instance, Jessie was robbed by one George Kirt. Then, on December 19, 1864, she was actually shot by some unknown man. Journalist Alf Doten noted in his diary on December 27 that Jessie "had to have her right arm amputated at the shoulder joint this afternoon—poor creature, she was just recovering from the taking of chloroform during the operation and was shrieking with pain— and in her delirium, calling on her mother . . ." Jessie apparently knew she would not survive the operation. In the three weeks following the surgery, she made sure her bills were paid, gave away her things, made a will, and even planned her own funeral. In late January of 1865, Father Manogue held last rites over Jessie, and she died on January 23. Her will left $5,294 to the Sisters of Charity, and she was buried in the Catholic cemetery. Jessie's funeral procession, Doten wrote, consisted of six carriages "filled with whores."[8]

Not all prostitutes coming to Virginia City had a checkered past. One of these, Martha Margaret Dickey, was with a handful of respectable young single women when she arrived in town circa 1864. Martha had escaped the oppression of her native Ireland, intended to marry well, and wanted to live a good life. She found her knight in shining armor in Horace Camp, a miner who had once owned Henry Comstock's Ophir Mine—for a mere twenty-four hours. The day after the purchase, Comstock later claimed, Camp had wrongfully sold the mine in a fit of depression. Comstock took Camp to court, successfully reclaiming the Ophir. Camp, meanwhile, shaped up and "set about staking as many claims in the vicinity of the Ophir as he legally could." At least one of the claims, the Yellow Jacket, paid off. That was in 1859. When Martha met Camp, he was on the verge of becoming very wealthy, and the two married. But the Yellow Jacket stopped producing. The newlyweds had enough money to open a saloon on C Street, but Horace Camp died a short time later. Left alone, Martha continued running the saloon but also began selling sexual favors on the side. Soon she was operating in the Barbary Coast district.

On a May night in 1867, Martha awoke to the sound of someone creeping across her floor. Famed harlot Julia Bulette had just recently been murdered, setting all of Virginia City's prostitutes on edge. Julia's murder lurched into Martha's mind as she summoned the courage to raise up and look around. The woman spied the figure of a man crouching behind her bed, a dagger in his hand. Screaming for help, Martha beat a hasty retreat out her front door. Witnesses ran to her aid, but found her room empty—but on the floor was a "cudgel," a short stick which was primarily used as a weapon. Julia Bulette's killer had not been found, and the local paper, the *Daily Trespass*, speculated whether he was the same man Martha saw in her room. About a week later, Martha recognized the intruder from her room on the street. His name was John Millian, and when he was arrested a local shopkeeper piped up and claimed Millian had tried to sell her a dress belonging to Julia Bulette.

Millian was found guilty of the murder and filed an appeal. The matter was still in court in October when a strange man appeared at Martha's and ordered a drink. Martha had poured him a glass of wine, when "suddenly he lunged at her, wrapped his hands around her throat and swore that he would kill her." Martha fought him off and he fled. For Martha, the threat was one of several she had received, she believed because of Millian. She showed the injuries to her neck to the *Daily Enterprise* newspaper, and expressed her willingness to testify against Millian during the appeal. Alas, the man was found guilty without her assistance, and hanged in 1868. Still, historians today point out that Martha's identification of Millian as the man she saw in her room hastened the public sentiment against him.

Even after Millian swung from the gallows, Martha remained uneasy. The 1870 census shows that she had moved in with saloonkeeper George Olffen and his wife, Louisa. Also in the house were four other prostitutes, Maggie Smith, Sus [*sic*] Duranda, Mercedes Navarro, and Mary Smith. By 1874, however, Martha had enough of both midnight marauders and Virginia City's growing number of laws prohibiting her kind. The lady packed her bags and moved on to the high desert mining community of Panamint, California.[9] Nothing more was heard of her.

Like Martha Camp, Rose Wilson turned to prostitution (and drinking) when her miner husband died, leaving the woman with children to raise. What became of the children is unknown, but by 1865 Rose was known as a "vagrant prostitute." When sober she was kind enough, but alcohol could turn her into a violent demon. When police found her passed out in the gutter, they often arrested her just to assure she had a warm bed for the night. One night, Rose was beaten by an assailant who then stole $3,000 she had hidden in her room. Rose was not the only one to fall victim to a beating and robbery. Also in 1865, prostitute Julia Shaffer (aka Julia White) was robbed of her jewelry, and Lizzie Hayes's skull was fractured after she was struck with a Colt pistol.[10]

Sometimes the shoe of violence in the red-light district was on the other, female, foot. Madam Rose Benjamin blew into town in about 1866 and ran four separate brothels on her property at 15 North D Street. The lady was discreet: Her niece was listed as the property owner, and Rose herself lived in a private home in a respectable neighborhood. She also hired one Phil Escobar to run her brothels when she was out of town. Upwards of seven girls worked for her at any given time. But Rose was a less than ideal madam. She was "hard on her girls," to the extent that three of them committed suicide while working for her. Two of the women merited entry in Alf Doten's diary in 1872: "2 whores at Rose Benjamin's corner of D St. and Sutton Avenue, committed suicide by taking laudanum this PM—I went to see them, one not quite dead, but died about 11."[11] The other, twenty-two-year-old "Scotch Laura" Steel(e), killed herself the morning after Rose threw herself a birthday bash in 1875. Born in Scotland, Laura was described as beautiful "with black hair and fair skin." She began her life in Nevada as the respectable wife of a saloonkeeper. For reasons known only to herself, she left her husband, changed her name, and took work at Rose's place. She had only been there six months when she died.[12]

The harridan Rose Benjamin was ruthless. Once, in 1877, she went so far as to file suit against one of her girls who had somehow agreed to give the madam her baby and changed her mind. Another time, a fifteen-year-old identified as Miss Duffy was found working for Rose Benjamin "because her home life was worse than life in a whorehouse." Rose evidently had no problem taking in young women, as evidenced by

NOT SO VIRGINAL VIRGINIA CITY

another teenager, sixteen-year-old Hattie Willis, who was discovered in her brothel.[13] But Rose was quite possibly at her worst when it was discovered that she had lured yet another very young girl into her brothel. The child, on a simple errand to buy some soap for her respectable parents, had been missing for four days. The *Virginia Evening Chronicle* reported that her father finally discovered her whereabouts, went to Rose's brothel, and "demanded admittance." Rose merely slammed the door in his face.

Before long "a crowd of over 100 men," hearing the father's cries, appeared in front of Rose's brothel. As the situation was explained to them, some onlookers began shouting, "Pull down the House!" and "Gut the den!" At last the girl was rescued and later explained that another girl named Frankie Norton invited her in to smoke opium. But she also revealed that she had already been using opium for around seven months. "I smoked in Chinatown and Gold Hill," she told a *Chronicle* reporter. "The places are open every night." When asked how many tokes of the stuff she took each day, the girl responded, "About thirty-five, but sometimes not more than twelve. If I don't smoke I feel sick; I want some now." The reporter also learned that the girl, as well as another thirteen-year-old named Brinton from Gold Hill who was being held captive in Rose Benjamin's brothel, were having sex with men there.[14]

City officials and citizens alike were appalled by what they discovered, but for some reason, Rose Benjamin does not appear to have been held accountable for her actions. Notably however, several fires broke out at her brothel property. One of them was set by a "vindictive former lover." Others were thought to have been set by Rose herself in order to collect insurance money. Curiously, the 1878 Virginia City directory lists her as a waiter at the Nevada Hotel. That same year, the madam finally married George E. Perkins and left Virginia City, no doubt to the relief of not just respectable citizens but also her colleagues in the red-light district.[15]

The 1870 census recorded 109 prostitutes and forty-eight "harlots" in Virginia City. Seven others were "actresses." One whimsical lady told the census taker she worked at a "hotel de refreshment." By 1871, the local married women had grown mighty weary of the soiled doves in their midst. The ladies were suspected of taking matters into their own hands by burning down the red-light district along D Street. A column in Carson City's *Daily State Register* explained that two women in particular were disgusted with their husbands "squandering their money and lavishing their favors on 'the fair but frail'" of D Street. The wives were assumed to be the ones who had caused "the same identical block of buildings" to be "laid in ashes three times in as many months." As the brothels burned, the "general stampede for the street was the most ludicrous scene any man ever looked upon" as a vast variety of men from all walks of life were seen escaping from the flames.[16] Prostitutes left homeless by these events were forced to move into other parts of the city, much to the chagrin of authorities. But fewer people were putting up with the demimonde damsels. In 1874, officials of the Virginia and Truckee Railroad ousted several shady ladies whose quarters were too close to their depot near D and Union Streets.

Efforts to quell the number of prostitutes in Virginia City failed to a great degree. Nevada's 1875 census documented 298 prostitutes and nine madams working in town. It is unknown if the number included seventy-five Chinese prostitutes located in Chinatown. Thirty-eight men were documented as living in brothels or with women in their cribs either as pimps, or perhaps customers. But these too gave way to yet another fire that destroyed the red-light district and much of the city later that year. The fire began in Kate Shea's boardinghouse on A Street after a lamp was accidentally knocked over. The ensuing inferno left folks wandering the streets "with such a look in their faces as men and women wear when they gather around a coffin to look upon one who in life was very dear, but who is gone forever." Most citizens were left homeless.

"We have not seen a business man who is not determined to resume as soon as a tent can be pitched," Virginia City's *Daily Territorial Enterprise* stated optimistically, "and not one who thinks of changing Virginia for another field. Amid what looks as if it ought to be enough to cause universal despair, there seems to be a brave confidence and unflinching determination to overcome the present misfortune."[17]

Virginia City did rebuild, and by 1877 the authorities had once again tired of the antics in the Barbary Coast and its low-end dives and brothels, which one editorial opined "should be removed or suppressed." A particular issue was the close proximity of the high school to the red-light district. Students were forced to walk along the bawdy portion of C Street where "prostitution flaunts its gay colors and there the coarse jest, the vulgar oath and the filthiest of conversation is heard at all hours of the day and night," said one newspaper. "It is time something was done to put a stop to all this, as now carried on in the principal street of our city, along which our girls, just blooming into maidenhood are compelled to pass and repass."[18]

The commentary might have been inspired, at least in part, by the antics of Ellen "Nellie" Sayers. Nellie's place was a bar with two bedrooms in the back at 146½ South C Street. Like the bawdy madam Rose Benjamin, Nellie's scruples were often nonexistent. The *Territorial Enterprise* once called her "the worst specimen of femininity to ever crawl down C Street."[19] In March of 1875, Nellie was involved in a three-way incident between herself, her lover Peter Larkin and Daniel Corcoran, the latter whom operated a similar establishment to Nellie's with his wife. Nellie lived with Larkin, but the man broke off the relationship and went to San Francisco. He soon returned with a "young, good-looking woman" named Susie Brown.

Nellie defiantly opened her own saloon right next door to Larkin's, perhaps as a means to get him back. But she was also having an affair with Corcoran, who was described by the *Gold Hill Evening News* as "a fat, good-natured, ignorant Irishman." The affair upset Larkin to a great degree, as well as Susie Brown, who soon saw that her man still wanted Nellie. Most surprisingly, Susie decided to move in with Nellie. It was the last straw for Larkin, who went into Nellie's one early morning, "heard a voice and went into the bar to check it out." It is there that he discovered Nellie and Corcoran together, and shot the man in the stomach. Corcoran died the next day and Larkin was hanged. Of Nellie, the *Territorial Enterprise* commented that, "a more unattractive female could scarcely exist. Low, ignorant, and drunken, and devoid of all personal charms, who was yet so valuable in the eyes of two men that gave their lives for her."

On April 5, 1877, Nellie Sayers made the papers again. According to the *Territorial Enterprise*, "Warrants were last evening issued on complaints made, and Miss Nellie Sayers and Mrs. Corcoran were arrested by Constable Norton and taken in before judge Moses for keeping disorderly houses." The next day, the paper told more: Mrs. Corcoran had pleaded guilty and was fined a dollar plus court costs. Nellie, however, fought the charge against her and demanded a jury trial. "She doubtless hopes to ring one or more of her 'friends' in on the jury, so as to procure a disagreement, if not an acquittal," surmised the paper. "This city and county have borne very much from this woman, but that does not forfeit her rights to a fair and impartial trial, which she will doubtless have before Judge Moses." The case was indeed "fair and impartial," which is probably why Nellie lost her case. Two months later, the paper reported that "from keeper of a house of common prostitution [Nellie] has descended to still lower depths of infamy, and became proprietress of a den of deeper disgrace, and is acting as procuress, for the frequenters of her place, but little girls, who are there [are] drugged with vile liquors and given over to debauchery." In spite of these charges by the paper, however, the worst the authorities did to Nellie was revoke her liquor license.[20]

The *Territorial Enterprise*'s claim was not without warrant. In June, the newspaper next reported on thirteen-year-old Maghey Gorhey who was drugged by her own mother. The child woke up to find she was being held at Nellie Sayers's place where she was forced to work as a prostitute. The *Enterprise* gave details on Maghey, who was "very small for her age and quite fragile. She says she had not had anything to eat for two days, living constantly on the liquor she had been forced to drink. There is no doubt she is telling the truth." Susie Brown, Peter Larkin's girlfriend from San Francisco, was still there too. It was revealed she herself was only fifteen-years-old, making her only thirteen when she first went to work at Nellie's. Armed with this information, the authorities of Virginia City followed through with their plan to abolish the brothels of the town. Some of the places, however, later reopened.[21]

It was not always a madam or a procurer who was responsible for luring or kidnapping young girls, but corrupt officials. In June of 1881 Madam Mercedes Rickey, who was "well-known in Virginia City," appeared in Carson City in search of her daughter. The girl, Emma, was thirteen years old. She apparently had disappeared, and what followed was one of the most crooked schemes, sprinkled with a dose of social reform, that the likes of Virginia City had ever seen. It all began when Carson City's *Morning Appeal* claimed on June 3 that Mercedes had told them Emma had disappeared some years previous and was presumed kidnapped. The madam had heard the girl had surfaced at the Orphan's Asylum in Carson City. The story took a darker turn when the *Appeal* revealed that Emma was not really the immoral woman's child, and that she had been "horribly treated" by Mercedes.

The paper's story that Mercedes had worked as a madam in Virginia City for some two decades was probably true, also that she was once worth around $200,000. She now owned only a row of crib houses on South B Street. Emma's real mother had died, the *Appeal* claimed, and her father had sold the child to Mercedes for twenty-five dollars.

Mercedes had spent a small fortune on Emma's education; the teen spoke five languages fluently and had been supporting her adopted mother by teaching French and German. But the child had run away on her own volition, and when she was returned to Virginia City she asked the court to protect her from Mercedes. "I am as yet not quite sure of her identity, or my own," Emma allegedly stated. "If the stories are substantial, I shall leave her permanently."

The *Appeal* further presented the girl as a victim of Mercedes, who "has had her in bondage and has compelled her to go from home on begging excursions and commanding her to bring home certain sums of money." Failure to do so resulted in Emma being "beaten in the most cruel manner, being bruised so that she could not get out of bed for as much as a week at a time." The beatings had left the girl crippled. That wasn't all: Emma also allegedly said she had been made to "sit on men's laps and to take liberties with their persons." The authorities, the paper said, had taken Emma to the safety of the asylum as her lunatic "mother" offered a reward to anyone willing to return the girl, and also threatened to poison herself. The following day, the *Appeal* reported further that Mercedes was insisting that Emma was her natural child, also that both mother and daughter were due to inherit a portion of a million-dollar estate in Cuba.[22]

Eyebrows certainly were raised at this last bit of news. They raised even more when Emma Rickey herself granted an interview to the *Appeal* that apparently revealed the amazing truth of the whole matter. While at the asylum, she said, Constable Ferguson and one George Brown had suddenly appeared and spirited her away. She was locked in a room, and her earrings and a finger ring were taken from her before she was deposited in the water closet of a train. The men told her that "a Spanish woman was coming after me to throw vitriol [a sulfuric acid] in my face." The "Spanish woman" presumably was Mercedes whom, Emma assured the paper, never abused the girl. "She sometimes slapped me on the hand when I deserved it," Emma said. "I was never whipped by her as badly as I have been whipped here [at the asylum]." The child also said she had attempted to send a letter to Mercedes, but was not permitted to do so. Mercedes, meanwhile, showed the *Appeal* reporter a letter verifying that both she and Emma were each due to inherit $25,000, and that the American Counsel in San Francisco only needed a copy of Mercedes's marriage certificate to a Mr. Rickaby [*sic*] as proof of her identity.[23] Mother and daughter were presumably reunited, and nobody seems to have been held responsible for what happened to Emma.

It would be nice to believe that the likes of Rose Benjamin and Nellie Sayers and corrupt policemen settled down some when a new ordinance in 1878 declared all brothels must operate only on D Street, but the law remained largely ignored. Another ordinance prohibited women from advertising their wares on the streets, as well as from their doorways or windows. Calling out to men passing by also was forbidden. Officer Jim Breen initially carried out the new rules with enthusiasm, but the good time girls eventually resumed their old tricks—such as when a "Madam Rachel" lifted thirty stock shares for the Mexican Mine from a mill laborer. And there was Black Hills Kate, who refused to leave town after being arrested for stealing several times and was subsequently jailed for one hundred days.[24]

Beginning in 1879, Virginia City's population of twenty thousand people began downsizing. In a letter from Ernest Marks in Gold Hill to prostitute Rosa May in Carson City, he mentioned how none of the girls on the line were doing well financially, nor were the men who paid them for sex. The situation was frustrating for all and resulted in more than the usual bar fights and an upswing in crimes. Yet all three bordello districts were still alive and kicking as of 1880. In addition, "badly built, cheaply run houses in Chinatown" still offered gambling, liquor, opium, and prostitutes. But the Barbary Coast remained Virginia City's biggest problem. There were only half a dozen or so saloons, but the district remained "the scene of gross profanity, lewd exhibitions, beatings, and murders."[25]

The 1880 census reveals more about the good time girls of Virginia City. On South D Street were four parlor houses, two with five girls and two with four girls. Prostitutes in all three of the districts included women working on their own and ranging in age from twenty-two-year-old Annie Higgins to thirty-nine-year-old Gavriel Valentine. Mary Doyle resided in the home of saloonkeeper Mollie Fralene. On E and F Streets were Mary Durant and Romez Galino, respectively, each of whom had children living with them. Other women lived in otherwise "respectable" lodging houses. Three women—Jenny Butler, Mary Sheehan, and Mary Vorhan—resided in one of them alongside gamblers and other people with more legitimate vocations. Most interesting is Alice Bryson, who appeared in the census on June 14 as a seamstress at 44 South F Street. Two weeks later, on June 22 or 23, the census taker inexplicably recorded her again, at the same address. This time, however, she was noted as renting a room at the lodging house of William Gaines and working as a prostitute. Also, nine men were recorded as living with prostitutes. Only the prostitutes of Chinatown were down in number.

Most of the parlor house ladies made ten to twenty dollars per customer at the time, paying 25 to 50 percent of their earnings to their madams for their room, meals, liquor, and laundry, as well as protection from both pimps and the long arm of the law. The districts continued operating in this fashion for seven more years before the wicked vixens of the Barbary Coast were finally chased out of the district. At hand was how valuable real estate in the district had become. That, combined with a shortage of usable property, led city officials to believe that cleaning up the Barbary Coast once and for all would allow for reuse of the property there for incoming, respectable investors. What nobody could know was that by 1893, Virginia City would downsize considerably as the local mines played out. Even the *Territorial Enterprise* newspaper ceased printing as people moved away. Still, it would not be until 1947 that prostitution would officially be outlawed in Virginia City. The industry would see a reprise in 1970, but the legal brothels around Virginia City today are located well out of the city limits.

CHAPTER 5

———•●•———

Cad Thompson, the "Good Sport"

Cad Thompson is an excellent example of a woman who entered the prostitution industry with success in business on her mind. She does not appear to have ever worked as a prostitute herself, preferring instead to run her brothels with a firm hand and lots of good sense. She did, occasionally, suffer arrests for "drunken and disorderly conduct," or "noise complaints" and opted for spending time in jail versus paying fines for such behavior.[1] At least one source claims that Cad's girls were treated well and there are no known records of suicides at her brothels. She even remained friends and corresponded with one prostitute, Jenny, for many years. Aside from the shooting of her paramour in 1867, the only other known violent incident at Cad's place was when Hugh Kerrin of Engine Company No.1 "accidentally" shot Zink Barnes in the leg at some unknown date.[2] Indeed, Cad was in business to make money, and was quite successful at just about everything she put her hand to.

Cad's beginnings are quite mysterious. Newspapers verify that her real name was Sarah Hagen or Hagan, and most historians agree she was born in Ireland in 1827. Another newspaper reported her name as Sarah Higgins. Whoever she really was, the woman was apparently a widow when she first arrived in Virginia City with her young son, Henry, in tow.

Prostitutes wishing to attend shows at Piper's Opera House were usually required to use a side door. Courtesy Library of Congress Prints and Photographs Division

There had been other children, and men, in her life: two children, bearing the last name of Mitler or Miller, had died in infancy. A third child, like Henry, had the last name of Thompson and survived to adulthood, but had died by 1897.

Upon her arrival in Virginia City, the lady—who would now forever call herself Cad Thompson—acquired or possibly built her first brothel on D Street near Sutton Avenue. The parlor house consisted of two stories with bedrooms for prostitutes upstairs, although one source states that Cad's employees were actually lodged in the basement. The parlor house was elegantly furnished with all the finest goods from Paris and San Francisco. The first time Cad made the local newspapers was in 1863. An article in the *Gold Hill Daily News* on August 9 reported that one John Dalton had been fined one hundred dollars for assaulting the madam at her bordello and threatening her life. But it definitely took two to tangle: Cad was arrested too, for disturbing the peace. And she and Dalton would carry on their stormy relationship for some years.

At least Cad had her fabulous parlor house, and when Virginia City decided to establish an official red-light district to keep ladies like Cad in check, the madam's place somehow fell just outside of the district but was allowed to remain in operation. Another advantage was that Cad's place, along with a handful of other women's brothels on D Street, backed up to Virginia City's saloons. Even so there are subtle signs indicating Cad was not so fond of Virginia City, mostly because the lady often took excursions away from town. The first time this happened was in 1865, via a Wells Fargo & Company stagecoach. Cad might have been on recruiting missions for fresh girls, but where she went and who she came back with remains unknown.

Cad may have been shrewd in business but she was, on at least one occasion, humiliated before the whole town. The Virginia City *Territorial Enterprise* of November 20, 1866, reported that a "number of 'rowdies' at 4 o'clock in the morning took Virginia Engine Number 1 from the engine company's house to the corner of D Street and Sutton Avenue. There 'they' took position at the cistern in front of the house of prostitution kept by Cad Thompson, got the hose all ready, set fire to a couple of barrels of straw on E Street which they had prepared for the occasion, and then causing the fire alarm bell to tap a few times, they at once smashed in the front windows of the house in question and commenced playing away with the engine as if for dear life, completely flooding the interior of the house with water." The newspaper "estimated the amount of damage by the water to be between one and two thousand dollars." Fortunately, only the furniture nearest the broken windows was "some what damaged," and Cad's fancy Dale and Co. piano in the parlor was protected "by an India rubber cover." The basement, where Cad's girls stayed, fared much worse. "There the plastering was all wet and will probably fall off," the paper said. "The bedding and furniture were also badly saturated with water pouring through the cracks of the floor."[3]

In the early morning scuffle, minor injuries were suffered by the piano player and others. Alfred Doten of the *Gold Hill News* also reported on the matter. "Some fellows took No. 1's engine about 4 o'clock this morning," read the article, "and washed out old Cad Thompson's whore house—gave her hell—created quite a consternation among the law and order portion of the community—not the end of it yet—We shall have to see who rules the city now, the rough or the decent men."[4] Amazingly, nobody was arrested even though it was known who the perpetrators were. The biggest concern seemed to be over the temporary theft of the fire wagon, which Doten lectured must never happen again.

Although Cad apparently expressed good humor about the situation (earning her the nickname the "Good Sport"), Doten did not. The newspaperman, who actually worked at several newspapers in the Virginia City area over time, was quite fond of the red-light ladies. When he wasn't writing articles about goings-on in the red-light district, he was privately penning more intimate details about the red-light ladies in his personal journal. Doten wrote frequently of his travels through the demimonde, visiting Cad's Brick House, as well as Bell Neal's place and Julia Bulette's crib. At Jennie Tyler's Bow Windows, he once entrusted the care of his dog, Kyzer, to a gal named Blanche. When "Little Ida" Vernon was found dead by the man in her bed of an apparent opium overdose, Doten wrote, "Rest in Peace Ida—she was her worst enemy."[5] Doten also wrote of observing a "big whore ball" in full swing at the Great Republic Saloon. And, he remembered a prostitute named Gussie who fell out of a theater box at the Music Hall and broke "a big hole in the floor with [her] head."[6] Doten's observations survive as some of the only firsthand accounts of Virginia City and its naughty occupants, including Cad Thompson.

The year after her parlor house was vandalized, Cad made the newspapers once more. On or about July 6, 1867, the madam was again fighting with John Dalton. Cad's place was now identified as being on D Street near Mill Street, a block from Sutton Avenue—indicating she likely had acquired a second brothel. Someone reported a gun had been fired, and a man was shot in the leg. Deputy Constable J.A. Hawkins and his "Kentuck" (a slang word for a longrifle) arrived at the house to see what the fuss was about. Both Cad and her man came to the door, but "opposed the entrance of the officer, using profane and abusive language." When Dalton pointed a derringer at Hawkins, the policeman left and returned with another officer named Harmon. This time the door opened and Dalton came out, still holding his derringer. When he raised it, Hawkins shot him with a revolver. Dalton staggered around muttering, "Oh God! I've come to an untimely end!" before sitting on the doorstep with the assistance of Harmon, and dying on the spot. One of Cad's girls, Mary O'Neill, would later testify she heard Dalton say, "You are wrong," just after being shot. In contrast another witness, Thomas Murphy, was nearby and said he heard Dalton admit he had "done wrong." As for Cad, the distraught madam claimed her man was murdered, that he didn't have a pistol, and that Dalton's enemies had schemed to do him in.[7]

With Dalton buried, Cad turned back to her business. She had to, for in 1868 the Virginia and Truckee Railroad was being extended from Carson City to Virginia City, and its new depot was located close to the Brick House. Possibly on a mission to find fresh employees, Cad hopped another stagecoach out of town. It was the first of many trips within a year's time, as the *Gold Hill Daily News* recorded her comings and goings twice more in 1869. The excursions might also have been an effort to drum up business along the road, for in 1870 Cad and her girls bore mention in the *Elko Independent.* "The 'Bloody British Blonds' [sic] passed east on Sunday last," noted the newspaper, which was likely referring to actress Lydia Thompson's traveling troupe of the same name. "They failed to set the Bay of San Francisco on fire." But the same article also reported that the "The Cad Thompson troupe has been more successful and is now performing at Virginia [City]."[8] More evidence of Cad's absence from Virginia City comes from post office records, which frequently named her on lists of "uncalled letters."[9] The madam must have found it refreshing when the Virginia and Truckee Railroad at last connected to the Central Pacific Railroad in 1872, bringing more single and lonely men from farther away.

From all indications, things were good for Cad until 1875. In February, however, she was sued by Andrew Allison over a house in the red-light district, and supposedly lost her case. Or did she? The *Virginia Evening Chronicle*, which said Cad's real name was Sarah Higgins, reported that a witness named Davis went to Allison's attorney, W.E.F. Deal, and told him something relative to the case that made Cad look bad. On the stand, however, Davis told an entirely different tale that benefited Cad. When asked by the attorney why his story differed, Davis explained that "what he had stated outside of court was false, and that he had been bribed by Allison to give such testimony." The *Chronicle* wasn't buying that explanation, however, and suspected that Cad had convinced Davis to retract his story.[10] The true outcome of the case remains unknown, but Cad and five of her girls, plus a Chinese servant, were identified in the 1875 state census. What none of them knew was that on October 26, Cad's Brick House would burn along with much of the red-light district.

One sidebar to the story of the fire includes an unsubstantiated tale that when Cad tried to throw out one of her girls, Mary Livingston, the woman refused to go. Cad beat Mary to a pulp before tossing her out anyway. Mary pressed charges, and gave such a convincing story to the all-male jury that the men set fire to the Brick House. Whether this occurred at all is largely up for speculation, and if it did, it was not in 1875 when Virginia City's fire swept through and destroyed much of the town after a lamp was overturned in a respectable boardinghouse. Cad and her girls were left homeless. What the madam did is hard to say, since the next time she was documented was in 1877, when she moved to the former brothel of Rose Benjamin at 15 South D Street. This house also was two stories high, and included a kitchen for making meals for the girls before they began their evening's work. Most sources point out that the new parlor house also was called Brick House.

Cad's new Brick House was finer than ever, but the madam was in for more heartbreak. In 1878 her son Henry, who had lived with her off and on, committed suicide on August 16. "Henry Thompson, son of Cad Thompson, keeper of a bagnio, shot himself in his mother's house this afternoon," reported the *Sacramento Daily Union* in California. "He will doubtless die."[11] Henry managed to cling to life for a few days; on August 24 the *Pioche Weekly Record* mentioned that "Henry Thompson, the young man who made an attempt to commit suicide day before yesterday by shooting himself in the left breast, was still alive last night. It is, as yet, impossible to say what may be the result of the wound, it being through the upper lung."[12] But young Henry did die, although his burial location is a mystery.

Sadly, there is no record of exactly why Henry Thompson shot himself, nor Cad's reaction. Surely the madam mourned over the loss of her son. Equally puzzling is this snippet from the *Daily Alta California* of October 20, 1878: "H. H. Toland has sued Sarah Hagan, Mary H. Thompson and Henry H. Thompson, in the Twelfth District Court, for an accounting in the matter of the trust of Henry Thompson, and asks to be relieved from his duties as a Trustee. The defendants were the beneficiaries under the trust, and the plaintiff asks the Court to discharge him and appoint some one else, and he asks to be awarded compensation for his services."[13] Interestingly, H.H. Tolland was a most prominent San Francisco physician with the University of California. Why was he put in charge of Henry Thompson's trust? Did he suspect wrongdoing with the trust? And, who were the other people named in the suit? These and other questions remain unanswered.

By 1879 Cad was in charge of another brothel, this one at 18 South D Street across from her other parlor house. The famed harlot Rosa May was working for her as of January, and was apparently left in charge of the house when Cad took another trip. In March, Cad was in San Francisco when she wrote to Rosa. "Friend Rosa," the letter began, "I received your letter and was glad to hear from you. I am still crippled up with rheumatism and have not been out to see a woman Lena Beck and that [*sic*] Emma and Lily from Carson called to see me last night . . . The weather has been rainy, cold, and disagreeable ever since I came down." Once done with the pleasantries, Cad got down to business. "Tell the Spanish woman to keep her house I don't want it," she told Rosa, "for if there is nothing in Virginia I will move my furniture down here as everyone seems to live in this place. I will try and get some women next week and run the house one trip and tell George that he need not mind whitening it until I see what we are going to do." Cad was obviously fed up with Virginia City. "I am sorry you have been sick," she wrote, "I don't wonder, that damp, dreary house would make any body sick, it makes me sick to think that I have got to go back to it." Notably, Cad ended her letter with "Give Harry's and my kind regards to George . . . yours respectfully. Mrs. C. Thompson."[14] Who was Harry? Was he the same Harry who was mentioned in Henry's trust suit? His identity, unfortunately, remains a mystery.

Cad may have wanted to remain in San Francisco, but she did not get her wish. By June she was back in Virginia City, where the 1880 census found her (as Caroline Thompson) at 18 South D Street. True to form, her occupation was documented as running a "house of prostitutes." Two young women, Annie Burnett and Kittie Raymond, worked for her. Also in the house was a Chinese servant, Ah Fung, and also Charles Young, a boarder whose occupation was listed as "lover." Notably, Rosa May had left Cad's employ.

Ever the gypsy, Cad left town again in 1881. But she was likely back in 1882 when J.C. Hampton told the town's Board of Equalization that it was he who paid taxes on a piece of property on lot 5, block 60—which "was in Miss Cad Thompson's name." Hampton requested a reduction in property value, which was $300, probably because it was a brothel. The Board reduced the value to $225.[15] Then, in 1883, Cad was once again in court when Bertha Neumann filed a lawsuit against her. Bertha accused Cad of taking her "trunk, books, papers and other articles," which the madam might have done because Bertha owed her money.[16]

Her business matters aside, Cad's ire was really raised in 1885 when someone tried to kidnap her dog. "While sitting at the second-story window of her establishment on D Street last Saturday evening, the widow Thompson observed a young man whom she recognized as the 'Barbary Coast masher,' holding a rope behind him and trying to coax her dog away, which was sitting in the doorway," reported the *Virginia Chronicle*. "Arming herself with a large bucketful of slops, she waited until the masher grasped the dog by the collar, when she emptied the entire contents of the bucket on his person. Adonis let go of his hold and lit out in the direction of the north pole, closely followed by the affronted dog and at least half a dozen fleet footed female denizens of the Thompson 'mayzong,' armed with mops and stove pokers."[17]

It was one thing to mess with Cad; it was quite another to mess with the madam's dog, and the incident might have even served as a breaking point for her. From that time on, news of the madam grew more and more scant, perhaps because she retired. Newspapers noted she had been on a trip when she returned to Virginia City via the Virginia and Truckee Railroad in 1889 and 1890. In February 1892 she left town again, but was back by May when she sold one of her D Street brothels to Jacob Tucker for a lousy twenty dollars. On March 23, 1897, the Carson City *Morning Appeal* reported that "Cad Thompson, who kept a notorious establishment on D Street in Virginia City for over a quarter of a century, died yesterday morning." In the tradition of the Old West, the newspaper had kind things to say about Cad. "Although a woman of the town, the [Virginia City] *Chronicle* says she possessed many sterling qualities. She was kind and charitable and her word was as good as gold in all of her dealings."[18] Other newspapers verified that the cause of death was "rheumatism of the heart."[19] Cad would likely be happy to know that her obituary was published as far away as Idaho and Reno. Yet where she lies buried remains unknown.

Cad left no living relatives. On April 21, the *Daily Territorial Enterprise* announced that the "estate of Sarah Hagan (Cad Thompson), deceased," consisting of her personal property, would be sold "by private or public sale."[20] By May Cad's former brothel at D Street and Sutton was owned by the California Bank when thugs broke into the place. A watchman, James Mahoney, lived on the premises and was in his room getting dressed to go to a dance when he heard someone in the house. Mahoney summoned the police, but by the time they arrived the intruders had left. It was discovered they had started taking up a carpet in one of the downstairs rooms when Mahoney's movements upstairs apparently startled them. A few months later, in August, the property was sold to a Mr. Wills, who said he planned to tear the house down and use the materials to build his own private home on his ranch near Glendale. Whether Wills got his wish is unknown, but about all that is left of Cad Thompson in Virginia City today are some fond, and fun, memories.

CHAPTER 6

————•◦•————

The Murder of Julia "Jule" Bulette

As happens when a western character becomes legend, stories of Julia Bulette and her tragic murder have grown to epic proportions. Writers have romanticized the lady with wishful thinking to the point of elevating her status to that of an elegant, gracious, and rich courtesan. She has been described as "young, beautiful, wealthy and adept at entertaining gentlemen with witty conversation in luxurious surroundings."[1] She has also been described as "a most beautiful creature, tall and willowy yet eminently seducible."[2] No matter how beautiful she was, in truth Julia was just another of Virginia City's red-light ladies who met with a bad end. Still, most historians agree she was well liked for many reasons, and citizens of Virginia City opined that her untimely death was one of the worst and saddest crimes the community ever saw.

Largely due to so many who have written about her, Julia's early life is a muddle of fact and fiction. Although her birth has been disputed by modern-day historians, an 1868 source verified she was born circa 1832 in London, England.[3] Writer Hillyer Best alleged she had some Black heritage in her blood, "about one eighth."[4] Yet another writer claimed that Julia was "an attractive woman of French extraction."[5] Any or all of these suppositions might be correct, but can hardly be verified by the only known image of the lady.

When Julia came to America is unknown, but she appears to have traveled to California during the gold rush and lived in various boomtowns for about a decade before relocating to Virginia City. In California she may have worked in San Francisco, as well as the mining town of Weaverville. That's one story about her beginnings, anyway. Another story is that by the 1860s Julia and her brother had immigrated to New Orleans, where Julia married a man named Smith from whom she later separated. In 1868, it was believed she did have an uncle who lived in New Orleans.

Wherever she had been, everyone agrees that Julia first appeared in Virginia City during 1863. She may have first worked in a higher-end crib, and when some new cottages were built at the corner of Union and D Streets, Julia rented one of them. Although it was sometimes known as "Julia's Palace" the brothel, which also constituted her home, was a simple, tidy two-room cottage. Her services were equally simple, and her clients often spent the night with her. Before long everybody in Virginia City knew Julia, and everybody liked her. She was a familiar figure around town and was fond of attending Piper's Opera House on a regular basis.[6] In time, she would become a special favorite of the boys at Virginia City's fire department.

Personalized services were not something every brothel client experienced, since most prostitutes needed to serve as many men as possible to make good money. Not so with Julia, who made her customers feel almost as though they were visiting a good friend for dinner and libations, with Julia for dessert. One source surmises that Julia often "overspent her resources by emulating the elegance of contemporary Cad Thompson's 'Brick House'."[7] And although her cottage was modestly furnished, at the time of her death it did manage to hold Julia's double mahogany bedstead, as well as a double spring mattress, a double hair mattress, and a "Double Decker" mattress. Julia's own bed was covered with a white bedspread and two feather pillows. Her bedroom also contained a mahogany washstand, a small "box stove," a chamber pot, and at least one of three trunks she owned.

Indeed, Julia's extensive furnishings also included a "red saloon table" and a parlor table, seven chairs made from black walnut or maple, two rocking chairs, a sofa, a large iron stove, two large parlor lamps, three spittoons, and two items identified as a "Mahogany whatnot" and "Mahogany Burcaw with glass." It is difficult to imagine how she managed to fit all of these items into two rooms, but manage she did. Fancy gilt cornices covered three of her windows, which were adorned with white lace curtains and window shades. On the floors were three Brussels carpets, an ingrain carpet, and a rug at the door. Only one gilt frame picture adorned the walls. Julia's household items included her feather duster, two washboards, and a bucket and mop. For the entertainment of her customers, there was a lot of assorted tinware and glassware, as well as fourteen towels.[8]

What did Julia charge for her services? Historians have followed the lead of author Hillyer Best, who claimed Julia charged upward of a thousand dollars a night—an exorbitant amount that even the richest miner surely could not pay. Best might have been figuring in the gifts Julia received from her admirers: "sables and bars of gold bullion, diamond trinkets and ruby eardrops."[9] Her only documented liquor bill averaged around thirty dollars per month and contained mostly wine, whiskey and brandy. Julia perhaps advertised her wares by taking drives in her "laquered carriage, the panel of which was decorated with a heraldic emblem."[10] The crest was described by Best as "an escutcheon of four aces, crowned by a lion couchant."

Of all of the things said about Julia's character, the truest is that she was indeed well liked. Among her friends was newspaper editor Alf Doten, who wrote about her in his journal. She was well known in social circles, attending local theaters but also the balls held by others of her kind. Her monetary donations to the town were many: She contributed heavily to funds for miners' widows, "made anonymous gifts to the poor, nursed miners ill from arsenic poisoning," and even made a donation to President Abraham Lincoln's Sanitation Commission.[11]

In many other ways Julia was a typical frontier woman, the exception being that she sold sex for a living. Locals grew accustomed to seeing her tending her roses, geraniums, and other flowers she had delivered to her by stage. Her earnings allowed for the hiring of a maid to clean her house, as well as a Chinese man to tend her fire. Even her manner of dress was modest; Julia preferred outfits resembling upper-class, respectable women. Notably she was quite the clothes horse, somehow squeezing dozens of ensembles into the trunks in her home. Julia's personal jewelry collection also was apparently quite extensive. In 1864, when she attended a show at Maguire's Opera House, it did not go unnoticed that she was "bedecked with diamonds and rubies around her neck."[12]

It is true that Virginia City's Engine Company No. 1 elected Julia as an honorary firefighter. Most historians believe the honor came "in return for numerous favors and munificent gifts bestowed by her upon the company, her taking always the greatest imaginable interest in all matters connected with the Fire Department, even on many occasions at fires working the brakes to the engine."[13] The honor might have been spurred by Julia's alleged love for Fire Chief Tom Peasley, who, according to writer George Lyman, was "a perfectly coordinated specimen of manly strength and grace. His profile would have honored a Roman coin." The couple often attended the theater together.[14] Peasley also owned the Sazarac Saloon and was quite the roustabout, bearing mention in the local papers for his involvement in various shootings and shoot-outs. Not surprisingly, Peasley was killed in 1866 during such an affray with one of his enemies, Martin Barnhart. There unfortunately is no record of how Peasley's death affected Julia. With or without Peasley's influence, the Virginia City fire department regarded Julia as their guardian angel. One year the firemen even honored her as Queen of the

Julia Bulette poses proudly with the fire hat given to her by Engine Company No. 1.
Wikimedia Commons

Independence Day Parade. She was given a fireman's hat, presented with a fire trumpet full of roses, and even rode in Engine Company No. 1's truck. An alternate version of this story says Julia was given a badge and even a uniform, which she donned to march in parades alongside the firemen. Either way, it was common knowledge that Julia willingly jumped on the fire wagon as it rushed to a fire, where she would "man the pumps and lend a hand on the brakes."[15] She was so proud of her honorary status that she had the only known photograph of herself taken with the fireman's hat.

Other heroics attributed to Julia included remaining in Virginia City during an Indian scare while other women fled to Carson City, cheering on a force of 750 men as they marched out of town to fight the Natives on Pinnacle Mountain, and cheering them again when they returned. She nursed the sick and helped out during outbreaks of smallpox, influenza, and cholera, sometimes nursing men back to health in her own home. In honor of all she did, the Mascot Mine was renamed for Julia after it caught on fire. The firemen joked that the flames, like Julia, "were too hot to handle."[16] In time, respectable women arriving in town looked down on the prostitute Julia Bulette. But her clientele changed little, and Julia continued receiving lavish gifts from many of them.

The last three months of Julia's life are interesting. She had been ill and had stayed with her friend, prostitute Annie Smith, in Carson City for a time. But she appears to have been in Virginia City during November and December 1866, when she saw Dr. C.C. Green, the resident physician for local prostitutes, several times. Notably, someone named Gertrude (likely Julia's friend Gertrude Holmes) paid a portion of Julia's doctor bill the day after Christmas. Gertrude Holmes was indeed a good friend, sharing meals with Julia in her own kitchen. The two also exchanged gifts, according to Gertrude, and were practically like sisters. Julia maintained a level of trust with Gertrude and also Annie Smith, who sent along a piece of gold jewelry to be repaired when Julia returned to Virginia City in late January of 1867. She also supported other women in her profession, willingly testifying against a man who had severely beaten another prostitute, Lizzie Hayes. Julia's testimony helped convict the perpetrator.

On January 19, the night before her death, Julia went to Piper's Opera House. Ironically, the two shows she wanted to see were "Willful Murder" and "The Robbers." Upon approaching the front door, however, Julia was denied entrance—quite possibly for the first time. She was instructed instead to use the side door with the other prostitutes and to sit in the balcony section designated specifically for red-light ladies. Offended, Julia left the theater and went home, stopping at Gertrude's place for a visit. She left around 11:30 p.m., telling Gertrude that she was expecting a client at midnight who would be staying the night. Julia next walked two doors down to her own cottage. Gertrude would later testify that Julia "did not tell me the name of the man who was to sleep with her; said he was a friend; a friend is generally spoken of among us in that way."[17]

It was never ascertained whether Julia received her expected visitor, but at five o'clock on the morning of January 20, a newspaper boy passed by Julia's house and heard a woman scream. Investigators later agreed that the boy likely heard Julia as she grappled with her killer. Later that morning, Julia's Chinese servant came to light her fire. The man later testified he saw her lying in bed, supposed she was sleeping, and left her be. Later that morning, around eleven o'clock, Gertrude Holmes knocked on Julia's front door, which was locked. Nobody answered. Going around back, Gertrude found Julia's back door open. Calling out again and receiving no answer, Gertrude went inside. Calling out three more times, Gertrude finally made her way to Julia's bedroom.

The scene was horrifying. Gertrude would later testify that Julia was lying naked in her bed, her discarded dress on the floor next to it. The sheets next to her were smooth, seeming to indicate that her midnight visitor had not spent the night. A pillow was over her face, and when Gertrude lifted it she saw the bed was soaked in blood. The woman panicked, began screaming, and fled. Soon, a crowd was gathering at Julia's, but it was J.R. Kaneen who next went in to view the body. According to him, Julia's body was "cold and stiff." A bloody stick of cedar lay next to the bed, and pieces of it were in Julia's bloodied hair. Kaneen also testified he saw "bruises and finger nail lacerations on her throat."[18]

The *Territorial Enterprise* gave more grisly details: Julia's head was saturated with blood, her hands were scratched, and there were two wounds on her forehead. "The bloody scalp wounds, it was deduced, came from an unsuccessful attempt to beat her brains in with a stick. The hand scratches were believed to be the result of Julia's attempts to fend off the murderer. The forehead wounds came from the cock of a pistol. Slowly and dreadfully, Julia Bulette had died, finally throttled to extinction by once friendly hands."[19] An autopsy, performed by Doctors Bronson and Gaston, concluded that the blows to Julia's head were not enough to kill her; rather, she had been strangled to death.

Julia's cottage also had been ransacked. The missing items were identified as "a set of furs worth $400, two gold watches and chains, several costly dresses, gold sleeve buttons, gold crosses, a long gold guard chain with miniatures attached and many other valuable articles of jewelry—the murderer had even torn the ear-rings from the ears of his victim."[20] The discovery sent chills through the townspeople, and fear through Virginia City's red-light ladies. One reporter called the murder the "most cruel, outrageous and revolting murder ever committed in this city."[21]

Julia's body was prepared for her funeral the same day. The services took place at the firehouse. Her mahogany casket was fine with silver handles, a gift of her admirers, and one source says the coffin featured glass panels and was pulled in a hearse by black horses with "nodding black plumed heads." On top of the coffin was an engraved plate, which was covered with a shroud bearing a flower wreath. After the services, the funeral procession was hampered by a horrific storm although dozens weathered the snowy conditions to take part.[22] The procession consisted of eighteen carriages filled with friends, as well as upward of sixty members of the fire department who marched along in full uniform as the Metropolitan Brass Band, or the Nevada militia (or perhaps both), played. The band stopped short of the road to the cemetery to allow the procession to go on ahead for another one and a half miles to Flowery Cemetery, the graveyard designated for outcasts like Julia that was located east of town. Reverend William Martin presided over her services. Afterward, the procession marched back to town as the band struck up "The Girl I left Behind Me."

Most interesting was that Julia's will had assigned not Gertrude Holmes, but prostitute Mary Jane Minirie as executor of her estate. Her probate papers clearly show that she was not as wealthy as legend claims, and that she didn't even have enough money to cover the debts she owed. One of her bills, from liquor dealer Thomas Taylor & Co., was for sales from October 16, 1866, to January 11, 1867. The extensive list of purchases included two dozen pints of ale, two bottles of port wine, champagne, a bottle of bourbon, a gallon of whiskey, a bottle plus a gallon of Suzerac brandy, a bottle of Jamaican rum, and two bottles of Claret wine.

She may have had little money, but it is true that Julia's wardrobe and jewelry collection was quite extensive. The most reliable list of her belongings comes from writer Alexandra Simmons-Rogers, who found notice of Julia's estate sale in Virginia City's *Territorial Enterprise* newspaper on March 17: "One blue plaid silk Dress; 1 red meire antique Dress and Body; 1 black silk Dress; 1 purple Dress; 1 silk Cape, trimmed with fur; 1 blue flannel shirt; 1 Silver Cup marked J.C.B.; 1 pair red silk stockings; 3 Chemises; 1 white silk Cord; 4 handkerchiefs; 1 pair of Gloves; 1 brown silk necktie; 1 fur Cape; 1 Fur cap; 1 fur collar;

1 fur Muff; 3 fur Muffs; 1 purple Hood; 1 Portmonnaie; 1 Gold Hunting Watch; gold Chain and Charms; 1 Watch Case; 1 jet-set Breastpin, Earrings, and Cross; 1 Silver Brick, marked Julia." Other newspaper articles listed more: "A diamond pin; a masonic emblem; coral earrings; twenty shirtwaists; fifteen jackets; eight dresses not described in the estate sale notice, among them a brown silk dress that sold at auction for $37.50; a red wool cloak and four other cloaks; two riding habits, one with a black velvet coat; a cashmere shawl; a small diamond ring; a matched pair of gold bracelets; and a locket and chain."[23] Author George Williams III found even more: thirteen pairs of "drawers," a "small dressing case with glass," opera glasses, a hair "dagger," a coral necklace, a gold buckle and belt, several more dresses, skirts and blouses, a brown wrapper, a gray Merino suit, numerous cloaks, coats and jackets, a parasol, and several pieces of lingerie—but only one pair of shoes and one pair of slippers.[24]

Julia's obituary is indicative of how the people of Virginia City felt about her. The *Territorial Enterprise* called her "fair but frail . . . being of a very kind heart, liberal, benevolent, and charitable disposition—few of her class had more true friends." The newspaper further lamented that "true she was a woman of easy virtue, yet hundreds in this city have had cause to bless her name for her many acts of kindness and charity. That woman probably had more real, warm friends in this community than any other."[25] There is little doubt it was true.

As people mourned the loss of their beloved harlot, authorities looked for Julia's killer. But it was not a law officer who found him. On May 2, Virginia City prostitute Martha Camp identified a French immigrant named Jean Marie A. Villain, aka John Millian, as the man she saw sneaking around on the floor of her room in the dead of night. Police Chief Edwards investigated, and finally located Millian's trunk, which had been stashed behind a local bakery across from Julia's house. Inside were several items: a set of enameled buttons, the silver brick with Julia's name engraved on it, a gold ring, a gold watch, a pair of red silk stockings, a breakfast cape trimmed with white down, a black silk dress, and the silver cup monogrammed "J.C.B." They also found the gold piece of jewelry Annie Smith had given Julia to be repaired.

Millian was duly arrested on May 25. The man spoke limited English, but was regarded by his fellow countrymen as a blowhard. He had worked at a Mr. Hall's laundry business in Geiger Gulch, and it was believed that he had done laundry for Julia. When Edwards confronted Millian about finding Julia's belongings in his trunk, the man initially confessed and asked the officer to kill him. He also said he wanted to be hanged immediately. Later, however, Millian recanted his confession. In an all-new account on April 23, 1868, told to his attorney Charles E. Long, Millian said that on January 19, he was passing by the International Hotel when two men identified as Jim Dillon and Douglass called him over and asked him "to help us do a little job tonight: there is money in it." Millian agreed and the men told him of their plan to rob Julia Bulette. "Now, you go down and go to bed with her and we will be there," Douglass told Dillon.

After Dillon walked off toward Julia's place, Douglass and Millian visited numerous brothels. Finally, Douglass led the way to Julia's, picked a lock, "and entered into a sort of vacant place there under Julia's house." Then he instructed Millian to wait and left. When he returned, he handed some "lunch" and a bottle of wine to Millian, who consumed the goods and soon fell asleep. Douglass woke him up a short time later, telling him, "It is time." Dillon was there too, and all three men left their hiding place and approached the front door to the house. Millian was handed a cocked revolver and told to stand guard at the bottom of the steps. The other man stayed on the landing as Douglass produced a key, unlocked the door, and went inside. The next sound Millian heard was "one smothered exclamation of distress," which was "lengthy and painfully expressed and in a subdued voice as if of a person being smothered." Soon Dillon and Douglass came out, the latter man carrying "the bulky plunder," which he handed to Millian. "Here, Frenchman," he said, "you take these, you have a room and a trunk."

Millian did as he was told. In the morning the men came to his room, "took the diamonds from their settings and sent him to sell them." He first tried a Mrs. Moch, who assessed the gems were worth one hundred dollars and said she would pay seventy-five dollars. Millian declined the offer and returned to his room. Douglass ended up selling them to Nye & Company, sharing some of the money with Millian. Douglass and Dillon, said Millian, had committed other murder/robberies. He also denied ever being in Martha Camp's house.

Everyone, including the local paper, took a stand against Millian. The public was gunning for blood, and they would have that of the little Frenchman. As newspapers and folks around town smeared his name, someone also remembered that Millian himself was at Julia's services and "had the audacity to walk in the funeral procession with a piece of crepe about his arm." As Millian sat in jail, one more item was reported to have been in his possession. A shopkeeper named Mrs. Cazentre of Gold Hill claimed Millian was the one who sold her a dress pattern that had belonged to Julia. Police took the pattern and made the rounds of local merchants. The item was "recognized by two dry goods merchants as one sold by them to Jule Bulette."[26]

Millian's trial lasted into 1868. In court, District Attorney Bishop reminded the jury that "Julia Bulette was found lying dead in her bed, foully murdered, and stiff and cold in her clotted gore. True, she was a woman of easy virtue. Yet hundreds in this city have had cause to bless her name for her many acts of kindness and charity. So much worse the crime. That woman probably had more real friends in this community than any other; yet there was found at last a human being so fiendish and base as to crawl to her bedside in the dead hour of the night, and with violent hands, beat and strangle her to death—not for revenge, but in order to plunder her of these very articles of clothing and jewelry we see before us. What inhuman, unparalled [*sic*] barbarity!" Did Bishop know about or shame the respectable ladies of the town who hastened to the jail with delicious meals for Millian? Probably, because when the ladies circulated a petition asking for Millian's impending sentence to be life in prison, the *Territorial Enterprise* shot them down. "We believe that the man will be hung," read the paper. "If he is not, we do not know where a fit subject for hanging is to be found." John Millian was indeed found guilty, and hanged. As was common in the West, the hanging would be one of the biggest social events ever witnessed in Virginia City. Postcards of Millian were sold as onlookers viewed the gallows on display in front of Benham's carpenter shop. Later, the gallows was moved to a hillside outside of town in anticipation of the event.[27]

On the morning of the hanging, the entire town of Virginia City readied to see the murderer swing. Crowds gathered at the courthouse. At 11:30 a.m. a carriage arrived, accompanied by thirty to forty Special Deputy Sheriffs and sixty National Guardsmen. The men parted the crowd and made a pathway to the courthouse. John Millian was quickly ushered out to the carriage and deposited inside as the shades were drawn. It took half an hour for the carriage to make its way through the throng to the gallows site. Schools, saloons, and mines had closed down and everyone in town made their way to the scene. The crowd, numbering four thousand people, watched as Millian was quickly taken to the platform and the guardsmen formed a square around the gallows. Priests, including Father Manogue, members of the press, and physicians were positioned in front. Millian "gazed earnestly" at the noose as his death warrant was read. Then he kneeled as the priests in attendance prayed for him.

When the sheriff asked Millian if he had anything to say, the man pulled a speech, written in French, from his pocket. In it, he denied killing Julia. He graciously thanked the respectable women who had assisted him in jail, and gave an especial thanks to a man named Mr.

Hall, who stepped up with his sons and shook Millian's hands. Upon finishing his speech, Millian next shook the sheriff's hands and kissed the priests who had prayed for him. A black hood was placed over his head and at 12:42 p.m. the trapdoor underneath him opened. Twenty-five minutes later, Millian was declared dead. His body was lowered into a coffin, but his burial spot remains unknown. Afterward, the saloons opened to record crowds.

That was the end of John Millian, but it was not the end of Julia Bulette, who very nearly reached saintly status as thousands remembered her in the coming decades. One of the last tributes to her occurred as late as 1946, when Gordon A. Sampson of the now failing Virginia and Truckee Railroad "reconditioned an old coach and named it the *Julia Bulette*." Sampson may have been paying tribute, but he also was hoping to attract more visitors to Virginia City.[28] And although the effort failed as far as the V&T Railroad was concerned, Julia has not failed Virginia City: Even today, the town receives visitors from all over the world who come to learn about its history, and its favorite harlot.

CHAPTER 7

---•◦•---

The Elusive Ladies of Ely

Ely's population today hovers around five thousand people. The remote city has long been a hub of sorts; US Highways 6, 50, and 93 serve as junctions for travelers on the way to other places. These lonesome highways were just trails back when Murray Creek Station, a mere stage stop at the mouth of Robinson Canyon, supported a tiny, budding community somewhere near the junction. One story of Ely's beginning goes that mining began around nearby Mineral City as early as 1864, with J.R. Withington controlling the local water rights and eventually relinquishing them when George Lamb laid out the townsite in 1870. At the time there were just a few cabins. Harry Featherstone, who ran the Murray Creek Station and post office, soon built a "real house" as well as a restaurant and small hotel. He later sold out to R.A. Reipe, who enlarged the hotel and named it the Ely Hotel. Ely, according to this source, was named for Smith Ely, president of the nearby Selby Copper Mining and Smelting Company.[1] A second source credits Vermont resident J.W. Long as appearing at Murray Creek Station circa 1878 and naming the camp Ely, either after his hometown in Vermont, a New York congressman, an Illinois miner named John Ely, or Smith Ely.

However Ely was named, one thing is certain: By 1880 a bevy of good time girls had found the town. That was the year that one of Ely's only surviving brothels today, known now as the Big 4, was built. First known as Rainey's, the place was owned by Tom O'Neil by the 1900s. O'Neil's paramour was Ruby Wells, who might have taken her name from a place name of the same moniker in Elko County. Ruby was in Ely as early as 1907, however, when she and bartender Charles Wells were accused of stealing $1,400 from the safe at the Old Resort Saloon. Both were discharged due to circumstantial evidence. Whether or not, or how, Ruby was related to Charles is unknown, but by 1912 Tom O'Neil was her man and her business partner. That year, the pair was arrested for white slavery and extradited to Utah for trying to import two young girls for prostitution purposes back in 1911. The girls, identified as Bessie Arlington of Ogden and Margarie Clarington, were brought to Ely by train but made the trip locked in one of the Pullman cars to prevent their escape.

Although Ruby and her paramour beat two other charges, Tom O'Neil pleaded guilty to another white slavery charge in 1914. The court did not take the crime lightly, and he was sentenced to fifteen months at Leavenworth Prison in Kansas. Back in Ely, folks pondered over O'Neil's decision to plead guilty until the *Eureka Sentinel* explained matters. "The plea of guilty in this case came as a surprise to his friends in Ely, but the supposition is that a compromise was effected with the Government, whereby charges against [O'Neil's] business associate, Miss Ruby (also under indictment for the same offense) would be dismissed."[2] O'Neil did his time and returned to Ely, where by 1920 he had given up the brothel business. The census found him living on Aultman Street with his wife, Alice, and working at his own garage. As for Ruby, she disappeared without a trace like so many of her kind.

O'Neil's brothel, meanwhile, remained in business under a series of names until the 1930s, when it was officially named the Big 4. The name was said to relate to "four prominent businessmen" who owned the place. The Big 4 was still in business as of June 1959, when a complaint

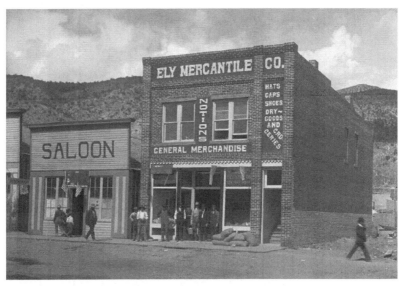

A typical saloon in Ely, Nevada, circa 1906. Wikimedia Commons

against the brothel was filed with the County Commissioners. The complainant was Charles "Babe" Fields, who wanted the "Big 4 Club" shut down because he saw it as a public nuisance. At the root of the problem was that the Big 4 was not only adding more rooms, but proposed catering "to business and professional people who do not wish to be seen publicly." The matter was discussed at a City Hall meeting. Local resident Boots Miller defended the resort, telling the council, "Ely needs more of these places." In the end, however, city officials decided that "while houses of prostitution may be necessary and proper in a community such as Ely, this is not a business which should be expanded or built up." Although Fields's complaint was the only one against the brothel, the Attorney General issued the order for the Big 4 to close, which it did—for a little while. By the 1970s, and quite possibly even before that, the Big 4 was open under the ownership of Tony Asena. Notably, Asena was one of the four owners from the 1930s when the Big 4 was so-named. The brothel remains open as of this writing.[3]

The Big 4 was not the only bordello in Ely during the 1880s. In 1887 the courthouse in the town of Hamilton burned (for the second time), and the honor of county seat was transferred to Ely. At the time, the town's population was around four hundred people. Soon, more brothels were opening on the west end of High Street at the very edge of town, between the city limits and 2nd Street. And when a copper boom coincided with the tracks of the Nevada Northern Railroad reaching town in the early 1900s, the district also boomed. By far, however, the larger district on High Street was more popular and became known as "Bronc Alley."[4]

In 1906 Bronc Alley spanned three blocks with several brothels, ranging from cribs to dance halls and saloons. Within a year, Ely's population had grown to over two thousand people with such amenities as electricity, two banks, two daily newspapers, schools, churches, and a number of shops. A year later, the 1907 Sanborn map showed a variety of brothels ranging from cribs to at least one house towering two stories high. Interspersed with these places were two dance hall/saloons, one of which featured rooms in the back and two small cribs. At #4-5 on the south side of High Street was a curious cluster of cribs and brothels sharing a common courtyard, with only one entrance from the street. There was a saloon too, which could only be accessed by entering the courtyard.

Although there is little doubt that Ely's red-light district was fraught with violence, there was only one known murder reported in the district during 1907. Constable Ed Gilbert went to arrest F.N. Saunders "for beating and threatening to kill Ruth Deardorff, his paramour and Ely prostitute." The constable found Saunders in a two-room crib at the Club Dance Hall on October 12. Ruth would later testify that Saunders was a known bad man, with a record stemming from his robbing of banks and trains in Texas and Indian Territory. George McClure, owner of the Three Deuces dance hall, also testified that Saunders had recently broken out of jail at Ardmore, Oklahoma. That night in the Bronc Alley crib, Saunders unfortunately got the jump on Constable Gilbert, shooting him in the abdomen and again in the back. As he fell, Gilbert managed to shoot Saunders in the head. The outlaw died instantly. Gilbert was taken to his cabin and then to the hospital at Dillon, but died from his injuries. They said Gilbert's funeral procession was nearly a mile long, and the largest of its kind at the time.[5]

By 1908 another smaller brothel district also flourished near the East Ely Depot, on the corner of 13th and B Streets. Today it is referred to as "Crib Row." Most of the property owners in Ely were men by 1909. A sewer plat for that year identifies Tom O'Neill, Charles Aubery, Jos. Dugan, Eugene Giles, Rockhill and Rickard, H.C.F. Brown, W.B. Graham, and J.W. Delmore as the owners of several lots containing brothels. The only two female property owners were Miss Ellen Hayes and Mrs. A.M. Gist.[6] More telling is the 1910 census, which identified the men and ladies of the red-light district as follows:

House No.	Name	Birth	Marital Status
216	Violet Gordon	1888, Illinois	Single
217	C C Brown (pimp)	1876, California	Single
218	Paul Cherry (fruit dealer)	1882, Illinois	Single
219	Charles Miller (pimp)	1882, Germany (immigrated 1891)	Single
	Myrtle Silverton	1885, Wyoming	Single
220	Blanche Cunningham	1886, Iowa	Single
221	Blanche Hetter	1885, Iowa	Single
222	Mas (female)	1882, Japan (immigrated 1903)	
223	Bernice Snow	1882, Colorado	Single
224	Marguerite Deschamps	1880, France (immigrated 1904)	Single
225	Marcelle Bellerue	1885 France (immigrated 1903)	Single

226	Louise Wilton	1884, France (immigrated 1905)	Single
227	D H Hayden (bartender)	1866, New York	Single
228	W L Hale (gambler)	1880, Missouri	Single
229	Marnie or Mamie Rich	1880, Oregon	Single
230	Rose Mitchell	1882, Minnesota	Single
231	Nina Brown	1888, Utah	Single
232	Ruby Lyons	1886, Utah	Single
233	Maude Ellis	1887, Missouri	Single
234	Helen Stanley	1886, Illinois	Single
235	Mike Porter (restaurant cook)	1871, Georgia	Single
236	Martha Stuart	1888, Ohio	Single
237	Charles Aubrey (bawdy house proprietor)	1871, France (immigrated 1893)	Single
238	Charles Osterlund (bartender)	1881, Iowa	Single
	C C Green (laborer)	1884, Kentucky	Single
239	J R Williams (engineer)	1857, North Dakota	Single
240	Pearl Britton	1882, Colorado	Single
241	Elizabeth Wave	1887, Belgium (immigrated 1907)	Single
	Carrie Wilson	1880, Missouri	Single
242	Sadie Gregory	1889, Mexico or Spain (immigrated 1892)	Single
243	Pearl Knight	1884, Illinois	Single
244	Lulu Dickenson	1884, Tennessee	Single
	Rutledge Dickenson (son)	1904, Minnesota	Single
	Dutreil Dickenson (daughter)	1905, Montana	Single
245	E D Samaine (carpenter)	1854, New York	Divorced
246	Nellie Thomas	1880, Indiana	Single
	J J Crawford (bartender)	1877, United States	Single
247	Ophelia Jones (laundress)	1880, Arkansas	Divorced
	George Fagan (porter)	1889, Arkansas	Single
	Howard Lawrence (laundryman)	1884, Kansas	Single
248	Irene Reed (laundress)	1880, Virginia	Single

There are some interesting aspects of the 1910 census. Most of the residents in Bronc Alley were single. Pimps C.C. Brown and Charles Miller, and bawdy house owner Charles Aubrey were listed as such at their respective addresses, but no women are listed at these places—possibly because the ladies worked in round-the-clock shifts while living elsewhere. And, although the women of Bronc Alley were documented as prostitutes (the exceptions being Ophelia Jones and Irene Reed), the word "prostitute" was later crossed out on the census sheet. Either the census taker had a change of heart, or someone objected to the use of the word when defining Bronc Alley's residents. Still, the census did record everyone in Bronc Alley as being residents of the "red-light district," indicating that Ely's demimonde was firmly in place.

After 1910, the ladies of Bronc Alley are harder to track. Only the 1912 Sanborn map tells the tale, with about as many brothels as in 1907 and few changes. Most of these brothels would burn down around 1920 after a fire began in the back of Reinhart's Dance Hall. The flames spread quickly, burning nearly every building in the block between High Street and the alley, including a Chinese restaurant—although it is unknown whether this was the north or south side. Three or four cribs on High Street and Second Street also were damaged. Property owners at the time were identified as Charles Aubrey, Robert Brady, and Hugh Wilson. For many towns of the era, that might have been the end of Ely's red-light district. But Bronc Alley was more resilient, and by the 1930s brothels had reemerged. Two of them remain in operation as of 2020: the historic Big 4 and the Stardust Ranch, which opened in about 1965.

CHAPTER 8

———•●•———

The Tarts of Tonopah

Tonopah sprawls over a small section of the Nevada desert in what is now known as the Tonopah Basin. The summer months bring warm temperatures and cool evenings, while winters can dip down below freezing. In this arid climate in 1900, prospector Jim Butler discovered some silver deposits. He eventually partnered with another prospector, Tasker Oddie, to file eight different mining claims that produced some of Nevada's richest silver to date. A mining camp soon formed and was aptly named Butler. By January of 1901 the population consisted of some forty men. Soon after the first stagecoach rolled through in March, the population grew to two-hundred fifty, and the Butler post office opened the following month.

Prospectors were not the only ones to take an interest in Butler. Five-year-old Minnie Belle Thompson was just one of many whose family relocated to town in 1901. The Thompsons first lived in a tent next to an alley, which was peppered with saloons and gambling joints. Minnie's father instructed her to step into the street when passing by them, to avoid anyone who might be coming out onto the sidewalk. At night, Minnie could see the back entrances to these places. Come nightfall, she recalled, "a lovely carriage would draw up at the back door of the saloon near our place. A half-dozen or so beautifully dressed Red Light

One of several small frame houses that survive in Tonopah's former red-light district.
Author photo

entertainers would get out of the carriage and enter via the back door. From then on until very late we could hear much laughter and dancing. The girls would 'never think' of going in by the front door."

In time, Butler's red-light district was established in an area along Main Street, bordered by Knapp, Oddie, and Central Avenues. Within the district were bars with dance halls and the usual assortment of brothels. Certain old-timers would later claim that there were roughly six hundred dance hall girls and prostitutes in the district. Visiting the district was the main pastime of the hardworking men who toiled in the mines by day and got staggering drunk in the red-light district at night. Most unfortunately, social diseases were rampant at this early date. Historian Bob McCracken described how "in the shower and change rooms at the mines one could see men whose genitals were missing or seriously deformed by venereal diseases." Even so, the good time girls of the town were long remembered for their generosity, especially "in times of need and tragedy," acting as surrogate mothers of sorts to their customers and even assisting young people of the town with their college expenses.[1]

In June 1901, the Mizpah Saloon was built a block or so from the red-light district. It was meant to be Butler's finest tavern "where at all times may be found the choicest of wines, liquors and cigars." There was a hotel attached as well where, according to the *Tonopah Bonanza* sometime after 1905, "the weary one can stroll in, state that he wants to be fed, bathed and put to bed, and all these things will be attended to for him."[2] The Mizpah must have been a boon to the higher class working girls of the town, who could sweep in, dazzle a customer at the bar, and hopefully lead him off to their quarters for some fun. In the red-light district proper, however, newspapers had much to say about the "he-prostitutes who live upon the earnings of these scarlet women, and like human vampires that they are, suck the life blood of their victims." At a meeting in June, police officers were duly instructed to "arrest every macque [pimp] in the tenderloin district."[3]

It was not a man who next appeared in the paper regarding the red-light district but prostitute Georgie Grant, who was arrested for disturbing the peace in July. Georgie's boyfriend was a painter named McGregor, who owned the woman's house. When an officer visited there in an attempt to collect a fire tax, which neither McGregor nor Georgie felt obligated to pay, he was duly insulted. Georgie, not McGregor, was arrested and fined twenty-five dollars. "This woman has created considerable trouble in Tonopah," noted the *Tonopah Bonanza*, "and it is to be hoped that this will be her last appearance in the Justice Court."[4]

By 1903, Butler's red-light district was clearly out of control. News items that year included a razor fight between two "dusky denizens of the red-light district," and the arrest of James Welch for shooting at a prostitute when she caught him stealing her wine.[5] County commissioner Egan and district attorney Richards ultimately decided to build a jail right smack dab in the middle of the red-light district, near Water Street. The structure replaced the original jail that had been built elsewhere in 1901. The idea seemed sound enough, but was employed for only a short time. When another jail was added to the Nye County Courthouse in 1907, the one on Water Street briefly served as a residence before it, as well as a matching stone row house, was converted to a brothel. It is fun to imagine the ladies who occupied the building as they tittered over operating out of the same place that was once intended to repress their profession.

Marjorie Brown was just a newlywed when she moved to Butler in 1904. Although she was a proper lady, Marjorie remembered the rouge-cheeked dance hall girls who "tripped across the street with long skirts held tight and hats loaded with plumes, often with parasols slung negligently over a plump shoulder." Notably, dance hall girls did not live in the red-light district, and Marjorie "never knew where they did live." Marjorie's husband, Hugh Brown, had an office in the Golden Block across from the Butler Saloon. On her visits to him, Marjorie could see inside the place where "women stood at the bar, foot on rail, with the men." Brown chastised his wife for watching them, commenting, "They're a dime a dozen. They're not even good-looking." But Marjorie disagreed, recalling that some of the women "were very glamorous."

Marjorie also remembered a couple of madams. One of them ran one of three houses she knew of, either "the Bijou or the Sagebrush or the Golden Nugget." Whichever it was, the brothel was of higher class, and the girls employed within were strictly forbidden from stealing from their customers. One day, Marjorie said, one of the girls was found with a certificate for ten thousand shares of the Mohawk Mine. She told the madam it was a gift from her customer. The wise madam, however, knew better and "cuffed the girl a bit just to teach her a lesson." Then she took the certificate and set out to find the customer, who had been "dead drunk" the night before and was still reeling with a hangover. Sure enough, the man had yet to realize the certificate had been stolen from him. The story of the honest madam circulated throughout town.

Another madam, Marjorie said, had "a very well-built and roomy house" on Oddie Avenue. When the lady fell in love with a gambler, she resolved to marry him and wanted a child of her own. The two married, and the madam's fine bordello "was picked up, perched crazily on Harry Hudson's freight wagon, behind a ten-mule team, and teetered up Main Street to the farthest end of town, where it was deposited on a nice flat piece of ground." There the couple lived in blissful wedlock. A few months later the former madam bore her baby and, presumably, lived happily ever after. Less fortunate was a harlot who died in the red-light district. The word on the street was that the girl had always wanted a wedding gown in case she ever got lucky enough to get married. Although she was single when she died, the woman's friends chipped in and bought a white satin wedding dress for her to be buried in. Marjorie Brown said she could hear the Miners' Union Band playing a funeral on Main Street as the girl's hearse carried her casket to the cemetery.[6] Matrimony was not often in the cards for women of the red-light district; in May 1904, Nellie Ruppert filed for divorce from her husband on the grounds of "failure to provide and drunkenness." The two had been married for some time and had a child together. It was noted that Nellie now lived in the red-light district and was asking twenty-five dollars per month for the support of her child.[7]

On March 3, 1905, post office authorities officially changed Butler's name to Tonopah. Just a month later, the Sanborn Fire Insurance Company mapped out the town. No less than twenty-five brothels were scattered along Corona Avenue north of Main Street, as well as a sizeable dance hall and saloon. Another dance hall sat across Main Street. Just northwest at what was then Mizpah Avenue at the corner of Central Street, were roughly two dozen or more brothels. All of these structures ranged from cribs sharing a common structure to finer parlor houses. Some small saloons and no less than two Chinese laundries (which likely also provided opium) dotted the landscape around these places.

The Sanborn map also shows a large unidentified building on the east side of Main Street between Oddie and Knapp Avenues that must have been the Big Casino. The combination betting hall, dance hall, restaurant, and saloon opened shortly after the map was made. Inside, a balcony above the dance floor contained cribs for the girls who likely did not live on the premises. Rather, they might have worked in shifts, dancing with men and enticing them into purchasing drinks at the bar before taking them upstairs. The girls made good money: 40 percent from the drinks they sold and half of what they made dancing. An official orchestra was in place by 1907, with professional "entertainers" being brought in from as far away as San Francisco. In time, the Big Casino claimed to be "the largest hurdy-gurdy house on the west coast."[8]

Later in 1907, a whole new kind of floozy suddenly appeared on the scene. Her name was Bina Verrault, and her story is quite interesting. Bina, described as "a lady of luminous dark eyes," was lately of New York. There, along with her childhood chum, Izella Brown, Bina had run a "love syndicate." The women claimed to be wealthy widows and seduced men—to the effect that they gave the ladies "fine clothing, jewelry and money."[9] Newspapers later explained that before embarking on her love syndicate venture Bina had married an artist, George T. Verrault, in Philadelphia back in 1901. Within a week of the marriage, however, Verrault had to bail his new wife out of jail for shoplifting. Soon after, Izella appeared for a visit. Together, the women went on a shopping spree and ran up a sizeable bill, putting it on Verrault's tab. Fed up, the man left Bina. The ladies next secured several fancy houses around New York and fitted them up "in expensive style." Using aliases, the pair took out classified ads, saying they were wealthy widows looking for a husband. Those answering the ads were encouraged to produce expensive gifts and money as a token of their love before being unceremoniously cast aside for the next victim.[10]

New York's state census of 1905 found thirty-five-year-old Bina residing in a prestigious apartment house at 114 West 73rd Street in Manhattan where she claimed she worked as a stenographer. She was masquerading as Mrs. Helen Hamilton when she and Izella first made the newspapers in August of 1906. Pennsylvania's *New Castle News* reported the women were running a "national matrimonial swindling bureau" with at least three victims. Two warrants were issued for Bina's arrest.[11] A week later, the *Syracuse Herald* in New York explained that one of the charges was made by a Syrian healer, Aballah Habbed, who charged Izella with paying only $75 for over $800 worth of goods he delivered. Bina made at least one court appearance, telling the judge that the money she received from insurance dealer Leo Kiesler was done so as a test of his love. When she was accused of taking his money, the woman retorted, "Do you blame me if I did? Here was this man, who told me he was manager of the foreign department of Mutual Life, with a $100,000 a year salary, a graduate of Heidelberg and a nobleman to boot. Fancy such a man bawling about $2,000, which he himself says is all he ever gave me. And then to find out he's only a clerk and of a family of swineherds! That my ideal? I guess not!"[12]

After that, Bina decided she had enough of New York, the courts, and the broken-hearted men she left behind her. Pawning a few of her diamond rings, she left town and surfaced in Tonopah about a year later. What the woman didn't know was that as much as there were wealthy men in Tonopah, the great Panic of 1907 was coming. Also known as the 1907 Banker's Panic and the Knickerbocker Crisis, the event took place after the New York Stock Exchange took a dramatic downswing that October, fueling a recession that bankrupted numerous businesses and banks across America. Nobody was spending money, least of all on a fading socialite with a shady past. Soon, Bina was drinking excessively and was "no longer attractive," according to the *Trenton Evening Times* back in New Jersey.[13] Most sources, including Bina's primitive grave marker in Tonopah's cemetery, state she died on October 31, 1907. Her recorded cause of death was "heart failure."[14]

Bina Verrault missed out on Tonopah's recovery from the panic and its continued success. Although the 1909 Sanborn map shows several vacant buildings once occupied by prostitutes, and a number of brothels situated on Corona Avenue, there were still numerous good time girls in town by the time the census was taken in 1910. But Nevada had just passed a new anti-gambling bill, an act which trickled down to the good time girls as authorities began scrutinizing them more closely. Due to these constraints, the number of women who were outright identified as prostitutes or dance hall girls in the 1910 census were fewer than the actual number of shady ladies in town. Only about thirteen crib girls and nine dance hall girls are identified, for instance (notably, twenty-three-year-old dancer Ethel Evans lived with a forty-year-old man, who might have been her pimp). Of the three madams (identified as prostitutes who owned their own home and employed other women), Birdie Smith and Harriet McCabe each had two women working for them. Frankie Hunt only employed one woman, but had a Chinese servant.

The number of Tonopah's working girls likely increased that fall, when mining activities increased with vigor. Places like the Big Casino, however, suffered hits by the anti-gambling laws too. The once grand resort was losing money, and by August of 1913 was in receivership in the federal courts. Because of this, the Big Casino more or less came under government ownership. One young lady had just moved to town to take a job there. When asked how she liked it so far, she quipped, "I should worry! I'm working for the Government." But she, and several others, became unemployed when the Big Casino was officially deemed a public nuisance and lost its liquor license. Somehow the "former man-agement" from the Big Casino's glory days was reinstated a short time later. Without gambling, however, never again would the Big Casino see the amazing profits it once netted.

Slowly but surely, a series of ordinances began limiting the activities of Tonopah's red-light ladies. One of them, in 1915, decreed that it would be "unlawful for public prostitutes or notoriously lewd or abandoned women to stand, sit, or frequent the sidewalks in front or near the premises they may occupy, or at the alleyway, door or gate of such premises, or to occupy the steps thereof, or accost, call or stop any person passing by, or to walk up or down the sidewalks, or to stroll about the city streets indecently attired, or in any other respects to behave in public so as to cause scandal or to disturb the peace and good morals of the people."[15] Only by following this and other ordinances were the ladies of the town able to stay in business. By 1917, when Tonopah's next Sanborn map was published, the girls had abandoned their digs on Corona Avenue but dozens of brothels lined Central Avenue, running between Oddie Avenue and beyond Knapp Avenue. Some of them were quite large.

As of the 1920 census, prostitutes were no longer identified as such in the census at all. Rather, women who worked as "entertainers" appeared, and only fifty-three of them were documented. Some of them worked for a "cabaret," while seven were employed by an "orchestra." All of the women lived on either Oddie Avenue or St. Patrick, Main, and Stoneham Streets. Some of them shared a house. The youngest entertainer was twenty-two-year-old Mildred Myles, lately of Oklahoma. The oldest was Marie Martez, a forty-seven-year-old widow from Illinois. There were four other widows in the bunch. Of the dozen who said they were married, none of them lived with their husbands. Many of the girls likely worked at the Big Casino, which was turned into a hotel later that year. The Big Casino finally burned in a 1922 fire, which destroyed the downtown area north of Oddie Avenue.

With the Big Casino gone, the cabaret girls looked elsewhere for work. Although national prohibition had been enacted in January of

1920, many towns simply disregarded the new law. Tonopah was one of them, although they did tone things down a bit. Still, when US District Attorney William Woodburn addressed the Lions Club in Reno in 1922, he noted that "in no place in the state except Reno and possibly Tonopah is there any good liquor left [in Nevada]. In every other place jackass brandy, which is nothing but poison, is being distributed broadcast."[16] Indeed, throughout the 1920s Tonopah remained a tourism destination, with places offering not only liquor but also live music by well-known bands from Reno and San Francisco. The entertainment venues offered free hors d'oeuvres, or sometimes a beef, pork, or turkey sandwich and a beer for just a nickel. Bars, dance halls, and brothels offered tokens, which often featured discounts, and were accepted by other businesses.

The red lights were still casting their seductive glow in Tonopah during the 1930s. One of the more memorable harlots to arrive in 1930 was Taxcsine Ornelas, who ran Taxcsine's Bar in the red-light district. Known for drinking beer from a champagne glass, Taxcsine followed the laws as needed and managed to remain in business for nearly twenty-five years. That was quite an achievement, given that Tonopah's mining activity had slowed considerably. But the town was, after all, a great stopping place between Las Vegas and Reno. A dozen bars—the Bungalow, the Cottage, Effie's Place, Fay's Place, the Green Lantern, Inez Parker's Place, the Lucky Strike, the Newport, Nigger Dee's, the Northern, the Silver State, and Taxcsine's—remained in Tonopah, as well as a sprinkling of brothels. As a boy, Solan Terrell was employed as a Western Union messenger. Although he was not allowed to deliver telegrams to the red-light district, Terrell would watch to see if the woman working the office was looking, steal the telegrams from their place in a drawer, and deliver them to the ladies of the line anyway. The women were always good tippers. But although the good time girls of Tonopah were allowed to shop and dine out around town, they were "not permitted to fraternize in the bars."

Times were changing in Tonopah. During the early 1940s, when the nearby Tonopah Air Force Base was under construction, city officials willingly made sure that all bars and brothels closed at midnight to assure workers would not be hung over for work the next day. But when one of the red-light houses burned, killing a soldier inside, the incident was enough to elicit a complaint. Soon after, Tonopah authorities began working to shut the district down for good.[17] But even that didn't seem to stop Mary "Bobbie" Duncan Himes, as she was later known, from moving into town around 1941.

Bobbie was Rachel Mary Ferro when she was born at her family's home in Billings, Montana, in 1915. Her parents, Matteo and Carolina Ferro, were Italian immigrants. By the time of the 1930 census, Carolina had died. At the young age of nineteen, Bobbie married Fred Franklin Fuller at Wolf Point in Roosevelt County. But the marriage had apparently fizzled by the time Bobbie first appeared in Tonopah. She initially was there for only a short time before leaving town for Lusk, Wyoming, where she worked under Madam Dell Burke at the infamous Yellow Hotel. How long she was there is anyone's guess, for by 1944 she was back in Montana when she married again, to Albert Duncan, in Cody. When that marriage was equally unsuccessful, Bobbie returned to Tonopah but kept her ex-husband's name.

Using the business savvy she had learned working for Dell Burke, Bobbie partnered with Madam Margaret Cox, formerly of a brothel known as The Willows. Together, the women moved "an old frame house to atop a long-disused dump from the old Buckeye Mine" outside of town, and named it the Buckeye. Bobbie eventually became the sole owner and madam. She also married a final time, in 1956, to Bill Himes, a retired navy man who co-owned the Pastime Club downtown. After the marriage, Bobbie continued running the Buckeye and became well liked and respected around Tonopah. She was known for donating money to schools and other causes, and prominent men attended her legendary birthday parties.

Bobbie's business was successful enough that in 1963, she was able to move several trailers onto her property to serve as a bar, a parlor, and rooms for her girls. The parlor featured tables and a piano for the entertainment of her customers, as well as a sunken, heart-shaped pink tile bathtub. The main house became her private home. Ten years later, the madam may have retired when she filed for social security. Bill Himes died in 1979; Bobbie followed ten years later. The couple is buried together in New Tonopah Cemetery.

Bobbie Duncan's time in Tonopah during the 1950s coincided with other brothels opening, although these were not as grand as those from previous years. And Bobbie was likely as alarmed as the other good time girls when, in December of 1951 at the Nugget Bar on St. Patrick's Street, prostitute Alice Nashlund was brutally murdered and Madam Inez Parker was severely beaten. Both women were taken to the Nye County Hospital, where Alice died on December 20. Her death certificate verifies she came to her death "by crushing of skull & brain by being struck on the head with a bar stool."[18] The culprit, reported the *Nevada State Journal* on December 28, was a miner named Raymond Millan. "An argument that preceded the beating is said to have involved a matter of prices at the bawdy house where the incident took place," reported the paper. At his preliminary hearing, Millan pleaded not guilty.[19] Still, the man was officially charged with the crimes on January 20, 1952. The outcome of Millan's trial remained unknown, but it didn't really matter; in June he was admitted to Nye County Hospital, succumbing on July 4 from "acute dilation of heart."[20]

Following Alice Nashlund's death, Nye County officials decided it was best to close the prostitution industry down for good. Among those put out of business was Taxcsine Ornelas, who, after years of leading a respected existence in the red-light realm, was upset at the "harsh treatment she had received from local residents who had once been more friendly to her." On May 21, 1954, the woman was "found lying face down in her bed, dead," of a heart attack.[21] Some folks "said that she died of a broken heart, having never recovered from the closing of her business following the Nashland [*sic*] murder," as well as the way she had been treated. Only when her room was inventoried were folks reminded of the lady's generosity: There were cards and letters thanking her for various acts of kindness. Some letters from "The Boys in the Stockade" at Tonopah's Army Air Base called her "The Little Desert Mother." Soon, people were remembering how many collections Taxcsine had taken up, mostly using her own money. And they recalled how she contributed to the purchase of a school bus and the building of a hospital for the army station. The kindly harlot was vindicated, at least for a little while.[22] Today, Taxscine rests in New Tonopah Cemetery beneath an intricate and lovingly carved wooden headboard.

CHAPTER 9

————— •●• —————

Good Time Girls of Goldfield

G oldfield lies some twenty-seven miles south of Tonopah. Although they are located in different counties (Tonopah in Nye; Goldfield in Esmerelda), the two are similar in many ways. Both experienced mining booms after the turn of 1900, spawning rapid growth and large populations. Both also attracted several prominent mining men, as well as an influx of prostitutes who became an integral part of their history. In Goldfield's case, the town was established after several gold mines were staked in the area. In October 1903, thirty-six mining men gathered and agreed to establish an official townsite. Alva D. Myers, of the famous boomtown of Cripple Creek, Colorado, was elected president.

Goldfield's link to Cripple Creek is interesting. Founded in 1891, the Cripple Creek District was the site of Colorado's last official gold boom. Over thirty-three millionaires and twenty-five towns and camps were generated, including the district's third largest city, also known as Goldfield. By pure coincidence, Myers Avenue in Cripple Creek and Myers Avenue in Goldfield shared a most ironic common bond: Both places eventually became home to their respective city's red-light district—although in Cripple Creek, Myers Avenue was named after city founder Julius Myers, while Goldfield's Myers Avenue was named for Alva Myers. Several other prominent men from Cripple Creek were known to have an interest in the Goldfield of Nevada, including Grant and Newt Crumley, who made names for themselves in Tonopah and Goldfield shortly after their arrival. Although Grant was known to consort with prostitute Grace Carlyle and other working girls in Cripple Creek, there is nothing to indicate he continued this practice in Goldfield. It is notable, however, that the Crumleys' niece, Lida Crumley Winchell, was a prominent madam in Prescott, Arizona, for many years. There is no evidence that Lida ever visited her uncles in Nevada. When she died in 1939 her sister Josephine, who lived in Colorado, claimed the body and received Lida's ashes.[1]

By about 1904, Goldfield was Nevada's largest city. Notable figures who came through town included Virgil Earp, brother of famed lawman and gunfighter Wyatt Earp, who was sheriff during 1905. The position was not destined to last; Earp, who had suffered debilitating injuries in the infamous shoot-out at the OK Corral in Tombstone, Arizona, back in 1881, suffered bouts with pneumonia and died in October. Had he survived, Earp would have found much to contend with in the way of lawlessness, as well as the soiled doves who had flocked to town and taken over a large portion of Main Street between Crystal and Myers Avenues. The Sanborn map for 1905 shows that no less than forty-three cribs, common bordellos, and lavish parlor houses were scattered throughout this area, as well as a large saloon and dance hall at the corner of Elliott and Main. One of these may have been the Jumbo Club, a fancy dance hall built circa 1905. Goldfield's tiny jail buildings, which hardly looked capable of holding much in the way of wrongdoers, were situated on First Street between Elliott and Myers.

Although Goldfield's red-light district would become quite sizeable in time, the *Goldfield News* seemed disinclined to report much about the goings-on there. Certainly it was not so much that there was no activity, nor that citizens of the town chose to ignore what went on there. Notably, one mining group named their company the Red Light Claim.

Still, reports on the women and others in the district were sparse. Only tidbits of news give any insight into life in and around the demimonde. The *Goldfield News*, for instance, commented in September 1905 that "Bacchus has many devotees in the Red Light district and worship at his shrine is frequent and sincere . . . There are all sorts of games for the delectation of visitors with the price; dance halls where bevys [sic] of frail damsels scantily attired as to length of skirt and height of corsage, stand ready to join patrons in the riotous measures of waltz and two-step, or to render efficient service in separating them from their coin; variety theaters where one may drink his fill of beer the while he listens to the mellifluous notes of the 'silver voiced tenor,' imported from Tonopah by the management at 'great expense.'"[2]

There was some hint of corruption in the district when, in late September and early October, Justice of the Peace William Bell, District Attorney Davison, and Constable Russell were indicted for extortion and blackmail against the local good time girls. They were, however, "discharged on account of the complaint being faulty."[3] And when Clara Rameriz, a "beautiful Spanish woman" in the red-light district, committed suicide in October, her death only rated page 12 news. All that was known about her was that she had once lived in Tombstone and Benson, Arizona. On December 29, when prostitute Mollie Fisher of Jake's Dance Hall died of some unknown illness, she too merited a mere mention.[4] More was told of a woman identified only as "May," who quarreled with a man "who has a number of aliases" and shot him. But the bullet only grazed the man's abdomen. It is interesting that May was not arrested.[5] Either her crime was considered too slight to merit jail time, or officials simply wrote it off as just another day in Goldfield's red-light world.

By 1906, Goldfield was booming. The local mines provided 30 percent of the state's gold production. There were roughly eighteen thousand to twenty thousand people living in town. The 1906 Sanborn map offers little more information, aside from showing that the red-light district was still active with numerous cribs and brothels. At the peak of its prosperity in 1907, Goldfield had forty-nine saloons. One source mentions The Den, a well-known brothel "attached to the Ajax & Martine Saloon."[6] Another says The Harem was run by Madam Dorothy Reed, who is said to be buried in the Goldfield cemetery. There also was Jake's Dance Hall, named for Jake Goodfriend, which served as a saloon with a brothel out back, across the alley. The stone building featured six small rooms, just big enough to hold a bed and a table. Each room had two doors, one leading outside for clients to use, and another that opened to a hallway leading to a common bathroom. Little else is known about the ladies themselves during this time, the one exception being Nana G. Long, aka Ray Raymond, who committed suicide. Nana was a young girl from Texas who, feeling that "life became a burden," shot herself in the head on May 10, 1908. She may have been heartbroken "because her lover had apparently abandoned her." Nana's father in Texas refused to claim the body, and the woman was buried in Goldfield's cemetery.[7]

The 1909 Sanborn map shows that the red-light district remained more or less the same in size that it had in 1905 and 1906. Yet the 1910 census reveals only a handful of prostitutes. On Main Street, Dell Aber, Dot Conley, and Grace William resided with several men, including saloon employees William Lacy and Arthur Turley. Laura J. Lujema and Ruth Davis lived at the home of saloonkeeper Victor Ajax. Arline Young was documented as the partner of saloonkeeper Thomas Wright, with prostitutes Charlottie H. Fisker, Dot Sarell, and several men also living on the premises. Canadians May Graves and Alace Sheffield lived with a saloon proprietor, John Kennedy, and his bartender, Hugh Hoekek. Next door, Gladys Munroe lived with saloonkeeper Wallace Buck. Prostitutes Maud Miller and Louise Martha each lived alone. In other areas of the town, Essie Mickie resided on Crook Street with roulette gamekeeper Samuel Kardonski. Finally, in yet another neighborhood,

Dorrisey Reed was recorded as head of her household, with Iva Brown working for her. Of these women, three had a collective five children from previous relationships or marriages who did not live with them.

It is notable that most of the women in the 1910 census lived with men who very well might have served as their pimps. Also the seeming shortage of soiled doves in Goldfield during 1910 was not unusual, for the town at that point was suffering from a marked decline in mine production. The population soon dipped below five thousand people as folks moved on to greener pastures. Then, in September 1913, Goldfield suffered a major flood that all but wiped out the red-light district. The flood did not, however, wipe out the red-light ladies—at least not entirely. In July 1916, the *Goldfield News* reported on Maud Barnette, "a colored woman," who was found "lying on the floor of her house in a pool of blood which was coming from numerous cuts on her head, face, throat and arms." Her assailant, "another colored inhabitant of the restricted district," was Flossy Edwards who had brandished a razor as the two women fought. What the argument was about nobody could say, but Maud was taken to the hospital for treatment while Flossy was deposited in jail.[8]

And there were more. During the trial over a kidnapping case in January 1917, the *Goldfield News* reported that court was temporarily adjourned when Justice of the Peace Arnold had "to go to the scene of the death of a woman in the red-light district." Her name was not revealed.[9] Soon afterward, Freddie Weeks created "a disturbance in a red-light dance hall" and was arrested. In jail, the man built a fire on the wood floor, which created some concern.[10] Then in May, R.L. Burnett was arrested for assaulting Lorena Nelson, "his reputed affinity." Burnett was released, but Lorena filed a second charge of assault. As police arrested both she and Burnett in the red-light district, they noticed another man breaking into a cabin. He was arrested as well. Such antics continued into 1918, when Owen Hickey was found guilty of robbing

An image of Goldfield's dilapidated red-light district was later captured for generating a tourist postcard. Courtesy Special Collections, University of Nevada, Reno

the Mozart Saloon and James Carr was tried for robbing the Star Saloon. The Star happened to be located in the red-light district, with the *Gold-field News* commenting that "many of the inhabitants of the district are in attendance at the trial, making a display of feminine charms that renders it difficult for the clerk of the court to perform his duties."[11]

Sporadic reports on the good time girls of Goldfield might have continued for several more years had it not been for a disastrous fire that burned most of the town in 1923. Goldfield, already in the early throes of becoming a ghost town, never rebuilt. At long last, any remaining wanton women packed their bags and left town. Today, there are three buildings still standing that are known to have been associated with the red-light district. Two of them are identified as "the [1905] Stone Row House" and "the Brick House," both located in the old red-light district itself.[12] The other is an original stick-built crib, which has been renovated and now serves as a unique Airbnb.

CHAPTER 10

—•◦•—

The Tragic Tale of Mona Bell

Murders in the red-light districts of the West occurred with alarming frequency. What with the violence and mayhem that accompanied the prostitution profession, it was not uncommon to see newspapers riddled with stories of women who met an untimely end in one form or another. Although suicides were regularly reported, death at the hands of another were often passed off as simply the norm in the red-light world. Plenty of good girls hooked up with bad men, at a tragic cost. But the sad killing of Isabelle "Mona Bell" Heskett (sometimes spelled Haskett) had a profound effect on the general public, enough to make front page news for weeks, even years.

Mona was Isabelle Sadie Peterman when she was born in October 1887 in Nebraska to Emery and Carrie Peterman. Her mother gave birth to nine children in all, two of whom had died by the time the Petermans appeared in the 1900 census at Lead, South Dakota. Emery worked as a teamster while Carrie raised the children. By the time Isabelle was seventeen, the family had relocated again, to Deadwood. Notably, Isabelle's aunt was Mary Baker Eddy, who was famous throughout America for founding the Christian Science movement.

Young Isabelle apparently had no time for her aunt's teachings, nor for her family, for that matter. Somehow she met, and subsequently married, Columbus Clinton Heskett, a farmhand-turned-gambler from Missouri. The union, which took place in Dawes County, Nebraska, on April 14, 1906, was done "on the sly." To wit, several entries on the marriage record appear questionable: Columbus Haskett is documented by his middle name, and said he was from Denver. Isabelle stated she was from Seattle, and that her parents were Ed Peterman and Jane Rach. The *Tonopah Daily Bonanza* would later verify that the pretty girl "entered into a life, with her marriage, the existence of which she knew not, but to the credit of Heskett, it is said he tried to shield her from the harm of it."[1] The article was likely referring to Heskett's occupation as a gambler, which for some reason took the couple to Arrowhead, Colorado. Founded circa 1904, Arrowhead was initially a railroad construction camp. By the time the name was shortened to Arrow, there were sixteen saloons and a bevy of brothels. But the town was already in decline by 1906.

All was good for about a year, until Heskett got into some sort of trouble. According to one source, he was running a saloon when he was jailed for forging checks and asked Llewellyn Felker, his bartender, to keep an eye on Isabelle. Another source says Heskett left town for a while and asked Felker to "take care of his wife until he found a safe haven and could send for her." By the time Heskett could do so, however, Isabelle had thrown her husband over in favor of Felker.[2] A short time later, in August of 1907, Felker and "Sarah Isabella (aka Sadie)" were arrested for being drunk and disorderly in Arrow's red-light district.[3] The *Daily Bonanza* would later report that the couple finally eloped one night while Heskett was not home, and headed to Nevada. But Felker was already married and his wife, the former Anna Goodwin, was in Longmont, Colorado, with no idea of what her renegade husband was up to.

To Isabelle, getting tipsy with Felker and running off with him to Tonopah must have seemed like a great adventure. But Felker was certainly no winner. A navy veteran from Vermont, his criminal career began in 1900 when he was arrested for shooting his brother-in-law, John Cunningham, to death in Butte, Montana. Felker claimed Cunningham had abused his pregnant sister, and believed the man was about to stab her when he pulled the trigger. Felker was arrested, attempted to escape in 1901, and was eventually sentenced to ten years in jail. He appealed, but as his second trial was underway he escaped a second time. This time he surrendered, was tried a third time, and was eventually acquitted in 1904.

Whether Isabelle knew of Felker's checkered past is unknown, but she appears to have willingly left Colorado with him as the couple headed for Nevada. She might have even giggled at the idea of Felker taking on two aliases, Fred Skinner and Fred Davis. As for Isabelle, she was rechristened Mona Bell. And when the said Skinner "put the girl into the dance hall here [in Tonopah], and she provided food and raiment for him that he might live the life of ease and comfort," Mona might have felt even extra special as the provider for her man.[4] Little did the girl know, however, that her life was destined to go downhill from there.

By November 1907, the couple was in trouble after they allegedly robbed one C.A. Cable of $410 "by force and intimidation." This apparently happened one night at the Merchants Hotel in Manhattan, located some miles northeast of Tonopah. When Cable awoke the next morning to find that his wallet had been cleaned out in its entirety, he wandered into the hotel lobby and "blew his brains out."[5] Skinner (as Davis) had also assaulted Judge Chambers in Manhattan. He was sent to jail, but Mona went free. Another source tells a different version of this tale, explaining that Mona had rented a crib in Manhattan, also that she did not rob Cable but actually lent him $5 after he had already paid her $20 for her services. It was a friend of Cable's who accused Mona and Skinner of robbing the man, and also arrested in the incident was a woman known as Mother Levy.[6]

With her man in jail, Mona appeared to have finally awakened to her reality when she wrote Skinner a letter on December 5. "My dearest," she wrote, "I can't get out this afternoon and am in my room darling, quite miserable. I am afraid, love, that isn't going to be settled." At those words alone, Skinner's eyes must have popped out of his head. But it got worse: "Now, sweetheart, I am going to leave in the morning," Mona wrote. "I think that it will be best. I will go away and get settled. There is nothing here for me you know. I don't think that they would let me alone if I went to work. But I will get everything in shape and will be able to send the money for the fine and enough for you to come on." Apparently Skinner had exhibited some jealousy in the relationship, for Mona also admonished him that "Dearest you should try to brace up and trust me. I wouldn't have gone this far if I hadn't have intended to stick to you. It is the thought of your unhappiness that makes it so hard for me. Now, darling, you will be out at the most in a week or so. I'll send the money to you made out in Wells Fargo. You can endorse them and pay your fine and come right to me. It seems the best way. You can come on the next train after you get out. A week isn't long and I'll have the money then."

Next came a most cryptic sentence in the letter, creating an intriguing puzzle that has yet to be solved: "Now darling the thing most sacred to me is our little Edith and as a guarantee of my faithfulness I am sending her picture from my locket, so that you can look at it and trust me and then give it back when we meet again," Mona wrote. Who was Edith? There is no record of her, and no documentation showing that Mona had a child. At any rate, Mona continued, "Now dearest if I can get any other work when I get into a new town it's no more tenderloin for mine. It doesn't pay. Then when you come you can go to work and all will be well. Sweetheart, I would love to have you go with me but it seems impossible. I've tried so hard to get the money. But love, the impossible is the impossible, and another name for money just now, so have patience and be good. No matter what anyone thinks of you I know you to be truly good. I know you have the most loyal heart that beats in a human breast and most of all, you are the only one in the world for me."

If that last rosy line made Skinner feel better, the next one likely did not. "Now, sweetheart, I am not coming up to see you," said Mona, "it is far too painful. I'll pray for you every night that the days may seem less long. I will go to sleep with your image in my heart, I will know you to be faithful to me and surely you can be satisfied for a few short days. The fine will be a little less then and I will make it somehow. Don't think that I've been contented one minute since you have been in there, for I've been on the verge of collapse all the time. But I've got to brace up and that is all there is to it. When you get out I'll be as sick as I want to. When you get discouraged, dearest, think of that little piece of poetry: 'Then let come what may, I've already had my day.' Surely we have been happy enough to make up for a few unpleasant days. The sun, you know can't always shine. We must take the sunny days with thankfulness and the rainy days our due. I am going to work down there and get you some kind of work and we will be quite happy. Things could have been much worse. I might have been in and that would be dreadful." The letter ended with another reference to Edith. "I am kissing little Edith's face darling, and she will carry my kisses with a short good bye. Surely she knows how closely she binds us together. Mona."[7]

As Skinner seethed in jail, Mona did make a move—to Rhyolite, some one hundred miles southwest of Tonopah. Settled in 1904, Rhyolite was rich with gold deposits. The town was promising enough in 1907, with electricity, hotels, shops, a school, an opera house, and, as expected, a sizable red-light district. The first woman to buy property there was Madam Mabel Vaughn of the Jewel Consolidated brothel near Amargosa and Colorado Streets, and shady ladies came to work there from as far away as San Francisco. Six thousand others also called the booming town home.

When he got out of jail, Skinner made a beeline for Rhyolite. Anxious to shed he and Mona's unsavory reputations in Manhattan and Tonopah, Skinner began going by the name Fred Davis, and Mona became known as Norma. All seemed well, and in early December of 1907, Skinner (as Fred Davis) opened a saloon. Mona, meanwhile, could find no respectable employment and finally took a job at the Adobe Dance Hall. Others observed that the young lady, "while pretty and jolly company, was as hardened a denizen of the red-light district as ever came to Rhyolite. She drank and smoked and swore like a pirate. Her vocabulary of profanity was picturesque to the limit."[8] And, it turned out, her life with Llewellyn Felker, alias Fred Skinner, was not nearly as rosy as she hoped it would be.

On the evening of January 2, 1908, Byron Demming was out barhopping with the couple. Constable Harry O'Brien would later remember seeing them at the Mission saloon where Mona was apparently working and had opened earlier that night. Later, after O'Brien had left, Mona "declined to drink," at which point Skinner "threw several glasses at her and also beat her with his fists, and when she fell to the floor, he kicked her, despite her pleas for him to desist," reported the *Tonopah Daily Bonanza*.[9] Demming would later describe how Skinner became angry that Mona had not finished her drink. When he told her to do so, the girl said she wasn't feeling well. At that point Skinner picked the glass up and threw it at Mona, hitting her in the shoulder. Mona managed to block another glass flying at her face with her hand. As she ran for the door, Skinner caught her and began kicking her as a stream of obscenities came out of his mouth. Instead of letting her go home, Skinner then commanded Mona to sit and have another drink before she was allowed to leave. Demming later testified that he did not help Mona because he knew Skinner had a gun with him, also that he was "a bad man. He did not care to risk his life when he knew that Skinner was armed."

Later, the two men walked to the house Mona shared with Skinner on Main Street. Mona, he said, came to the door in her nightgown. As Demming departed Skinner called him back and asked if a man named Wright had given him $20. Skinner, said Demming, suspected Mona of robbing Wright for $180. But Demming had not received any money from Wright, and showed Skinner his pocket change as proof. Then he went on home, shortly thereafter hearing what sounded like several shots. Being unsure of whether the noises really were gunfire, Demming declined to investigate. Skinner would later claim that when he came home, he shared a pint or so of liquor with Mona before confessing that he wanted to return to his wife. He claimed Mona "went wild" and attacked him, also that in the past, Mona had threatened to kill him if he tried to leave her.[10]

The next thing anyone knew, Constable O'Brien saw Skinner running toward the Mission saloon in his underwear. He was screaming, "I want to make a confession!" but blew right by O'Brien and ignored commands to stop. The officer chased Skinner to the Exchange Bar, which was closed, and caught him as he tried to force the door open. Skinner told O'Brien that he "only had a short time to live" and wanted to write down his confession. "Norma shot me; I shot Norma and then shot myself," he said. "She was not to blame. I want to tell my wife and relatives in Colorado that Norma was not to blame." O'Brien hustled Skinner to the office of Dr. J.A. Wilkinson as the man switched his statement to "I shot Norma, then Norma shot me and then I shot myself. She was not to blame."

O'Brien left Skinner with Dr. Wilkinson, summoned two deputies, and went to the house Skinner shared with Mona. The sight was quite disturbing: "On opening the door the body of the woman was found kneeling beside a cot as if in prayer. An examination disclosed the fact that she had been shot three times in the back. Her nightgown was covered with blood and a pool had collected on the floor by her side. Death had been almost instantaneous." O'Brien instructed the deputies to go back to Wilkinson's office and keep an eye on Skinner while he went to find the coroner, Judge Kelleher.[11] Dr. Wilkinson, meanwhile, was treating Skinner's wounds with the assistance of George Myers. The doctor was in another room when Myers asked Skinner what had happened. "We had a fuss and I shot Norma with the soft nosed bullets," Skinner replied. He also wanted to know whether his wounds were fatal. When told they were not, Skinner "shut up like a clam and refused to discuss the case any further." Then he stood up suddenly, and when Myers stood too, Skinner back-handed him and ran from the office. Myers and Wilkinson set out in pursuit, following Skinner back to his house.[12]

When O'Brien, his officers, and Kelleher returned to the house, they found Mona's body where it had been as Skinner frantically rooted through a trunk looking for something. The man jumped up as Kelleher and O'Brien entered the house, ran into a back room, and emerged with a rifle. O'Brien was quick to disarm him and ordered him to get dressed. Upon putting on his trousers and shoes, Skinner knelt beside Mona's body and "attempted to kiss her face." Then he finished dressing, only to suddenly run to a shelf where he picked up a revolver. This too was taken from him as he laughed and declared the gun wasn't even loaded. Before being taken away to jail, Skinner knelt down beside Mona once more, "and secured a lock of the woman's hair."[13]

Later, undertaker J. Bacigalupi shared his findings. Mona, she said, "was covered with bruises as if she had received a beating. One eye was black and there was a long gash over the same eye that evidently had been inflicted by a blow."[14] The public in general was furious when they heard about Mona's terrifying life with Skinner and what he had done to her, to the extent that there was brief talk about lynching the man. Authorities sought out Clinton Heskett, who had been searching for his wife for some time. Heskett hurried to Rhyolite, where he was treated "with utmost kindness."[15] There are some discrepancies regarding what happened next. Some sources state Mona was buried in Haskins Cemetery near Rhyolite, while others state she was taken to her parents' home state of Washington and buried at Crown Hill Cemetery in Seattle. Because her burial is marked in both places, Mona may have initially been buried in Rhyolite until Heskett arrived, at which point her body was exhumed and taken to Seattle.

As Skinner went to trial, the public must have been surprised when his wife Anna suddenly showed up in town. With her was her mother, and it was reported that Anna was "supporting herself by sewing and also trying to earn money to be used for the defense of her husband."[16] Anna also attended Skinner's trial religiously, and it is hard to say just what she felt when, in March, her husband was found guilty of murder in the first degree. He was sentenced to life in prison. Upon hearing his sentence, Skinner merely displayed "that sarcastic smile that he continually wore throughout the trial." His attorney immediately motioned for a new trial, which was denied. It wouldn't be the last time Skinner demanded a retrial. Throughout 1909 he wheedled at the court until at last, in October, a new trial was granted.[17]

Through all this, Anna Skinner (as she was identified by newspapers) remained in Tonopah, as evidenced by a January 1910 report in the *Tonopah Daily Bonanza* that she contracted blood poisoning as a result of wearing tight shoes. Fred Skinner's second trial began in Carson City the following month, after being fraught with problems finding a suitable jury and making a change of venue. Apparently public sentiment against the murderer was so strong, not to mention Skinner's seedy reputation, that his attorney worried he would not receive a fair trial in Nye County. Judge Averill denied the request, perhaps feeling that enough nonsense had already taken place and that Skinner deserved what he had coming to him. Notably, Anna Skinner was not the only woman in the courtroom. The *Tonopah Daily Bonanza* would later report that "for the first time during the present trial, there were a number of women present

The ghost town of Rhyolite sometime before 1920, just a few years after Mona Bell was murdered. Courtesy Orange County Archives

yesterday and all were intensely interested."[18] Mona Bell's tragic death had apparently struck a chord with the ladies.

If he thought the jury might go easy on him, Skinner was dead wrong. Of particular interest were Skinner's confessions to Officer O'Brien, made within minutes of each other. Although he initially said *"Norma shot me*; I shot Norma and then shot myself," Skinner admitted just a few minutes later that *"I shot Norma*, Norma shot me, and then I shot myself."[19] Nobody seemed surprised when the man was found guilty again, and sentenced to fifty-five years in prison. It may as well have been another life sentence, seeing that Skinner was now thirty-three years old. Naturally he vowed to appeal his case.

By 1911, Anna Skinner finally had enough. A small, seemingly insignificant article on page four of the *Tonopah Daily Bonanza* announced that the woman, who had relocated to Carson City, was now seeking a divorce from her husband. The truth was, Anna found someone else she wanted to marry. As soon as her divorce from Skinner was final, Anna scurried to Reno where she wed F.R. Davis and, presumably, lived happily ever after. As for Skinner, the convict tried to escape from prison on various occasions. The first escape happened in September of 1912 and was successful for a few weeks until Skinner was recaptured at his sister's house in San Francisco. The second attempt was thwarted after the warden discovered a revolver hidden inside one of Skinner's leatherworking tools.

In spite of his escape attempts, Skinner kept applying for parole, which was denied again and again until 1923, when at last he was released into the custody of his brother in Los Angeles. By some miracle, Skinner eventually found someone else to marry him: Ruth Ardell Russell. The couple was united in Oklahoma. The marriage wouldn't last; after Skinner was arrested for bootlegging and assaults in Las Vegas throughout the late 1930s, Ruth divorced the man in 1938. Skinner was in Washington state when he finally died in 1962. His burial place remains unknown. As for the memory of Mona Bell, her story was told in writer/producer Ted Faye's documentary episode of "Weird Tales" in 2011.[20]

CHAPTER 11

————— ◦●◦ —————

Viva Las Vegas

Today's Las Vegas is a true oasis in the desert, seemingly dull by day but exploding into a virtual firework of color by night. Oodles of casinos, food buffets, entertainment venues, and other hot spots run twenty-four hours a day as visitors flock to the city year-round. Little do people realize, however, that Nevada's "Sin City" goes all the way back to the days when it was no more than a primitive, hot and dusty spot in the middle of the desert. In this remote place, almost anything went when the city was first founded in 1905. Writer Marie Katherine Rowley would later note that the "attitudes of local officials toward prostitution in the Las Vegas area shifted dramatically from open acceptance in 1905 to total disdain by 1955."[1]

Las Vegas was originally intended as no more than a railroad town along William A. Clark's San Pedro, Los Angeles and Salt Lake Railroad. The opening of saloons and bawdy houses were a given, since miners from the Bullfrog and Goldfield mining districts often sought relaxation in town. Almost immediately Las Vegas's Block 16 on First Street, between Ogden Street and Stewart Avenue, was designated as saloon row as lots in the district "sold quickly and for the highest prices."[2] Most of the saloons (initially eight in all, according to Sanborn Fire Insurance maps) had brothels attached to them. The district was conveniently located only two blocks from the railroad depot, and only a block from the main drag on Fremont Street.

Like other communities throughout Nevada, Las Vegas authorities were allowed to oversee and regulate the sex trade as they saw fit. Thus, news of the good time girls of the town rarely made the newspapers—at first, anyway. By 1906, authorities were busy fine-tuning the way they felt Block 16 should operate. In July Sheriff Johnson, Deputy Murphy, and District Attorney Horsey issued warrants for men found to be "living and consorting with a prostitute." Only two men were actually arrested. At issue too were some "high board fences," which were built between the back doors of the saloons and the entrances to the cribs. In this instance, it was observed, "most of the 'ladies' refused to stand for the indignity of being compelled to climb the fence for their drink, and have departed for other pastures, where lumber is higher and crusading officials are not in action."[3] Two months later the Las Vegas Age, which had reported the story, predicted that the attempt to separate brothels from saloons would "soon cause the local brothels to cease operation permanently."[4]

The newspaper was wrong; soiled doves of all ages continued flocking to Las Vegas. One of them, Gabrielle Wiley, was just a fledgling good time girl when she arrived in Vegas in 1906. At the age of fifteen, Gabrielle found herself orphaned in San Francisco, with no other way to make a living. The girl first hitched a ride to Oakland with an older woman before catching a wagon heading east to the Nevada goldfields. Once there, Gabe was said to have been forced "into the life of the submerged." She began cruising from gold camp to gold camp, waiting tables by day and working as a prostitute by night. At the infant town of Las Vegas, Gabe met and married her first husband. But the husband, whose name remains a mystery, was shot to death in about 1908 and Gabe was forced to move on. She eventually landed in Arizona, where she became a reigning madam in Prescott and became known as the "black widow" due to the untimely deaths of her various husbands and consorts.[5]

Young ladies like Gabe were welcomed by the saloon owners in Las Vegas. The *Las Vegas Age* described in glowing tones the Arizona Club whose owner, Jim McIntosh, furnished the place lavishly with mahogany furniture, lead-plated glass and "deep red wainscoting."[6] The bar was big and fancy, meant to impress patrons that included visitors from out of town. One resident said that visiting the Arizona Club "was just like going to a museum, almost."[7] In about 1909, McIntosh sold the property to Al James, who added a second story in which prostitutes could ply their trade. Still, there was occasional trouble with the men who drank at places like the Arizona Club and patronized the brothels of Block 16. In 1910, Joseph Goldie got into trouble after he stole a horse from a nearby ranch, sold it to someone, and spent most of the money in the red-light district.

As in other towns in Nevada, Las Vegas suffered a setback in 1910 when the state outlawed gambling. The ban would remain in place for over twenty years as the gaming halls figured out other ways to make money. Also, there may very well have been a brief shortage of girls. In the 1910 census only saloon owners James Franklin, Henry Farrell, and William Burkhart reported one or more unattached women living with them. The ladies' occupations were listed as "none." Either Las Vegas's good time girls had moved on, or they were living elsewhere while working out of the series of cribs on First Street. Still, according to at least one source, the illicit ladies of Block 16 continued serving "the ranchers, railroad workers, and railroad passengers who traveled through the tiny town."[8]

Today, more remains about the history of Las Vegas's red-light district itself than the ladies who worked there. One known madam, Pilar Santa Cruz, opened the Red Front Saloon sometime after 1910. Pilar appears to have been successful, remaining in business for decades. The 1920 census shows five women working for the madam, who was documented as managing a "soft drink parlor." The ladies of the house ranged in age from twenty-one to thirty-four years of age. Two of them came from Mexico, while the others were born in Pennsylvania, Poland, and Italy. Also in the house was a porter, Allin Ontonio, and Lusa Munz, a twenty-three-year-old whose occupation was not given. Years later, after prostitution was outlawed, Pilar converted her place to a rooming house called Liberty Lodgings. She died in 1947, leaving $50,000 in real estate to her brother and some nieces, and a home in Los Angeles to a friend identified as Concha Ruiz.[9]

By 1912, women of all nationalities were working in Block 16, sometimes sharing the same brothel. This alarmed the authorities to some degree, as well as the *Las Vegas Age*, which pointed out that Block 16's brothels were less than eight hundred yards from the nearest church. A grand jury recommended that the city relocate the red-light district, but nothing came of it. Still, Las Vegas's sex industry was highly disapproved of by some. One of them was railroad owner William Clark himself. In 1914, Clark invested in the all-new smelter town of Clarkdale, Arizona. The *Goldfield News* was quick to point out that "no red-light district will be allowed in [Clarkdale] and only a few liquor concessions will be granted. The town is to be policed by Mr. Clark's own men, so there will be no politics in the department. As everything in the town will belong to Mr. Clark, and he owns thousands of acres surrounding the town, objectionable characters can within 24 hours be escorted far beyond the city limits."[10] Clark's intentions in Arizona were justifiable enough, for the *Goldfield News and Weekly Tribune* reported in December that "a half-breed Italian" named Dan Castellana shot prostitute Lillian Roberts in Las Vegas before killing himself. "The woman will probably recover," said the paper. "The motive for the attempted murder and suicide is not known."[11]

Very little else was reported about Block 16 until 1919, when prohibition brought out the best in bootleggers and speakeasies around Vegas. Probably realizing that outlawing prostitution would just cause the working girls to go underground, the city chose instead to try to regulate the business. Somewhere between twenty and forty women worked in the industry throughout the 1920s and 1930s. The 1923 Sanborn map for Las Vegas shows a much smaller red-light district than in previous years. There were no visibly large brothels; instead, a series of cribs were bunched together on the east side of First Street behind seven different "soft drink salons." There were thirty-six cribs in all. Except for an adobe rooming house across the alley, there were no other buildings on the block.

The good time girls were now strictly relegated to Block 16 and were required to get "regular health checks" from a local physician. The ladies were given a certificate to show police if they were deemed healthy; those who were not were forbidden from working. Police were kept abreast of who could and who could not work.[12] Then, in 1929 the state of Nevada proposed building a nine-foot fence around the entire red-light district, accessed by "a maximum of two gates," in every town with a population of eighteen hundred or more.[13] Las Vegas residents numbered over five thousand.

Even lots of rules and a nine-foot-tall fence failed to hide Vegas's red-light ladies from the public. "Of course, those who come looking for dirt and sensation, can find our gambling houses, bootleggers and red light just as they could in their own home town," commented the *Las Vegas Age*, "or just as, possibly, some of us do when we visit other places."[14] And when District Attorney Harley Harmon was "caught in a compromising position with a woman from the red-light district and accused by her, in a sworn statement, of criminal conduct," the accusatory eyes of America became focused on Las Vegas.[15] In answer, the city talked of donating the land upon which Block 16 was situated for the construction of a new federal building. "The donation of this land to the government would necessitate the immediate removal of the red-light district from its present location," explained the *Las Vegas Age*, "and change that section into valuable business property."[16]

At the same time as the proposed doing away with Las Vegas's red-light district, the Bureau of Reclamation was readying to build the famed Hoover Dam some thirty-seven miles distant. Laborers would live in the newly built Boulder City just a few miles from the dam, with the caveat that gambling, liquor, and red-light ladies would be prohibited from operating there. "Instead of a boisterous frontier town," said the far-away *New York Times* of Boulder City, "it is hoped that here simple homes, gardens with fruits and flowers, schools and playgrounds will make this a wholesome American community."[17] Prostitutes may not have infiltrated Boulder City, but there was nothing to stop the town's male inhabitants from flocking to Block 16 in Las Vegas. In addition, miners and railroad workers also patronized the brothels. The city, however, simply viewed this as good business revenue. The girls of the row received so many clients in the way of dam workers that they even began to accept company scrip in lieu of cash payments, even though the scrip was only redeemable in the company stores of Boulder City. Whether those stores knew whether some of their female shoppers were women from Block 16 is unknown.

By 1930, Las Vegas had switched gears. When the census was taken in April, the ladies of Block 16 appeared to be doing just fine. Thirty-nine or so women present were either documented as dancers in a cabaret, or else having no occupation. But city officials were becoming more stringent. Women were now forbidden from soliciting business "in the street or in other bars or resorts." The ladies were also discouraged from spending their "leisure time" outside or in front of their places of work, the exception being during Las Vegas's hottest months. Prostitutes now lived in back of their brothels, renting their rooms by the week but keeping all of their earnings instead of sharing them with a pimp.[18] Because their living quarters were accessible by the alley, many ladies likely entertained gentlemen from the privacy of their small apartments as well.

Meanwhile, the building of an all new red-light district was proposed east of Las Vegas, outside of the city limits and "close to the main highway" leading to Hoover Dam. The *Las Vegas Age* gave the opinion that "the red light should move itself and not wait until forced out by the city." Also that "the authorities should not allow the new red light district to establish itself where it will still be an offense to public decency. The new site should be as far as possible removed from our main highways, and if possible it should be so placed that it is not in the direct hue of high class residential improvements."[19] But city officials remained adamant about their choice of location, and the arguments about the red-light district continued into 1931. When the state of Nevada officially lifted the ban on gambling that year, the ladies no doubt prospered even more. But in March, when it was rumored that two prostitutes were selling liquor without a license, the police raided the house they shared.

As construction of Hoover Dam continued, the highway leading to it began seeing more red-light activity behind the new Railroad Pass Club south of Henderson. Prostitutes were suddenly everywhere, it seemed, and even more visible after violence broke out in Block 16 in March of 1932. The *Las Vegas Journal* reported that a man, possibly a pimp or boyfriend of a working girl, severely beat a laborer from the dam. Other dam workers retaliated by fighting and committing other acts of violence. Some prostitutes, perhaps frightened by the goings-on in Block 16, started doing business in hotels around town, including along Fremont Street. Police soon had their hands full, what with trying to get rid of pimps while driving the girls back to Block 16. It wasn't an easy fight, as the old district also had expanded somewhat into Block 17 with women of all cultures working in the saloons and resorts there. Disapproving authorities were quick to make arrests. But there was more: At a locale known as Four Mile, located the same distance from the downtown area, even more brothels popped up.

Finally, in November 1932, frustrated city commissioners passed Ordinance 194, which outlawed soliciting sex on the streets and in rooming houses. More pointedly, Las Vegas outlawed prostitution within the city limits for the first time ever, although Block 16 was left unmolested. But the arrests continued. Three women were jailed in 1934 for soliciting. "We've rid the city of the colored bootleggers," a municipal judge told them, "and now we're going to start in on you girls."[20] It was a losing battle at best; as late as 1939, women were still soliciting outside of Block 16, and those within the district were selling liquor without a license. In June, Mayor John Russell charged seven men and women with not having a liquor license, and such a bold group had surely never appeared in court before as the defendants. Jack Irish, owner of the Pastime, along with Earl Noon from the Arizona Club, Babe Roan of the Honolulu Inn, and Bessie Williams of the Arcade told Judge Gus Blad just what they thought of the proceedings, as well as their proposal to move their trials to a later date because they were just too darn busy running their businesses at the moment. Amid the verbal tirades, it was discovered that Mayor Russell forgot to officially charge the resort owners with a crime. The haughty defendants were set free.

During the 1940 census, Las Vegas's wild women were again operating out in the open. At least twenty-three women blatantly told the census taker they were employed as prostitutes. About a year later, attorney J.R. Lewis bought the Arizona Club and began a serious campaign to close down the brothels of Block 16. Mayor Howell Garrison was cornered, and threatened with a recall if he did not follow up. The argument went on for months. "It is my belief that the closing of Block 16 will bring about an undesirable situation in Las Vegas," Garrison explained. "Were it within my legal power to do so I would not approve the closing order."[21] Thus Block 16 was not vacated when the city revealed an all-new plan to form a new red-light district outside the city limits in an area called the Meadows. The fight began afresh, especially when military officials began sweeping the nation clean of its soiled doves as World War II loomed on the horizon. Las Vegas was no exception, and at last city officials had no choice but to comply. Besides, property owners in the Meadows were objecting to the new red-light district anyway. In turn, Block 16 madams like Babe Roan and Bessie Williams were suing others for evicting them. The fights for and against prostitution raged on for several more decades.

One of the last houses of prostitution from the old days was the Roxie, located in the Four Mile area and opened in 1946 when Las Vegas began pushing for tourism. Although authorities vowed to close it too, somehow the Roxie never shut its doors. The owners were Edward Clippinger and the love of his life, Geneva Helen "Roxie" "Jean" Mills. Clippinger was a native of Chicago, was relieved from serving in World War I due to his left ring finger being amputated, spent time in California's San Quentin Prison for selling illegal hooch in 1928 (where his occupation was listed as that of an interior designer), and once owned a brothel in San Bernardino before moving to Vegas. Clippinger divorced his wife to be with Roxie, who had apparently worked in the Meadows. As early as 1945 the twosome leased property at Four Mile before opening the Roxie a year later. Together the couple weathered the occasional raid, but made good money and even managed to take at least one vacation to Hawaii in 1953. The following year, however, they were charged with white slavery and tried in California. Then it was revealed that the Clark County sheriff, as well as a county commissioner, had been taking bribes for the Roxie to remain open. The Roxie finally closed for good in 1955. Clippinger and Roxie retired to California where Clippinger died in 1966. Roxie died in 1989. Today Block 16, the Meadows, and other places of prostitution are officially no more, and the industry is outlawed in Las Vegas's city limits.

CHAPTER 12

The Good Time Girls of Utah

As early as 1776, Catholic Fathers Francisco Atanasio Dominguez and Silvestre Velez de Escalante first viewed what was to become Utah. Next came trappers and fur traders, followed by the first Mormon emigrants, led by Brigham Young, in 1847. Mormonism would soon run rampant throughout today's Utah. Ten years later, US president James Buchanan attempted to overthrow Young as governor of Utah Territory. Over the next year, thousands of troops would pour into the territory during the infamous Utah War of 1857, bringing with them the inevitable "camp followers"—women who willingly sold sex to soldiers and others. Amazingly, these prostitutes were among those who actually "influenced economics, politics and lifestyles" in pioneer Utah.[1]

The presence of prostitutes in Utah was no doubt reviled by respectable members of both the Mormons and the non-Mormon Gentiles—the latter whom did enjoy arguing that any man sporting multiple wives put those women in the position of prostitute as well. This feeling was even felt by many Mormon women who shared a common husband. Others were of the opinion that plural marriage was comparable to enslavement, even though the Mormon Church maintained that women were not forced into multiple marriages. Furthermore, they stated, the first wife of any marriage had final say as to whether her husband could take on

A tongue-in-cheek supposition: Soiled doves used any mode of transportation available to get to Utah. Author photo

additional wives. But while Mormon women may not have been forced into polygamy, a good number were heavily pressured into doing so by the church, their husbands, and their neighbors.[2]

As politicians argued over the rights and wrongs of multiple marriages versus the prostitution industry, the soiled doves of the West doggedly made their way to Utah. Political and social ethics mattered little to them; rather, the ladies saw that there was money to be made. Even fledgling Salt Lake City, the Mormon capital, didn't scare them away. The naughty ladies took up residence in Salt Lake as well as more remote areas like Camp Ford and Camp Floyd. At the latter place, seventeen saloons and numerous prostitutes operated in nearby "Frogtown," also known as "Dobieville."[3] Frogtown's population eventually grew to "a thousand or more inhabitants, all gamblers or whores."

During the 1860s, especially after the establishment of Fort Douglas (also called Camp Douglas) near Salt Lake City, prospectors discovered valuable minerals in the canyons to the southeast. Shortly after Camp Douglas was established in 1862, the usual camp followers arrived. One day a soldier named McCoy, who had landed himself in the territorial penitentiary, received a visit from a woman claiming to be his wife. But General Connor, who oversaw the pen, recognized the woman for what she really was. "It's that old strumpet, Mrs. Hall, that keeps at the mouth of Dry Canon," he said. The warden approached McCoy about the matter who answered, tongue in cheek, "Mr. Warden, you introduced her as my wife, and I understand that you Mormons have a way of marrying by proxy, and I accepted the ceremony."[4]

Battles over the morals of prostitution between the Gentiles and the Mormons continued to occur with great frequency. Writer Orson Whitley discussed the idea of prostitution versus polygamy as early as 1870. "I am challenged again to prove that polygamy is no prevention of prostitution," he wrote. "It has been affirmed time and time again, not only in this discussion, but in the written works of these distinguished gentlemen around me, that in monogamic countries prostitution, or what is known as the social evil, is almost universally prevalent."[5] Although larger cities tended to better support the Mormon culture, many of Utah's mining towns did not. At Park City, just thirty miles east of Salt Lake City, the town gleefully made much money from saloon licenses and prostitution fines. Only one initial complaint was recorded, when the *Park City*

Record reported that respectable citizens were fussing about the "shirt-tail factory" in the residential section of town. The madam of the place, reported the paper, was given thirty days to move. She relocated to a place near the "green house."[6]

In Park City, periodic fines of $40 per madam and $20 per prostitute were made in lieu of a license being issued. Raids on the red-light houses were sporadic, and most often made when city coffers were low. In 1899, Madam Francis Foster paid a $10 fine. Her girls, Margaret Henderson, May Mitchell, Hazel Morris, Hilda Richardson, Bessie Scott, and Louise Wilson, paid $5 each. Ultimately, a 1907 ordinance banished Park City's red-light district from its more visible location along Main Street to the nearby community of Deer Valley. Everyone, from the girls to the law, seemed to like it that way. The streets of Park City remained safe, while the red-light district was discreetly located away from the general public. By 1910 the district at Deer Valley spanned sixteen houses along Heber Avenue. Customers there and at other places typically paid $2.50 for a visit, or $10 if they wanted to stay all night. At either location, the red-light occupants continued to pay regular fines to the city.

Being removed from the public eye somewhat, Deer Valley could be wild; tales are told of a madam whose unruly customer once poked a revolver into her breast. The gun misfired and both escaped injury, but the man was arrested. Another time a young customer tried to leave without paying and was held at gunpoint while his lady of the evening demanded not one but two timepieces he had on his person. The boy complained to police but no action was taken. Gambler Fred Flint told of telling his longtime prostitute lover it was time to part company. The girl suggested a final drink together, only to collapse on the floor and die. Further investigation revealed the girl had tainted Flint's cocktail with a heavy dose of arsenic and drank it by mistake.

Prostitution was present in many other places by the 1860s. In 1865 the silver mining town of Alta, located just west of Park City, was founded. Twenty-six saloons and six breweries soon popped up, the two most popular being the Bucket of Blood and the Gold Miner's Daughter. There were also numerous houses of prostitution. Alta Nell, Patsy Marley, and Kate Hayes were the reigning madams. Patsy in particular must have been one tough cookie, for she was reported as having won a prize fight at Alta in 1873. But Patsy also was much loved by the mining men of the town, to the extent that the eastern-facing slopes from Grizzley Gulch and almost to Catherine Pass were named for her. Kate Hayes had a mining claim, the Kate Hayes or the Katie, named for her in 1878. One, or perhaps all, of the ladies operated out of what was known as the "Cat House."[7]

Another town, Corinne, was settled in about 1870 near the confluence of the Union Pacific and Central Pacific railroads in Box Elder County. By the time Corinne was just a few months old, there were already nineteen saloons, two dance halls, and an amazing eighty prostitutes. Notably, Corinne was a non-Mormon city and strongly discouraged Mormons from settling there. There was also Ophir, another 1870 silver-mining town located in a "narrow dusty canyon" which was soon "lined with tents, saloons, brothels" and other businesses.[8]

Utah achieved statehood in 1896. It would take some time, however, for the wild west towns in the new state to settle down as gentiles continued using prostitution as a tool against polygamy. Finally, in 1913, respectable women from all religions began putting their foot down regarding the good time girls of Utah when the female members of the Progressive party organized to clear Carbon County of its soiled doves. Dozens of prostitutes vacated the county during the fall, although the endeavor remained only a limited success. In March of 1914, a page one article in the *Carbon County News* told of the death of Mrs. J.R. Mattingly, a prostitute of Carbon whose Oak Bar and brothel was south of the Continental oil tanks. An autopsy revealed bruises and even a cystic tumor, but no internal injuries. The coroner concluded that the lady must have died of poisoning or perhaps heart disease, since she had been taken ill some thirty-six hours before—even though one of her girls told investigators that Mrs. Mattingly had been beaten and kicked by one of her customers some four days previous. The body was shipped to Salt Lake City, and no more was said about the matter.

By 1917 Utah had several dry counties. Bootlegging soon became a national pastime, especially after nationwide prohibition was enacted in 1919. It was only natural that gambling and prostitution accompanied the illicit vice. Small handfuls of brothels continued running. In Vernal, a Mrs. Canady's bordello was busted in June. Canady, the court charged, had been running a brothel "in a back room of the Hub Building for six weeks or more." Witnesses testified that when men entered her place, the woman would lock the door and pull the blinds down in the interest of being discreet. Several of her customers were subpoenaed for her trial, but all of them testified they visited Mrs. Canady for legitimate business purposes only.

After the trial, Mrs. Canady next relocated to the home of Mrs. Rock Labrum in Maeser. Mrs. Labrum apparently did not object to Mrs. Canady's continued solicitation of men and young boys for prostitution. But Maeser was too small for such a business, which became so notorious that Canady was taken to court again. One witness, a nineteen-year-old customer, testified that he and a buddy were enticed into Canady's and paid her for services. She was shut down again, and sentenced to sixty days in jail. Women like Mrs. Canady had no choice but to move around, a lot. Although bootlegging and prostitution were kept very much on the sly, women especially were subject to arrest when they were caught.

Efforts to squelch the sex industry continued, especially with the influence of the Mormon church. After 1919, newspapers either declined to or could not find enough information to publish articles about Utah's wayward good time girls. One of the only exceptions was the work of

Carbon County attorney Reva Beck Bosone, who eventually became the first Utah woman elected to Congress. Bosone recalled meeting her first prostitute when the raids against red-light districts and prostitutes were taken more seriously during the 1930s. The woman was an attractive blonde who "was pretty and well dressed, but looked hard as nails. This was the first time in my life I had met a prostitute. My heart was pounding for I was really nervous," Bosone remembered.[9] In 1936, Bosone again made history as the first woman in Utah to become a judge. And by 1937 she had overcome her reservations about facing prostitutes. When Leda Chavez appeared before her for allegedly stealing a dress from a beauty salon, the young woman claimed she had legitimately purchased it. "If the dress fits you, you can have it," Bosone proposed. Leda soon reappeared before her, wearing the item in question. "The judge took one look," reported Washington, D.C.'s *Evening Star*, "and sentenced her to 15 days in jail."[10]

During World War II, military efforts were increasing to squelch the prostitution industry once and for all. American troops were returning from Germany and other places, sometimes bringing with them venereal illnesses they contracted while abroad. Similarly, unregulated areas where prostitution thrived across the nation were suffering similar issues. The efforts across the United States included making prostitution a crime, rounding up prostitutes, checking them for venereal disease and treating them, educating the public, and, most important of all, closing all brothels in every city. The effort was a limited success, and prostitutes in some areas continued working well into the 1940s.

CHAPTER 13

---•●•---

Sin in Salt Lake City

As early as 1852, religious leader Orson Pratt explained that prostitution could be "prevented in the way the Lord devised in ancient times; that is by giving to his faithful servants a plurality of wives by which a numerous and faithful posterity can be raised up, and taught in the principles of righteousness and truth."[1] Polygamy might have been alright in Pratt's book, but to non-Mormons, it was an outright sin, and while prostitution also was wrong, having more than one wife was no way to abolish it. The subject of prostitution versus polygamy continued throughout the 1850s as Salt Lake City was settled. In spite of Mormon president Heber Kimball's threat to abolish any prostitutes or their cohorts that might infiltrate Salt Lake City in 1854, the sordid ones did come. And, as early as 1856, even Mayor Jedediah Grant admitted that "some who profess to be 'Mormons' are guilty of enticing and leading girls to prostitution."[2]

Mormon sentiments against prostitution in Salt Lake City were strong. Police captain Hosea Stout recorded in 1858 that some men had gone to the house of one male resident "and dragged him out of bed with a whore and castrated him by a square and close amputation."[3] Not even this brutal attack, however, remained for long in the memories of men seeking female companionship. A gentler approach was taken when

Salt Lake City incorporated in 1860. Section 22 of the new municipal code included the right "to suppress, or restrain bawdy and other disorderly houses," and to "punish vagrants, mendicants, street beggars and prostitutes."[4]

Although initial visitors to Salt Lake City noted only a few brothels and saloons within the city's small neighborhoods, the coming of the Utah Central Railroad in 1869 likely caused a marked increase in the influx of prostitutes. No one is sure just when an official red-light district was designated, but the bawdy neighborhood was in place by the early 1870s when the district was well established on Commercial Street (now known as Regent Street). Further evidence of the red-light ladies in the downtown area came in 1872, when several women were hauled into court. Among them were Cora Conway, Kate Flint, Sady Hulbert, and Nettie Hutchison. Both Nettie and Sady testified that since being fined a few days prior, both women had quit the business. Their cases were dismissed. The brothels of Kate and Cora, meanwhile, were destroyed before a large crowd. Brigham Young, according to the *Corinne Daily Reporter*, was among those who "stood looking on grandly exempt from havoc touching the many stinking bagnios over which he is ruler."[5] Clearly, even those against the prostitution industry were equally unhappy with Young.

As for the women themselves, Dr. Jeter Clinton made his feelings very clear on the matter of prostitutes infiltrating Salt Lake City. "Now for these women, the low, nasty street-walkers . . . the low, nasty, dirty, filthy, stinking bitches—they stink—that will invite strange men into their houses and introduce them into the family circles," he seethed. "They ought to be shot with a double-barreled shot-gun."[6] Yet the city now fairly thrived on the fines received from Salt Lake City's prostitution industry, which was regulated as best as possible. The ladies perhaps knew they had the authorities over a barrel, for they were growing quite bold. In September of 1878, Madam Lou Wallace, the "well known

Salt Lake City's busy Commercial Street, circa 1870.
Courtesy Library of Congress Prints and Photographs Division

courtesan," made the papers for paying $25 for a ticket to a baseball game between the Deserets and Cincinnati's Red Stockings. Lou also "brought three others paying the regular price of $1 for each," reported the *Salt Lake Herald*.[7] In all probability, the ladies dressed in their finest just for the game, much to the chagrin of the authorities and the general public. So much for remaining on the down-low.

In 1876 Salt Lake City saw the arrival of Matilda Turnross, aka Emma Whiting, alias Emma DeMarr. Born in Sweden in about 1860, Emma came to America in 1873. By 1876, at the tender age of sixteen years, she was in Salt Lake City working under Madam Emma Davis. Later, in 1882, Emma and her sister Alvie (Christina Elvitina Turnross) partnered on a brothel in Bellevue, Idaho. In the fall, they returned to Salt Lake together after having made over $3,000 in Bellevue. The ladies bought a two-story adobe house and resumed running a brothel together. When Alvie married in 1883 she left the business to Emma. Two years later Emma was arrested along with several other madams for keeping a house of prostitution. She was fined $99. Twenty-four other prostitutes, some of whom surely worked for Emma, were fined $50. Next, in 1886, Alvie suddenly reappeared and sued Emma with claims she had been defrauded. Emma appears to have played dirty. She insisted that her maiden name was DeMarr, although Alvie revealed it was Turnross. She also claimed that Alvie had signed over everything to her and even presented a letter in court from her mother to ascertain that Alvie was older than she was and therefore old enough to sign over her half of the business. In reality, the letter was forged by Emma's brother, but because of it, she won.

Emma, it appears, would do anything to maintain control over her brothel queendom, and that included working with and assisting other madams. Around the time of Alvie's lawsuit, Emma also was reported to have gone "out to try and rustle up the amount necessary" to bail another madam out of jail. Over the next two years, Emma continued acquiring brothel property around her adobe house at 243 South Main Street. She also married, in 1888, to a saloon owner named Charles V. Whiting. Two years later, a case was dismissed against Emma for running her Main Street brothel because she had actually leased it out to another woman. In 1891, Emma leased the house again, to Minnie Barton. This time she was immediately indicted for leasing a brothel. Whether Minnie continued leasing Emma's brothel is unknown, but it is known that she died the next year.

In 1897 Emma charged Charles Whiting with calling her "a bitch, a damned whore and a damned son of a bitch," and giving her a severe beating.[8] Yet the couple resided, perhaps off and on, at 243 South Main until 1898. In the meantime, they began investing in real estate while

Emma leased most of her property to other madams. She eventually took some of her businesses back, but Madam Ida Walker was leasing Emma's property at 243 South Main by 1900. Emma and Charles moved out of the house and continued investing in other properties for the next several years. Finally, in 1909, Emma sold all of her property for $120,000 to William Ferry, who became mayor of Salt Lake in 1915 and supported prostitution regulation. When she died in 1919, Emma left most of her estate to Charles Whiting. The rest of her money went to her two sisters and a brother and his three children.

By 1880 Salt Lake City had five houses of prostitution. The census lists eighteen prostitutes, all of whom likely worked in these houses. Among them was Sadie Noble, who worked for Madam Ida Bell. Two years later Sadie was running her own house, but closed after a raid in 1886. Her employees were believed to have left for Butte, Montana. As for Sadie, she decided to get some muscle behind her. Upon traveling east she married saloonkeeper and ex-Mormon John Finley Free and had a daughter in Iowa. By 1887 Sadie and her new family were back in Salt Lake, where she sold her old brothel and invested in new properties beginning in 1889. Sadie now called herself Susie Free and used her financial holdings to purchase bordellos for other madams to run. Her leasers included Jessie Blake in 1892, who fled town owing everyone money a few months later. During the financial panic of 1893, Susie had to sell some of her lots and mortgaged her furniture several times before losing most of her money altogether in 1895.

During the 1880s Salt Lake's red-light district was still mostly located along Commercial Street and also Franklin Avenue. There were few objections to the district by the predominantly white authorities, and it is notable that the neighborhood was largely populated by minorities. Chinatown was located in Plum Alley paralleling Commercial Street. Other houses of vice were operating on West Temple Street between First and Second, and on Second South Street. These houses only existed in these areas a short time, but later popped up again during the 1890s. Everybody, it seemed, knew where the red light hung—including certain officials. In 1885 Brigham Young Hampton, the Mormon leader's adopted son, decided "to expose the moral hypocrisy of the people who are hammering us" by pointing fingers at federal officials who were known to cavort with prostitutes. Hampton set up a pseudo-brothel on West Temple Street and hired two women "detectives" to entrap officials. Police watched the goings-on through holes in the walls and netted upward of one hundred guilty men. In a most humorous turn of events, however, the men who were convicted in Mormon court were acquitted by a higher non-Mormon judge, and Hampton was sentenced to a year in jail for running a brothel. Still, authorities continued their tirade against the red-light district, especially as society went after both polygamists and prostitutes.[9]

The *Salt Lake City Daily Tribune* reported on a more legitimate bust in March of 1885. "Mesdames Flint, Davis, Demarr, Lawrence, Nobel and Grey were fined $99 each for keeping houses of prostitution," said the paper. "Of the twenty-four inmates of the houses of ill-fame, fifteen were fined $50 each."[10] By 1886, such arrests were routine. In one instance, police "arrested several dozen prostitutes, fined them a maximum of $50 each, gave them physical examinations, and released them."[11] Another long-awaited raid took place in June, with between twenty and thirty women being jailed for prostitution. The *Salt Lake Herald* expressed hope that these and other arrests would eventually do away with prostitution altogether, even as they noted that the ladies "have prepared for 'license day'" with "great regularity." The paper further encouraged the authorities to "let [prostitutes] be taught that it is not their widely earned money that the city wants, but that they will either cease their degraded practice, leave the town, or so hide their business from the public that it shall not be an offense, because its existence will be unknown."[12] Certainly the ladies themselves had a good laugh at this oxymoron of sorts; how could they make money selling sex if nobody knew sex was for sale?

The arrests continued. There were "some six brothels, forty tap rooms, a number of gambling houses, pool tables, and other disreputable concerns, all run by non-Mormons" in Salt Lake City during 1886, according to the *Deseret News*.[13] During one of the raids (perhaps the one in June), it was noted that authorities thought "there wasn't much money" in the industry, and so had waited for the women "to lay up boodle enough to make it worthwhile to effect a capture."[14] But if there wasn't much to be had in the way of fines in 1886, that misnomer was largely disproved by the 1890s when thirty-five bordellos thrived in Salt Lake. Now, the red-light district included Commercial Street and Victoria Alley a block to the south, and Franklin Avenue. Madams were now fined $50 per month while their girls paid $8.50. The fines also were still accompanied by required health exams.[15]

Naturally, newspapers delighted in giving details of the women's arrests and fines when they could, and watched eagerly for times when prostitutes got in trouble for something other than working in the sex trade. In 1892 Martha Turner, formerly of Chicago, was accused of attempting to defraud Minnie Barton. Minnie had leased her house from Emma DeMarr in November of 1891 but fell deathly ill. Martha came to Minnie's side in her last minutes in February of 1892. She later claimed the sick woman had turned everything over to her, an estate worth over $12,000. The administrator of Minnie's estate, however, argued that the madam had been much too ill to sign anything. In the end the Utah Supreme Court found that Martha and Helen Smith, aka Helen Blazes, had coerced Minnie into signing the document.[16]

While women of the underworld were usually identified outright by newspapers when there was trouble, men were seldom identified unless they were prominent citizens—even though common businessmen often owned brothels in the cities where they lived. One of them,

Gustave S. Holmes, constructed two buildings at 165 and 167 Commercial [Regent] Street in 1893. Over time Holmes also owned the fancy
Knutsford Hotel, was a director for the National Bank of the Republic,
and invested in various mines. His Commercial Street buildings served
as legitimate businesses on the ground floor, with brothels functioning
upstairs, a practice that was still in place as late as 1909 when Holmes
was said to be "the fifth or sixth largest taxpayer in Salt Lake County."[17]
Today, Holmes's building at 165 Regent Street remains the only former
brothel left standing in the area.

More red-light women were noted in the newspapers during the
1890s. In about 1894, Essie Watkins appeared in the red-light district
fresh from Dallas, Texas, where she had worked for Madam Lizzie Hand-
ley. In Salt Lake, Essie aspired to be a madam, but soon after setting up
shop one of her girls killed a customer. Authorities also took umbrage
with Essie, who was white, because she dared to employ two Black prostitutes—but also because she boldly attempted to open a brothel in the
Salt Lake Times building. Essie was ousted almost immediately, and next
tried her luck at Kate Flint's former brothel on East Second South. Her
circumstances did not improve; Essie mortgaged her belongings seven
different times during a two-year span and was forced to borrow $800
from her mother. The year 1897 was her undoing when she was convicted again for stealing another prostitute's property and for not paying
her fines. Essie left her furnishings and bills in Salt Lake and disappeared. Essie was not Salt Lake City's only bad girl; during 1894 a Black
madam named Nellie Davis was found guilty of abducting a woman for
purposes of prostitution but was released since the woman was "not of
previously chaste character." Madeline Mortimer, another madam, was
also arrested for grand larceny and keeping a house of prostitution.[18]

Authorities were up in arms over their wicked women by 1895. "I
think the best plan is to put them [prostitutes] in one locality as much
as possible," commented Salt Lake Police Chief Arthur Pratt, "and

keep them under surveillance. The evil cannot be suppressed, but it must be restrained and kept under strict police control. It is a more difficult problem to handle when the women are scattered out than when they are kept together." While officials debated over Pratt's statement, the red-light ladies stubbornly continued business, as did several more businessmen who had started investing in bordello properties. One of them, Stephen Hayes, was a merchant, real estate speculator, and—like Gustave Holmes—a director at the National Bank of the Republic. Hayes financed the construction of a building at 169 Commercial Street in 1899. The structure was designed by renowned architect Walter Ware. For some years the bottom floor functioned as a saloon run by city councilman Martin E. Mulvey, with a plush parlor house upstairs. The brothel contained a central parlor surrounded by ten small bedrooms, each large enough for a bed, wash stand, and "one or two chairs."

City officials finally officially began seeking ways to restrict prostitution to one district beginning in 1903. Doing so would assure that the presence of shady ladies all over town would "not be a constant blot." Houses of ill fame were beginning to spread beyond Commercial Street and included several brothels on Main Street, as well as Helen Blazes's new parlor house at Seven South Street. At issue was how and where to move the district from the public eye. Mormon Church leader Nephi W. Clayton suggested moving the district "to the far west of the city," while the *Salt Lake Tribune* supported an idea to "open up a new street into the interior of some of the downtown blocks."

John J. Held, who became a sports illustrator and cartoonist for the *Salt Lake Tribune* in 1905 at the young age of sixteen, recalled the red-light district in Salt Lake City when it was located on Commercial Street: "Within the street were saloons, cafes, parlor houses, and cribs that were rented nightly to the itinerant 'Ladies of the Calling.' Soliciting was taboo, so these ladies sat at the top of the stairs and called their invitation to 'C'mon up, kid.'"[19] Held's uncle earned money installing electric bells in the parlor houses of Salt Lake City, and there is little doubt the boy became more familiar with the red-light district than most kids. The bells, he said, were for visitors who came to the house and were "admitted by a uniformed maid or an attendant. The luxury of these houses always included a 'Professor' at the piano. There was none of the brashness of the mechanical piano; those were heard in the saloons and shooting galleries of the street."[20]

Held also remembered two prominent madams, Miss Ada Wilson with her lavish house on Commercial Street and Miss Helen Blazes. Held's father, a printer, produced business cards for the two madams. "They demanded the finest and most expensive engraving, and the cards were of the finest stock, pure rag vellum," he said.[21] From about 1897 to 1908, Ada operated on the upper floor of the Brigham Young Trust Company building at 33 Commercial Street, whose owners had allegedly been unable to find more suitable renters. Vice-president Brigham Young Jr., however, was not buying that story. In January of 1897 he resigned in a fit from the company for letting Ada move in. At a meeting four months later, however, Young was convinced to rejoin the company.

With the matter settled Ada turned to the task at hand, which was converting the office space above the trust company into a lavish bordello—to the tune of $15,000. When it was ready, she sent out engraved invitations for her grand opening to prominent citizens, the city attorney, and even "high officials of the LDS Church." Author Jeffrey Nichols speculated that the men were unaware the invitation was to a brothel until they attended the affair. There is at least one indication that Ada cared for and looked after her employees. In 1899, she adopted a four-month-old baby whose mother was one of her girls. That same year, Ada began calling her brothel The Palace, and advertised it as such (in big bold letters) in the city directory. The brazen lady drummed up additional business by riding around town "in a dogcart drawn by a Hackney pony." Later, in 1907, Ada furthered her parades on the streets with a "chauffeur-driven automobile."[22]

Beginning in 1909, Ada switched addresses to a place at 253 South West Temple Street. Residing with her in 1910 were housekeeper Rose Desmond, twenty-seven-year-old Edith King, who said she worked as a hairdresser, and eighteen-year-old Caren M. Marriger, who had no occupation. By that time, Ada said she had been married for eight years and had one child who did not live with her, but nothing else is known about her family. In 1911, when Salt Lake City made the biggest effort to close its houses of prostitution, Ada changed the name of her place to Lee Apartments, and presumably ceased selling sex. It was the last time she appeared in city directories. Salt Lake City's wayward women, however, would carry on in the City of Saints for several more years.

CHAPTER 14

———•●•———

Ada Carroll, Inaugural Strumpet of Salt Lake City

The ordeal with Ada Carroll all started when, sometime around 1855, William J. Drummond was hastening to Utah to take a new job as Associate Justice of the Supreme Court in Salt Lake City. Everyone had high hopes for the man who, according to the *Chicago Weekly Times*, was "a gentleman of the highest manners, strict integrity, and high legal and literary attainments."[1] On the way to Utah Drummond visited Washington, D.C., where he met with Utah's territorial delegate, John M. Bernhisel. In short order, Bernhisel expressed his opinion that Drummond was a "pleasant gentlemanly man."[2] So when Drummond finally showed up in Utah with his wife, nobody thought much of it. It was not long, however, before it dawned on Drummond's colleagues that Mrs. Drummond was not all she seemed.

Back in 1850, Drummond was employed as a lawyer in Illinois and seemingly lived in blessed wedlock with his wife, Jemima. The 1850 census verifies that the couple had five children, ranging in age from one year to nine years old. The family at large, including Jemima's siblings, were inclined toward embracing the Church of Latter-Day Saints and Mormonism. Whether Jemima planned to join her husband in Utah remains unclear, but Drummond was indeed alone when he set out for Washington, D.C., to receive his credentials and instructions before moving on to Utah. But Drummond's activities while at the nation's capital included visiting at least one bawdy house, where he met Mary Fletcher, alias Mary Carroll, alias Ada Carroll. Ada, who hailed from Baltimore, had previously been married to a schoolteacher named Charles Fletcher in Maryland. Her mother also lived there, identified only by her last name, Ridgley. But Ada apparently had found married life rather dull, preferring instead to work as a prostitute, possibly in Maryland, before relocating to Washington, D.C.

LDS church member William I. Appleby later investigated Ada as a means to expose Drummond. He claimed that when Drummond first met her in Washington, D.C., he fairly drooled over his lady love. "My Lord, is it possible I am going to love a whore?" he said to her. "You are the same person I saw a few nights since in a dream." Love he did, and Ada soon agreed to join Drummond on his excursion to Utah in April of 1855. For the journey, Ada carried a whopping $2,000 (nearly $59,000 in today's money). The couple's first stop on the trip was Baltimore, where they spent the night at the Eutaw House. The next stop was at Independence, Missouri, where Ada was introduced to a Colonel Hall as Drummond's wife. Hall apparently thought nothing of the matter, throwing a dinner party and inviting other respectable parties to come meet the Drummonds.

Was Ada beautiful or even refined? One source refers to her as "Skinny Ada," but describes her as "a ravishing beauty whose only physical defects were a slight lisp and a split in one of the fingers of her left hand."[3] Appleby verified that one of Ada's fingers was "separated in the middle joint of her left hand," also that she had "a slight impediment in her speech."[4] The people who met her as she traveled with Drummond seemed to overlook these anomalies as the couple moved on to Utah, where everyone initially believed Ada was indeed married to the impending Justice. As for Drummond, he noted that "so far I have been most kindly treated, not only by Gov. Brigham Young, but by the Saints at large." Ironically, however, Drummond also observed that "Far too many Utahns [*sic*] were 'basely corrupt.'" It was an interesting statement to make, considering that Drummond was waltzing around Salt Lake with a painted lady on his arm. Yet he jumped into his new job with a vengeance. Within three months of his arrival, he was tattling to US Attorney General Caleb Cushing about how bad the Mormons were and trying to help replace Brigham Young as governor of Utah Territory.[5] It also was noted that Drummond freely made loans to others, using Ada's money and charging upward of 30 to 40 percent in interest until they were repaid.

Drummond also began blatantly criticizing the territory's court system and certain local laws, and claimed Utah had no right to incorporate its own cities. Hosea Stout, who initially "found His Honor W. W. Drummond & lady all well and in good spirits patiently awaiting our arrival to Court," was shocked at the proceedings. "After thus abolishing, setting aside, diverting from their obvious meanings nearly all the laws of Utah," Stout wrote in his diary, Drummond "most graciously supplied [in] their place . . . the laws of the US, the common Law, and his own [court rulings]." Drummond next proceeded to the trials surrounding the killing of US Captain John W. Gunnison and seven others by some Pahvant natives back in 1854. Surprisingly, his first case was the trial of Levi Abrams, who was accused of killing a Pahvant, which in turn resulted in the murder of Gunnison. Abrams was found not guilty, and as the trial went on it was apparent that Drummond exhibited considerable prejudice against the Pahvants, disallowed other defense attorneys from presenting their cases, and exercised other questionable tactics that soon had others wondering about the new judge.[6]

Drummond's worst offense, according to those in the courtroom, coincided with Stout's observation of Drummond's supposed wife waiting to enter the courtroom with him. For whenever court was in session there was Ada, sitting right beside Drummond, a highly unusual occurrence in Utah courtrooms. Sometimes, they said, the woman would confer with Drummond over the case and even nudge him on the knee to indicate the number of years in prison he should give convicts. She also had the mouth of a sailor. Drummond's associates were soon whispering about the strange, ill-bred "wife" who liked to bang her husband's gavel. Worst of all, according to onlookers, was that Drummond "would unburden himself of tirades against 'the deplorable Mormon practice of plural wifery.'"[7] And yet Drummond was still married to Jemima, even as he sat with his pseudo-wife Ada in court andopenly discussed the various cases with her as they came before him. This apparently went on for some time, as it was at least a year before Drummond's actions were finally questioned with any degree of seriousness.

The jig was up when Jemima Drummond's relative, Silas Richards, appeared unexpectedly in Salt Lake City for a visit. Upon meeting Ada, Richards inquired, "Is the wife you had in Illinois still living?" Drummond answered, "Yes, but I have been divorced from her."[8] The wily Drummond either knew Richards was coming, or had already prepared for any confrontations regarding his relationship with Ada; when he was questioned further, Drummond showed Richards and others an alleged divorce document from Illinois. Ada herself further explained that Jemima was the one who initiated the divorce, not the other way around. Did Ada know the document was a fake? Perhaps not. Either way, Territorial Secretary Almon Babbitt, who frequently visited Washington, D.C., eventually revealed that he knew Ada was a "notorious prostitute" there. Soon, scandalous truths, half-truths, and rumors were floating around Ada and her man. One visitor to the court even unabashedly called Ada a "strumpet, [whom Drummond] calls wife falsely." A letter to Jemima Drummond solicited the response that her husband had departed for Utah and "instead of leaving us plenty, he left but little." Even so, Jemima stated that "I never have nor never will get a divorce from him."[9] Now Salt Lake citizens eyed Drummond with suspicion and shock. The Justice who so vehemently argued against polygamy was himself a polygamist!

With his secret officially out, Drummond was pummeled with questions and judgments from the people of Salt Lake City pertaining to Ada Carroll. Drummond refused to admit guilt, and refused to step down. But there was more: In his investigation, William Appleby pointedly accused Drummond of other misdeeds. "Did you not speculate in purchasing runaway negroes, from Missourians returning from California, buying and selling horses, Indian claims, land warrants, loaning at enormous usery, [sic] etc., instead of attending to the duties of the office to which you were appointed?" he thundered.[10] Then there was still the matter of Ada, who "caused all of Utah to ring with [Drummond's] shame," according to historian Orson Whitney.[11] The woman appears to have taken a brief retreat when Appleby sneered, "Have you returned home to your 'divorced' wife again—please inform us where you left 'Ada,' and how much you made by using her money, and if she got profits, or any of the principal?"

In the course of his investigation, Appleby also found that in January of 1856, Levi Abrams had said something derogatory about Ada, and that in response Drummond had sent his "negro, Cato" to assault the man.[12] That same month, Drummond was brought up on charges for false imprisonment and lewdness, but details of his case remain unknown. What is known is that Drummond submitted a scathing letter of resignation in March, charging that Brigham Young had basically "set aside the rule of law in the territory," and also that the Mormons were disregarding both Congressional law and the Constitution.[13] In turn, Young said Drummond "transcended his authority, and demeaned himself very much like a dog or wolf, vicious and brutal, whining and snappish, vain as a peacock and ignorant as a jackass."[14] He also called Drummond "a rotten hearted loathsome reptile."[15]

When Brigham Young's buddy, "Wild" Bill Hickman, angrily announced he would "deal [Drummond] a painful bodily injury," the

Justice decided that Salt Lake City was too small for his liking. With Ada in hand, he skedaddled to Mottsville, near Carson City in today's Nevada.[16] There, in Mott's barn, Drummond stayed long enough to hold the first session of the US District Court on behalf of Utah Territory—until he heard Hickman was coming after him. The couple lit out again, traveling to San Francisco and boarding a ship headed for the East Coast. In 1857, the *Latter-day Saints Millennial Star* concluded that "Drummond's reports have been proved by US officers and other incontrovertible testimony to be false—utterly false—without even a shadow of foundation." As for Drummond, he had disappeared altogether. "Whether he still lives in unlawful intercourse with 'his dearly beloved,' Ada Carroll, we have not been informed," reported the *Star*.[17]

Apparently, nobody else knew what happened to Ada either. She simply vanished, perhaps taking up with another gentleman who was equally beguiled by her charms. As for William Drummond, the 1860 census found him working as an attorney in Chicago. His career didn't last: In 1863 he was accused of bungling the kidnapping case of a Mrs. Moody. Two years later, Jemima Drummond found him and, despite her early claim that she would never divorce him, successfully secured one anyway. Next, in 1885, Drummond was found guilty of stealing some postage stamps and spent some time in the Illinois House of Correction. Drummond's days as a respected attorney and Associate Justice were truly over. In 1888, newspapers reported he had died "in a low groggery, in one of the most squalid districts in Chicago," his clothing in tatters.[18] That was the end of William W. Drummond, illicit lover of one and winner of none.

CHAPTER 15

———•◦•———

Kate Flint, Maiden Madam of Utah

O f the gaggle of good time girls to infiltrate Salt Lake City, Catherine "Kate" Flint stands out as one of the most professional madams among them. She also is often credited as being Utah's first official madam. Kate told census takers at various times that she was born in Ireland or Tennessee in 1847. Where she spent her early life remains a mystery, but her career in Utah began with a primitive "tent saloon and gambling palace" at Weber Station, a remote Pony Express station in the northeast section of the state, sometime before 1869. A year later she was in Corinne, the notable "Gentile Capital of Utah."[1] The 1870 census found Kate employing three girls: Flaura Fairchild, Eliza McMarrie, and Mary Ray. Kate, who owned her property, was listed as "keeping house," while no occupations were listed for her girls. Kate's neighbors, Mary Clark and Angie Dungan, were also listed as "keeping house." In all probability, Kate, Mary, and Angie constituted Corinne's early red-light district.

By 1872, Kate lived in the far more profitable city of Ogden, where she was known as "Gentile Kate"—likely a moniker she took while living in Corinne. Her house at 150 25th Street became widely known and she was well-liked, at least by shopkeepers. Indeed, Kate quickly became "a respected part of the business life of the town, a speculator in real estate,

Western photographer William Henry Jackson captured this image of Corinne right around the time Kate Flint arrived in town.
Courtesy National Archives & Record Administration

the most liberal customer of the stores and an unofficial great lady." Prominent men knew to go to Kate's when they were in town. Her ladies dressed in their finest gowns and jewels for the occasion, and it is not hard to imagine what fine food and grog, not to mention entertainment, the madam might have offered. Kate also ran a strict house, and "no one was ever swindled at her establishment; no one was ever disorderly."[2]

Kate did not remain in Ogden very long. By April of 1872 she had moved again, to Salt Lake City. They say she opened the first official brothel on Commercial Street, right smack dab in the middle of downtown. She was almost immediately arrested in August for prostitution and fined $15. But when the city attorney complained that Kate and others like her simply continued operating whenever they were fined, a Judge Clinton ordered Kate's house, and that of Cora Conway, "abated." The decision was carried out by police officers, who went to the houses and "systematically destroyed their furnishings." Surely the destruction was intended to cause embarrassment, for a large crowd gathered in front of Kate's brothel to watch the proceedings.

Did anyone offer to help the women whose belongings were ruined and whose houses were likely made inhabitable? The answer is unknown, but Kate managed to regain control over her brothel rather quickly. Cora Conway did not, however, and went to work for Kate and other madams. Both women sued Judge Clinton and the police department. Kate testified that the men not only destroyed everything she owned right down to her underwear, but that $1,000 in cash was missing besides. Kate made sure to point out that she would probably not get a fair trial if any Mormons were on the jury, because the men named in her suit also were Mormons. In deciding the case, it also was pointed out that what happened to Kate should have happened to any man keeping more than one wife—the difference being that the said husbands claimed the women sleeping with them as wives, whereas Kate did not claim her clients as husbands. She was awarded $3,400.

Gentiles at war against the Mormons even went so far to allow Kate and other prostitutes to vote in local elections, especially those aimed at abating polygamy. This upset the Mormons to a great degree, who pointed out that while Kate and other women in the prostitution industry were allowed to vote, "the polygamous Saints could not." Prostitutes like Kate, however, could really care less about the polygamy argument, except when they were dragged into the fight. The madam refused to play games with anyone, no matter how important they thought they were. But her obstinacy only made her more susceptible to newspaper articles about her. Kate's name appeared in papers four times in 1872, twice in 1873, four times again in 1874, and a whopping six times in 1875.[3]

Undaunted, Kate refused to leave Salt Lake. When she was arrested in 1873, she immediately filed an appeal. And in 1876, she allegedly got even with the two-faced Brigham Young. According to one writer, the

Salt Lake Tribune reported on November 2 that it "was rumored yesterday, that Mrs. Catherine Flint had purchased Brigham's closed carriage, and would have his coat of arms erased and her own substituted." Some sources say this did not happen until 1877, after Young's death. Either way, in the days following Kate boldly drove the carriage up and down the streets of Ogden, well aware that some folks knew where the vehicle came from. And, it is true that Kate sued other prominent men and that the courts agreed with her at least some of the time. In 1877, for instance, she sued Jeter Clinton over some unknown dispute. Surprisingly, Mormon city council member Henry Dinwoodey recommended deciding in her favor.[4]

As strong and bold as she was, Kate was not immune to the many hardships faced by red-light women. One of them was fire. In March 1880, the *Salt Lake Herald* reported on a conflagration that broke out after a miner knocked over a lamp in the room of one of Kate's girls. By the time firemen arrived, the house was engulfed in flames. "At the time," said the paper, "the inmates were nearly all in undress and so rapidly did the flames spread that some of them are said to have only been able to escape by running out in their night clothes." Only a few pieces of jewelry and clothing and "one or two pieces of furniture" were saved out of the elegantly furnished parlor house. "The loss of furniture, wearing apparel, jewelry etc.," the paper reported, "is roughly estimated at from $10,000 to $12,000." The next morning, more pieces of jewelry were found, but Kate's extensive silver service and other items were "melted out of shape." Kate immediately began "casting about" for new property on which to resume her brothel business. The *Herald* expressed tongue-in-cheek concern when she first selected a building "on a place in the rear and close to the [Salt Lake] *Tribune* office." Kate made her offer, only to be outbid by the Walker Brothers, who swooped on the property "to prevent the proximity of a house of such character to their large building." But the effort cost the men some money, to the tune of $25,000.[5]

Enter D. Frank Connelly, Kate's knight in shining armor whom she married sometime during 1880. Connelly was an educated man who formerly worked as an express messenger and mail agent in California, Idaho, and Montana, and whose main interest in Salt Lake City was horse racing—and Kate. In all possibility, Connelly began as a favorite customer, maybe even a boyfriend, and it was he who now outright purchased a lot in Block 57 along Second South Street and immediately deeded it over to Kate. The two-story adobe brothel that emerged was called "The Mansion." In reporting Kate's good fortune, the *Herald* could not resist poking fun at her again with a not-so-quaint little poem:

> *She wore the prettiest, frizzled, hair*
> *Of yellowish golden sheen*
> *Her style, it was so debonair,*
> *And haughty was her mien*
> *Her actions grace in every move*
> *Her walk! oh heavens gait!*
> *In fact, a creature made for love*
> *But alas her shoe was 8![6]*

Fortunately, Kate was a good sport. Three weeks later, she herself placed an advertisement in the *Herald* even though the paper often insulted her: "LOST between the post office and Main Street, a Silver Portemonnaie [wallet] with papers which are of no value to anyone but the owner. A handsome reward will be paid to the party leaving it at Miss Kate Flints."[7] The ad appeared but once, leading to the assumption that Kate recovered her item.

Although Connelly was "particularly courteous and gentlemanly in his bearing to everybody," even he could not stop Kate from being arrested in April along with several other good time girls. The *Herald* named Kate, along with madams Ida Bell, Jule Brunker, Em Davis,

Annie Stafford, and another woman identified only as Blanche as being hauled into court.[8] The madams were each fined $99, while their girls paid $30. In the 1880 census, Kate was keeping house on Commercial Street with two other women, Zoe Howard and Annie Clifton. Both girls were eighteen years old. Also, Kate told the census taker she was single. More telling were Kate's neighbors: Music teacher Orson Pratt and his large family lived on one side, and a washing house run by Shun Ling was on the other. Kate, it would appear, was still the reigning brothel queen of Commercial Street, and probably preferred it that way with no competition around her—although her quarters might have been temporary as she built her new brothel on Second South Street.

Kate's name appeared in the *Herald* again in July. That time, an employee named Inez apparently slipped out of the brothel during working hours and got married. "Miss Flint has been heard to state that she had not missed the girl for a time," the paper reported, "but afterwards learned that she had made her exit over a fence, sent in for her hat by a colored girl, and when she got it said she was going to get married." The newspaper also had much to say about Inez, "the Calcutta girl" who had "first been a Mormon, then a Methodist and finally what she has been for three weeks past, a *nymph du pave*." As if that weren't scandalous enough, Inez's new husband was "a very young man of respectable parents." But the article declined to name him "in view of the possibility of there being a mistake." After spending an hour or so at Kate's, the newlyweds checked into a local hotel. "They claim that they are to receive their marriage certificate at 9:30 this morning," the *Herald* said. "The story is a pretty rich one and may cause some trouble."[9]

At least the *Herald* seemed to exonerate any wrongdoing on Kate's part for Inez's marriage. And when, in January of 1881, someone threw two bottles of something "foul and filthy" through the transom at Kate's new Second South Street house, the police promised to look into it. As for Kate, she continued dutifully paying her $99 fine every few months. In August, she also paid a tax amounting to $47.93 for sidewalk improvements. And when the room of Em DeMarr (who would soon become a madam herself) was robbed of $375 as the girl, the madam, and the other employees of the house were attending the theater, police duly arrested the culprit, George Myrton.[10]

In 1882 Frank Connelly again helped Kate by buying the adjoining lots to her new house for her in May of 1882. By then the lady was nearly a household word in Salt Lake circles: Whoever and wherever someone visited a shady lady, they were now commonly referred to as having "been to see Kate Flint." Naturally the police were at Kate's house often. Aside from their occasional raids to bring her in to pay her fines, scoundrels just couldn't seem to keep away from the madam's fancy parlor house. On a July night in 1882, pistol shots were heard coming from the direction of Kate's brothel. In "the expectation of gazing on a goury corps [sic]," several people ran to the scene. Instead they found a young man standing in the alley, who said that two other men had fired a pistol and ran off. A search of the man's clothing, however, revealed a pistol "which was yet warm and in which was an empty cartridge." He also carried a box full of bullets, save for one which was missing. After the suspect was arrested, it was discovered that he was a disgruntled employee of Kate's who had recently been fired. The next day, the *Salt Lake Herald* reported the man had been discharged "for some unaccountable reason" after telling the police that "he did not know the pistol was loaded and was so near drunk that he did not know what he was doing."[11]

Much more gruesome was the fatal quarrel between two neighboring prostitutes, Nellie Wilder and Jessie Walton. One October night in 1882 a Black servant for the girls, identified as Jenny, had gone out for some bread. Returning to the house a few minutes later, Jenny saw Kate Flint who told her "to run as fast as she could to the house, as Nellie Wilder had been shot and was left there alone." Jenny ran to the house the girls shared and "found her mistress lying limp and dead by the side of her bed. She was of course warm but there remained no spark of life and the blood which had gathered in a clotted pool on the floor told that the wound which caused her death was in her head."

The story unfolded that, during Jenny's absence, Jessie had appeared at the side door of Kate's brothel, saying, "Save me, Nellie Wilder shot me and I shot her too." Kate and one of her girls caught Jessie just as she fainted and brought her into the house. A Dr. Disbrow was summoned, and found that Jessie had been shot in the arm. Jessie was delirious, muttering that Nellie had shot at her four times. "I will go to Miss Kate's! I will! Don't shoot at me again Nellie or I'll kill you!" she cried out in her hysteria. It sounded like Jessie's shooting of Nellie was self-defense—except that she was wearing Nellie's cloak and also had Nellie's purse when she appeared at Kate's. Nellie's real name, it was ascertained, was Nellie T. Malone, and she had brought over $4,800 with her to Salt Lake City. Police grew suspicious and arrested Jessie.[12]

In the coming weeks Jessie, visibly shaking and twitching, would testify that she met Nellie in Denver just a week before coming with her to Salt Lake. Nellie had a quick temper, Jessie said, adding, "I have seen her fly in a furious passion over almost nothing." Jessie also claimed Nellie shot herself. She did not remember being at Kate's. But there definitely was more to her story. Before long, both Jessie and a Dr. Driscoll were accused of murdering Nellie for her jewelry. Jessie's claim of wanting to go work for Kate Flint was apparently a ruse; Kate herself would testify that she had never even seen Jessie before the night of the murder.[13] Jessie's case came up before the grand jury in mid-November. To everyone's surprise, the *Salt Lake Herald* gave the outcome on November 18 that "The grand jury ignored the indictment of murder against Jessie Walton, and the defendant and sureties were discharged."[14]

More trouble would come: In August of 1883, Officers Smith and Salmon heard some women screaming "murder" and "help" from Kate's house. Upon their arrival, they discovered that an unseemly gentleman had been ousted from the brothel for causing trouble, "and the further he got out the madder he became." Outside, the man picked up two rocks, wrapping one of them into a handkerchief in his hand. Next, he talked another man into helping him crash through the door. "Just at the particular moment, however," explained the *Salt Lake Herald*, "when he was about to make a wreck of the whole establishment and convert the inmates into gory corpses," the officers intervened "and made a complete change of programme." The offender was hauled off to jail, fighting the officers the whole way. He was fined $25.[15]

For a while, things were normal at Kate's. But on July 10, something happened that would absolutely break her heart. The madam was hosting one of her late-night, elegant dinner parties. Husband Frank was there, cheerfully eating his dinner and chatting with others. Suddenly, however, the man was "attacked by terrible convulsions, which seemed to double him up completely." Quite before anything could be done for him, Connelly died right there in Kate's dining room. His obituary in the *Salt Lake Tribune* come morning confirmed that Connelly's "many of his friends will hear of his death with regret." The man was indeed well-liked. "He was always fair and honorable in all his dealings," said the *Tribune*, "and was particularly courteous and gentlemanly in his bearing to everybody and under all circumstances and he leaves not an enemy behind him." The paper did note that he "was addicted to the use of liquor periodically, and this was perhaps one of the causes of his sudden death."[16]

The *Salt Lake Herald* merely reported, way back on page eight of the paper, that the "funeral of Frank Connelly, a sporting character who died on Wednesday night at Kate Flint's house, will take place at the Liberal Institute on Saturday at 2 p.m." It was up to the *Tribune* to describe Connelly's funeral, which "a great number of his friends and acquaintances" attended. A Baptist minister, Dr. DeWitt, presided over services, after which eight pallbearers "conveyed the casket to the hearse, the casket being of the most elaborate and beautiful design." Thirteen carriages made their way to the gravesite, where Connelly was buried in a casket costing upwards of $350. Numerous bouquets and "a large number of floral wreaths, anchors, and hearts" were laid on Connelly's grave at Salt Lake City's Mt. Olivet Cemetery. Neither newspaper mentioned that Connelly's beloved widow was Kate. Perhaps they didn't know, but Kate made sure they did. A small card of thanks in the back of the paper read, "Will you permit me through your columns to express my thanks to the kind friends who assisted in the funeral services, and those who by their presence and otherwise contributed toward the respectful demonstration on the occasion of my late husband's obsequies. To all sincere thanks. Mrs. D. F. Connelly."[17]

For over a month, Kate grappled with Connelly's probate. In the end, his estate totaled $1,750, including his diamond jewelry, a gold watch and chain, clothing, a buggy, and his prized racehorse, Greenback. Petition papers show Kate's wanting, or needing, to sell most everything. She did, however, keep Greenback, who was put under the charge of her hired hand, Harry World. Presumably Kate entered the steed in other races, for she later tried to purchase other racehorses as well. She also bought Connelly a most elegant tombstone in 1887. As usual, the *Salt Lake Herald* noted that "Madame Kate Flint" paid for the monument, but once again failed to mention she was Connelly's widow. But the monument spoke for itself. The paper reported that it was a statue of "Hope" and that "when finished the monument will be over eleven feet high, the statue resting on a block of marble supported by four marble columns. A marble steed about eighteen inches high with a rider will form a portion of the whole. The figure of Hope weighs over 1,200 pounds. Its transportation alone cost $200 and the expense of the whole monument will be something over $1,000."[18]

Sadly, the papers and others almost immediately exhibited a lack of respect for the grieving widow. Just two months after her husband's death, an article appeared in the *Salt Lake Herald*: "At midnight last night a number of individuals appeared in a hack in front of Kate Flint's establishment on Second South Street and began making a disturbance and engaged in a general scrimmage. The officers on duty interfered to quell the miniature riot when they were assailed and one of the party, who gave his name at the City Hall as Williams, drew a self-cocking pistol and threatened to shoot. He was promptly arrested and taken to jail where he will rest until tomorrow, when he will be required to answer to the police magistrate for his reckless conduct." A few weeks later, Latter-Day Saints president John Taylor included Kate and "her sisters of sin" in one of his many long rants. Kate remained stoic, dutifully paying her fine in October for herself and her employees, who were identified as "Miss Jenny, Agnes Carroll, Mabel Kirkham and Miss Panzy."[19]

Kate put up with a lot. In February of 1885 she was in the papers again after some of her customers got drunk and prank-called the firehouse to report the brothel was on fire. Later that month, Salt Lake police began an official "war on prostitution." The officers "quietly visited" six brothels, arresting some thirty-one women, which, of course, included Kate and her eight employees. "The swearing with which the officers were greeted was something no male imagination could conjure up," reported the *Salt Lake Herald*, "but it was suddenly quieted when the ladies were informed that the additional charge of profanity would be booked against them." Next, a prominent Salt Lake City businessman, Abraham Cannon, was alarmed to discover his own brother, Frank J. Cannon, "had succumbed to the wiles" of Kate and her girls. In his diary, Abraham later told of his frantic search for his brother, and that the "horrible information I obtained was that he was in Kate Flint's establishment and that his associations with that notorious prostitute are well known to several police officers. He has been drinking deeply and spending money very lavishly on fast women. Some of his suppers are said to have cost him $35." But Frank also owed Kate money, a debt that Abraham settled with the madam to prevent any scandal.[20]

The war on prostitution in Salt Lake City continued, with Kate's name frequently coming up in the papers. But the authorities didn't go after the madam right away, preferring to first harass her employees—and clients—beginning in January 1886. In an article with the headline "A Starter," the *Salt Lake Herald* focused on Harry World, Kate's faithful employee who cared for Greenback. "Mr. Harry World, a gentleman who has figured considerably before the public as *charge d'affaires* of Madame Kate Flint's establishment, has been indicted by the Grand Jury for being an inmate of that palace of infamy and papers were placed in the hands of a deputy to serve," the paper reported. World got wind of the impending charge and disappeared. The affair must have unnerved Kate, for in March, she was reported as purchasing the brothel of Mollie Price in far-off Leadville, Colorado.[21]

Kate never did move to Colorado. In June, the *Herald* named "Joseph Miller an employee of Mr. Henry Wagoner," as the man arrested at Kate's the previous May for "visiting a house of prostitution for the purposes of lewdness." Although Miller initially pleaded guilty, his attorney was quick to point out that the man had only a limited grasp of the English language. Miller was granted a new trial, to which his lawyer responded by demanding a jury trial, which he got. But testimony showed that when Miller was found in the room of Florence Kennedy, he was merely "lying back in a chair taking it easy," not engaging in sex. His attorney then provided an interesting commentary on Kate's palatial parlor house. The Mansion, he said, "was a model and most desirable place of residence and the inmates were second only in purity to the angels themselves." Next came testimony that "there was no evidence to prove that Miss Flint's house was such as was complained of." Other witnesses basically said the same. The case was continued.[22] Unfortunately the outcome remains unknown, but the authorities were hardly through with Kate Flint.

Four days after Miller's arrest, a second arrest took place during which another of Kate's employees, Lottie Perkins, was accused of "being a vagrant and a common prostitute." As with Joseph Miller's trial, Lottie's attorney demanded, and received, a jury trial. The first witness against her claimed that Lottie worked at a nearby brothel called "Black Jule's," which was "bad beyond all description" with nightly orgies, "perpetual singing, yelling and other antics." Three police officers also testified that Lottie was "considered bad." The defense answered the charge with testimony by Kate's housekeeper, Mrs. M.M. Morton, who clarified that Lottie did not work at Black Jule's, and was employed as a mere chambermaid for Kate. Mrs. Morton testified that Lottie's job was to greet and admit gentlemen at the front door, and although the fifteen rooms in the house were "occupied by ladies," Lottie had no inkling of what they did. Kate's other employees, a woman named Lily Reed and the Chinese cook, Jimmy Lin, also confirmed that Lottie was a chambermaid and nothing more. Lottie herself denied all the charges, stating she "was not on the streets, had never been drunk on the streets," and had "never been consorting with soldiers." The jury did not believe her, however, and found her "guilty with a recommendation of mercy." And although there was talk of an appeal, the *Salt Lake Herald* doubted that would happen.[23]

When they ran out of customers and innocent employees to arrest, the authorities finally put Kate herself on trial. The *Salt Lake Herald* noted on June 19 that "the trial of Kate Flint and her maids has been set for 2 p.m. today when unless again postponed, they will receive their reward." The newspaper clearly was out for blood, and fired back when a Denver reporter named Pat Lannan appeared on the scene with the promise to "show Salt Lake what metropolitan reporting was." Lannan apparently had published something to the effect that "the city authorities were dallying with Kate Flint's case out of favoritism for her." The *Herald* fired back that "had the howling idiot who wrote this taken the trouble to inquire he would have found that the Flint case has been postponed from day to day to suit the convenience of Judge McBride, the 'lady's' lawyer."[24]

It is true, McBride had delayed as much as possible, and with good reason: His client's business was at stake. At last, however, the courtroom managed to wrangle Kate and her "maids of dishonor." McBride asked for them to be discharged, claiming that "the court had no jurisdiction to try such cases, that it was an indictable offense, and should be brought in the name of the people of the Territory of Utah." He was denied as the court planned to call one of Kate's good time girls, "the winsome Kitty," as a witness. The *Herald* noted that Kitty had already appeared the day before, "clad, besides her usual habiliments, in a confident smile and several thousand dollars' worth of diamonds. An envious policeman counted no less than forty large diamonds in addition to several other jewels, all of which would seem to indicate that she had but very little to complain of in regard to hard times."[25]

Kate apparently beat the charges against her, but before long an all-new court case in October shook her palace of sin. This time "a somewhat dazed looking cowboy" named McCurdy, who owned a ranch in Nevada, had come to Salt Lake City for a little fun. In his effort to "paint the town red," McCurdy met a girl identified as Claudia Le Roy at Kate's brothel. It was love at first sight, to the extent that the rancher asked Claudia to come live at his ranch with him. Ever coy, Claudia agreed but explained she had some debts to pay first and successfully asked the gullible cowboy for $45. Next, Claudia showed McCurdy a letter from her father, who was dying somewhere back East. She wanted to visit him, and asked for another $100 to make the trip. Once again, McCurdy gave her the money believing that when she returned, she would go to Nevada with him. Claudia even offered him her trunk, which was filled with "rich dresses and hats," as collateral. McCurdy agreed to keep the trunk for the girl, and "had it carted away to his abiding place at some stable."

Before Claudia could board the train, a young horse racer named Charlie Traynor appeared on the scene. Traynor knew Claudia, and he knew just what kind of girl she was. Somehow the boy got wind of her plan and immediately went looking for McCurdy, whom he told was being played by Claudia. For $20, in fact, he could prove it. McCurdy agreed to the deal and hurried to have a second look at Claudia's trunk. Sure enough, it was filled with nothing more than straw and some bricks. Next he went to see Claudia herself, demanding his money back. The girl just laughed at him, telling him "that was her business, to beat men all she could."

McCurdy went in search of justice as Claudia hurried to secure a closed carriage bound for the train station. She made it as far as Elko before she was arrested. Later, Traynor would explain that he took McCurdy's money because "he hoped to make something out if it, and besides, it wasn't right to see the old man swindled." In court, Claudia would claim that Traynor was angry "because she had refused to pay his expenses to San Francisco." Madam Kate accompanied Claudia to court, where the girl said she had planned to follow through on her promise to McCurdy and had no idea how her trunk came to be filled with straw and bricks. When she was found guilty and fined $500, the girl gasped, "Oh Miss Kate," and buried her face in the madam's shoulder. As for McCurdy and Traynor, they too were held with a bond of $200 each. "It will not be uprising if principal and witnesses, too, await the action of the Grand Jury in the penitentiary," surmised the *Herald*.[26]

The shameful case of Claudia Le Roy was Kate Flint's undoing. Not a week went by before the madam and others of the red-light realm were arrested during one of their Saturday night soirees and deposited in jail. The authorities had had it up to their ears with the demure sign in her second-story window reading "For Rent." They'd had it with the antics of Claudia Le Roy and others. This time, they meant business. Upon entering Kate's officers rounded up the madam and three girls, identified as Claudia, Gertie Titsworth, and Kittie Allen. Customers from some nearby brothels were arrested as well. In court later that evening, Kate explained to the judge that Gertie was not employed by her and was only there to see her sick mother. She was finally allowed to leave on the promise she would return with bail money, which she did. Her case was set for the following Tuesday.[27]

Kate was clearly tiring of the tirades against her by the police. In court, she began by pleading again for the release of Gertie Titsworth, which was granted. But she also "made strong promises as to her intention of closing up. She had considerable property she said, and just as soon as she could dispose of it she would leave town." The ears of the court perked up at this news, as it was the first time Kate proposed closing her Mansion. But she was fined the usual $99 anyway and, also for the first time, was sentenced to ten days in jail.[28]

The authorities were foolish if they thought it would be easy for Kate to liquidate her property. As of December her brothel was still open, likely because the madam was making as much money as she could before quitting the business. Notably, only one girl was in the house in March when night watchman Thomas Thomas noticed some curtains on fire on the second floor of the Mansion. When Thomas and a Mr. Leaker tried to gain entrance, the girl initially said she could not let them in—until they informed her of the flames. Kate, who had stepped out, returned to find the men dousing the fire with buckets of water. They had been joined by Louis Cohn, to whom Kate handed some of her most valuable jewelry before aiding the others in extinguishing the fire. In the end, the bedroom sustained about $200 in damage. But that particular room had been unoccupied for weeks, and it was speculated that someone saw Kate leave the house, snuck in through the window, and perhaps lit a match with which to see before accidentally setting the fire.

The fact that at least one bedroom had been unoccupied for some time, and that only one other woman was present when the fire began, seems to indicate that Kate had nearly ceased doing business. Her valuables aside, the loss of income may be why two men, attorney Samuel A. Merritt and farmer Bergen DeMott, loaned the madam money in July and September 1887. She did finally sell the Mansion, in February of 1888. Even the *Salt Lake Herald* was astounded at the selling price of $32,000. The paper commented that the money "sounds so much like a fairy tale that we do not vouch for its correctness." Kate also still owned her building at the corner of Fifth South and Fourth East. In 1890 that property was valued at over $17,000. There is no record of her running a brothel at the address, and by 1892 most sources agree the lady had finally retired when she was living at 140 West North Temple.[29]

In 1895 Kate now resided at a place on Social Hall Avenue. She was not in business but did retain her relationships with her friends, madams Susie Free and Essie Watkins, who stayed with her for a time. Others knew where Kate was too. In January of 1896, Kate was in her room when she became faint from what was later assessed as a slight overdose of morphine. When she awoke the next morning, some diamonds she had left on her dresser, valued at $1,000, were missing. The theft was reported to police, and a few days later Kate heard a knock at her door. Opening the door, there was her diamond necklace and two bracelets hanging from the doorknob, with "two of the most valuable stones" missing. Kate suspected a well-known sporting man who had been down on his luck, but he was never caught.[30]

What happened to Kate Connelly, alias Kate Flint, the illustrious madam of Salt Lake City's largest and fanciest brothel? One source says she left Salt Lake in the early 1900s, and what became of her is unknown. But she must have gone somewhere familiar to her, hopefully living out her life in quiet comfort with the last of her riches. The last mention by newspapers of Kate Flint in Salt Lake City was in 1898. A *Salt Lake Tribune* reporter was recalling a time long ago, when a mortuary opened next door to Kate's Mansion. A policeman happened by, and asked Kate what she thought of such a place opening right next to her. "Oh, that's alright," she quipped, "sin and the wages of sin ought to go together."[31]

CHAPTER 16

———◦•◦———

"Hell 'n Blazes" at Helen Blazes's

S ometimes one must just start over. At least that is the way Helen Blazes felt about life. Of course, Helen Blazes was not her real name, and it is presumed that she took it from a popular euphemism of the late 1800s. There is a Lake Hell 'n Blazes in Florida, for instance. The nickname was also assigned to various "outlaw" horses in the wild west. In 1886, the *Los Angeles Herald* made mention of a racehorse of the same name. And then there is mythological Helen of Sparta, touted as the most beautiful woman on Earth, who was addressed in this little ditty:

> *Then Virtue packed her grip and ranged*
> *To other scenes and phases;*
> *And Helen, queen of Sparta, changed*
> *Her name to Helen Blazes.*[1]

For Helen, born Lillie Taylor Armstrong in 1858 in Ohio (or perhaps Pennsylvania), the spunky Helen of Sparta might have served as an inspiration later in life. In 1877 she married a promising medical student, Leander Melancthon Hutchison, who had only recently graduated from Muskegon College. A year later Lilly gave birth to her only daughter, Leona Blanch, and the young family began moving around the

Midwest. Most unfortunately, however, the Hutchison's marriage would prove less than ideal as Leander began exhibiting strange and sometimes violent behavior.

The couple had moved to Olathe, Kansas, by 1882. But in March that year, a fire destroyed Leander Hutchison's entire medical library and the research specimens he had painstakingly collected. Then in October, Lillie somehow got blood poisoning and little Leona was reported ill. The following month, Leander erupted into a terrible fit of anger and literally chased Lillie from their home. She was forced to stay the night at the American House as police watched over her husband to keep him from "doing any violence to himself or others." Afterward, Lillie came very near to filing for custody of Leona and leaving her husband, but the two reconciled after he promised to behave.[2]

During 1883 the Hutchisons moved, first to Kansas City, Missouri, and again to Andarko, Oklahoma. They were apparently back in Olathe in December of 1883 when Hutchison was jailed after he returned home from a trip and almost immediately shot a man named Bob Young. By 1886 he and Lillie were officially separated when Leander remarried, although Lillie did not officially divorce him until 1890 when she was in Denver. While there, Leona was sent to live with her aunt, Louise King, and Louise's husband, George. Helen eventually left Denver and headed farther west. There is evidence that Helen kept in touch with Leona, but the nature of their mother-daughter relationship remains unknown.

When she first surfaced in 1892 in Salt Lake City, Lillie had officially cast off her old name in favor of a new one: Helen Blazes Smith. Where or why she came up with the name Smith is unknown, but for the next three decades, she would become one of the wealthiest and most brazen madams in town. She was known for conducting herself in a conservative manner, serving only wine to her wealthy clientele. She loved watching baseball, and was a particular fan of Lefty O'Doul of the Pacific Baseball League. And she loved making money, lots of it.

Helen's first residence, 243 South Main, was the former brothel property of Emma DeMarr, aka Emma Whiting. Before Helen came along, Emma had hired Minnie Barton to run the place. In February 1892, Minnie died of an unknown ailment. Sitting at her deathbed were Helen (as Helen Smith) and Martha Turner; Martha would later claim that Minnie signed all of her properties, from Minnie's personal belongings to the lease on her brothel, to her. The court found otherwise, claiming that Martha and Helen had exercised "crafty, avaricious, and selfish" ways to get Minnie to sign over her property. Even so, Helen was able to purchase the furnishings at Minnie's, and used it as collateral to borrow $1,500 from Martha in April. There is evidence that Helen was a working madam (a proprietress who serviced customers alongside her girls), for she later told newspaper writer Harold Ross, "Jesus Christ, kid, cut out the honey. If I had a railroad tie for every trick I've turned, I could build a railroad from here to San Francisco."[3]

By the time Helen Blazes went into business, Salt Lake City had been dealing with its good time girls for quite some time. By December of 1892 Helen was on the police station's radar when she, along with a Madam Mulvena and fourteen prostitutes, was arrested. Helen and Mulvena each paid a $50 fine. The money mattered little to Helen, who was already making good money at her new brothel. Once, in 1893, she advanced $400 to two of her employees for their dressmaking and board expenses. The ladies left for Denver instead, and Helen successfully had them arrested and returned to Salt Lake City. One of them, Nellie Conley, was later committed to the state insane asylum for repeated morphine use. As for Helen, her name was soon known to everyone. Once, when a common prostitute was denied a floor seat at the Salt Lake Theater, the girl argued that "the Madame of two forty-three" was already seated on the floor. She, of course, was referring to Helen's 243 South Main Street house, and it was no doubt the madam who enjoyed floor seating while the other prostitute was bounced.[4]

Indeed, Helen kept her nose clean. She paid her fines for herself, as well as the six or so girls who usually worked for her. Doing so was just part of the business. But when two more new recruits from back East, Ida (aka Freda) Pulman and Cecil Gray, made off with a $300 advance and some of the other employees' clothing, Helen again went after them. The girls were arrested in Ogden and brought to the jail in Salt Lake City. In court, with several members of the demimonde looking on, the incensed madam asked the court to take $187 in clothing belonging to Freda, sell it, and apply it to the balance the girls owed to her. The request was apparently granted, for next, Freda sued Sheriff McQueen for "the return of certain wearing apparel, a silver toilet set, an album and other articles valued at a total of $125 and alleged to have been wrongfully seized by Deputy Sheriff O'Brien, and for damages in the sum of $150." The defense "claimed that the articles in question were exempt from execution" and produced the items. Justice Kesler "made a critical examination" of the goods and said he would get back to Freda later that afternoon.[5] It is unknown if he did.

As for Helen, it was business as usual. She followed the ebb and flow of Salt Lake's demimonde and agreed, at least temporarily, to move her business to Franklin Avenue with the other red-light ladies when the authorities demanded it in 1894. Even there, however, police were quick to pounce and raided Helen in July. She was charged a $50 fine, and each of her six girls were charged $25. The same thing happened in December, with the good time girls paying a combined total of $476. But when they arrested Helen and others yet again in February of 1895, Helen put up a fight. Like other madams, such as Essie Watkins who declared she was "not going to do any business until this affair blows over," Helen also shut down briefly. Even so, the *Salt Lake Herald* reported on February 1 that Helen and two of her employees, Flo St. John and Miss Cleo, had been arrested at 4:45 a.m. that morning. The women were charged with keeping a house of ill fame. An alleged customer, "John

Doe," was fined and released as Helen paid her fine of $17, plus $8.50 for her girls. In court, however, Helen vehemently pleaded not guilty. "I have not done any business for a week," she told the judge, "and it isn't fair to pull us just for nothing."[6]

Helen's case was set for that afternoon. Whatever happened in the courtroom angered the madam even more. Thus, it was not surprising that a small ad appeared in the *Salt Lake Herald* on February 10: "All persons having claims against Helen Blazes can have same settled by calling 166½ West South Temple street." The address was Madam Sadie Noble's former fancy parlor house. Sadie's furnishings had been quite lavish, one bedroom containing "a black walnut bedstead, dressing case, wash stand, and wardrobe; a patent rocker; an oak chair; a towel rack; a zinc heating stove; a window shade with a pair of lace curtains and black curtain pole; a Brussels carpet; a seven-piece toilet set; a box spring mattress, two feather pillows, one pair of blankets, and one quilt."[7] It is presumed that when Helen moved in, she furnished the house with equally fine items.

There is little doubt that Sadie Noble's former bordello ran just fine under Helen's management. And if the court wanted their fines, her brazen advertisement told them where she could be found. To further her point, Helen declined not to appear for her court case on February 2. "Helen Blazes lost $17 by not appearing," tattled the *Salt Lake Herald*. But the newspaper forgot that Helen had already been wrongly assessed a fine, and when the red-light houses were raided again later that month, the *Herald* was forced to acquiesce. "Helen Blazes, Flo St. John and Miss Cleo were dismissed," the paper reported, "it appearing to the satisfaction of the court that they paid a fine last month when they were not carrying on their illegitimate business."[8]

Helen had demonstrated her unwillingness to be taken advantage of by city officials, but she needed some muscle behind her. In June of 1895 she was in Golden, Colorado, when she married Richard H. Dreyfuss, a sometime bartender. Like any ceremonial husband—men who married prostitutes as a means to help them deal with authorities and appear respectable—Dreyfuss did not live with Helen until much later in the marriage. Rather, his place of residence over the next several years included various hotels and apartments in Salt Lake City while he visited his wife on the sly. Helen's new man emboldened her further. When she was fined on October 30, she and her four girls, Reta, Louise, Olive, and Harriet, pleaded not guilty in court the next day. "This maneuver of Helen's is a new one for members of her class," reported the *Herald*, eyebrows up, "and the result of the trial today will be awaited with interest." The paper was even more shocked when Helen "succeeded in refusing to pay police taxes, as have others of her ilk, by declaring that she has ceased to conduct a house of ill fame."[9]

Why did Helen claim she wasn't running a brothel? The answer may lay in a *Salt Lake Tribune* story about George Israel, an unfaithful husband who ran off with a woman identified as Mrs. Belle Dieter the previous June. A city attorney for Phoenix, Arizona, the married Israel met Belle and quickly developed "a case of mad infatuation." But Belle also was married, and when her husband threatened Israel's wife, the latter successfully had him thrown in jail. Then he took off with Belle Dieter. In Gunnison, Colorado, Belle began to regret her decision and wrote her husband "a very pathetic letter" asking him to take her back. Yet she kept traveling with Israel through Grand Junction and over to Salt Lake City, where Belle briefly became "an inmate of Helen Blazes's resort" around October 14.

Belle's husband, meanwhile, followed the couple to Salt Lake and filed charges of adultery against them. Belle and Israel fled again, through Idaho and back to Utah, through Ogden and finally to Park City, where they were "taken to the penitentiary" and brought to court. "Israel and his charmer . . . chatted to each other almost incessantly, apparently oblivious of the espionage of the court attendants," said the *Tribune*.

The paper described Israel as "a large, coarse-featured, slovenly-looking man about 40 years of age. Mrs. Dieter is quite small, a blonde, and a very handsome woman." In the end, US Attorney General Howat "concluded to resubmit the case to the grand jury."[10] The outcome of the case remains unknown, but Helen appears to have felt empathy for Belle Deiter, successfully cleaning up the mess she left behind. By refusing to admit she was in business, she might have been able to assist Belle in court, too.

Of course, Helen moved around a lot, especially during the times she denied running a brothel. In 1896 she relocated again, to a brand-new building at Number 7, Victoria Place. She almost immediately endured a raid in February when the authorities, tired of everyone disregarding city ordinances forbidding prostitution, raided the entire demimonde. Fifty-six women and twenty-six men were arrested, including Helen, her four girls, and "one male inmate." The following month she was arrested again, along with Madam Ida Walker and each woman's respective employees. A third arrest occurred in September when Helen, "with one of her fairies," was brought into court after cussing at a Mrs. Rippey. In court, the insulted woman repeated what Helen said to her. "The sound of it paralyzed the court room, and Helen looked around at the startled habitues with a sweet smile," the *Herald* reported. She was fined $20 "for her fine flow of rich colored invective."[11]

The *Herald* did not care to comment on Helen again until 1899, when two of her girls, Norma Perkins and Miss Murphy, "drank a few goblets of something" and decided to take a ride in a rented rig. "Norma shot past Officer Simpson on Second South with a wave of her hand and a merry ha ha!" the newspaper reported. The wily officer simply waited until the rig passed by again, jumped in, took the reins, and drove the wagon directly to the police station. The giddy girls "thought it was a huge joke" until the desk sergeant asked for their names and demanded $10 from each to assure their appearance in court. The walk back to

Helen's surely sobered the ladies a bit. Later in 1899, three respectable young waitresses, Mary Douglas, Helen Morton, and Sarah Jones, went out for the evening with a couple of "young bloods." The boys, Jimmy Kahn and H. J. Gump, talked the girls into visiting Helen's house where all five were arrested for "entering a house of ill fame." Kahn and Gump were sent to find bail money for the girls, and were "out until an early hour."[12]

The police were at Helen's parlor house again in March of 1900 after miner James Mullard of Park City, along with his friend, were entertained by two of the madam's girls. Mullard admitted he and his friend were already tipsy when they wandered into the brothel and ordered three bottles of beer. Some champagne came with their order, but Mullard claimed, "I don't know who paid for or who ordered it." Mullard's friend had left by the time he realized he had been "drugged by one of the women." In this dazed state, Mullard was "hustled" into a hack by two women and taken to what the *Salt Lake Herald* identified as the "State Street road house." Mullard remembered little about the girls except that "one of them was named Rita and she kept her face heavily veiled." The next afternoon, Mullard awoke to find the ladies gone and his pocketbook empty beside his head. Luckily, the bartender had seen the girls with the pocketbook. Mullard tearfully explained all this to police, claiming that he had $160 in the wallet from "three months hard work and sobriety in the mines about Park City."

An angry Helen Blazes told police she absolutely would not have her name connected to the incident. Mullard, she said, spent over $100 at her place, giving $20 each to three of her girls and spending the rest on wine. He was not, she said, drugged in the brothel. "The girl who caused this trouble will have to get out of town just as soon as this is settled," she seethed. But the *Herald* pointed out that similar robberies allegedly had taken place at Helen's. Three months prior, a man from Montana had $300 stolen from him, which was recovered. The paper also pointed out that most victims "are unwilling to have their names appear so that there is the utmost secrecy. The women do not greatly fear so that they become bolder."[13] The word "bold" was indeed an understatement for Helen Blazes. When some drunks got into a fight on a train platform in May, it was she, "brilliant in diamonds and gaudy colors," who "tossed one pugilist to the side like a baby, and steered the other away."[14]

The 1900 census, taken in June, shows that Helen had nine prostitutes working for her, as well as two servants:

Helen Blazes's Employees, 1900

Name	Age	Birthplace	Marital Status
Vera Ashton	25	California	Single
Cleo Hill	25	California	Single
Lillie Hopkins	21	Missouri	Single
Neita Johnson	20	California	unknown
Leona Jones	22	California	unknown
Violet Marton	20	New York	Single
Bessie Stone	24	California	unknown
Charlotte Taylor	28	California	Single
Mable Woods	25	California	unknown
Luttie Shelton (servant, Black)	26	California	unknown
Alice Walker (servant, Black)	30	Texas	unknown

The thief Rita was gone, just like Helen said she would be. But managing nine girls and two servants all crowded together in one house must have been difficult, especially when one of them was naughty and wound up in police court. But as much as the police had to investigate matters such as the robbery of James Mullard, they did respect Helen Blazes in a sense. In July, it was announced that troops from the Ninth Cavalry were leaving to go fight the war in China. One of them, John Giles, was quite in his cups when he was spotted by Officer Randolph as he staggered down Victoria alley "with the air of a bad man," cussing and making threats as he went. The women of the alley heard the noise, and a few of them poked their heads out of their windows to see what was happening. Giles "snapped his unloaded gun" in their faces as he stumbled by. Randolph watched until the soldier wobbled through the door of Helen's parlor house, came in behind him, and "snatched his gun from him. The disarmed soldier immediately flew into a fury and began to abuse the officer and raise a racket in general." By that time another officer, Smith, had arrived. The policemen marched the drunk man to the police station, "much to his chagrin and greatly against his will," according to the *Salt Lake Herald*. He was not drunk at all, he mumbled, and was only there to say goodbye to his wife who was employed as Helen's cook. A fellow trooper soon appeared and took him away to the train station. Helen was not charged in the incident.[15]

Beginning in 1901, Helen unaccountably began appearing in city directories once more as both Helen Blazes and Helen Smith. It is only a guess that she reserved the latter name for her business transactions, to remove herself from the more notorious Helen Blazes everyone knew. Masquerading as Helen Smith would go on for a few more years, although Chief Paul of the police department seemed to be easing up on the ladies during December of 1902. When questioned by the *Salt Lake Herald* about the robberies and revelry taking place in Victoria Alley, Paul commented, "Now some of the houses are run respectably. Helen Blazes runs her place pretty well, I am told, but I haven't been down there, only once, since I have been chief." He did say, however, that "I do believe Victoria alley is a nasty, nasty, nasty place."[16]

How could the *Herald* let a comment like that go? It turned out they couldn't. Five days after Chief Paul's commentary, an even bigger rant about the red-light area was launched by the newspaper. When Mayor Thompson was interviewed about the matter, crib owner Joseph Snell was brought up. Snell was deriving much of his "fat income" from the red-light ladies, charged the paper. Thompson responded that he had spoken with the man, who said "he is perfectly willing to rent his

VERY BAD.
Steel Ayres—How do you like my new song?
Helen Blazes—It needs ventilation.
Steele Ayres—In what way?
Helen Blazes—The air is bad.

The Deseret Evening News *poked some fun at Helen Blazes in a 1902 issue.*
Courtesy Library of Congress Prints and Photographs Division

property to respectable people, to families, but he cannot do so as long as neighboring property is rented for immoral purposes. The houses run as Helen Blazes', Ida Walker's and the place known as Three Deuces at 222 South State are in the same vicinity as the property owned by

Mr. Snell, and he could hardly rent to respectable people under those circumstances."[17]

Joseph Snell took umbrage to the disparaging remarks concerning his so-called fat income. In a letter to the editor of the *Herald* on December 22, Snell explained that he had been in the real estate business in Salt Lake City for some twenty years. He also verified that he would indeed find respectable renters on Victoria Avenue were he not surrounded by the likes of "Helen Blazes, Ida Walker, Em Demar, Cleo Starr and others, also the French and Italian women over the saloon at the corner of State and Victoria Avenue." Instead, he said, "I was compelled to rent the premises to any person applying or have the property sold for taxes." Snell's description is interesting, as it gives a glimpse into what the demimonde on Victoria Avenue contained: "eight houses of five rooms each and three double houses of eight rooms each, all of which are let furnished and the said property is now occupied by twelve tenants, and the rentals are less than one half that charged to transients on Second South street. The property is all connected with the sewer and the sanitary conditions are in good order. The avenue is brilliantly lighted by two arc lights."[18] Snell may have objected to his renters, but he certainly seemed to have wanted to make them comfortable to the point of leasing his buildings complete with furnishings.

Helen and the other red-light ladies surely read these articles with interest, and caution. But most of them stayed right where they were. In about 1905, John Held Jr. would later remember, Helen and Madam Ada Wilson both paid handsomely for the calling cards they purchased from his father, who ran a print shop. Held also remembered visiting the houses of the madams, probably to deliver their business cards, and learned the popular tune "Frankie and Johnny" from Helen's "colored" piano player.

Helen did eventually relocate—or at least expand—to a new parlor house near the corner of Seventh South and Main Streets. She also took a trip abroad in 1908. The *Salt Lake Herald* reported hopefully that she "has departed for Europe. Her establishment here has been sold. Miss Blazes will probably never return to Salt Lake." But back she was in 1909, when she returned to find that the lessee of her house on Victoria, Harry Robinson, had in turn rented the property to Madam Edna Prescott, who opened a new parlor house. Helen sued Edna for using the property for "immoral purposes." Edna vacated the next day, "taking her furniture and owing six months rent." But Helen wasn't done, suing both the madam and Robinson for $1,200 in back rent. Soon the Western Furniture Company, which held a lien against Edna's furniture in the amount of $800, jumped in to contest Helen's own lien against the goods. The suit dragged on until May of 1910, when Edna claimed that she had rented the house directly from Helen, and that Robinson had only acted as an agent for the transaction. Robinson agreed, and Helen was apparently made to pay all court costs regarding the dispute.[19]

By the time the suit was settled, Helen had quietly moved into another new house at 669 South Main, where she apparently had retired and would remain for the rest of her life. Gone were her glory days as the reigning boss madam of one of the finest parlor houses Salt Lake City would ever see. And at long last her husband, Richard, could live with her. In addition to the couple, the 1910 census records boarders Joseph Cunningham, Alvin C. Shaw, and Lavina Shaw living in the house. Unfortunately, however, there were still plenty of people around who remembered back when Helen Blazes was raking in the bucks and buying plenty of expensive jewelry and baubles. In September of 1913, the *Salt Lake Tribune* reported that "no trace has yet been found by the police of the burglars who took jewelry said to be valued at $4,000 from the residence of Mrs. Helen Dreyfus, [*sic*] 669 South Main Street Thursday night. Mrs. Dreyfus said last night that she despaired of ever getting back her jewelry, or the handsome silver-mounted toilet articles that the burglar secured from the dresser of her bedroom."[20]

By some miracle, Helen did get some of her jewels back. Six months after the robbery one "William Ross, alias Joe Clark, alias George Moore" was apprehended in Portland, Oregon, for the robbery.[21] He escaped his initial arrest but was finally recaptured and returned to Salt Lake City. Sadly, he had disposed of all but about $800 worth of Helen's jewelry. There was more trouble; the 1914 city directory noted that Richard Dreyfus had moved to Los Angeles, and the 1920 census listed Helen as Lilly Dreyfus, divorced. Only her maid, Ada Smith, lived with her. Ten years after that Helen was still alone, living with a different maid identified as Harriet Hoff.

In January 1932, Helen was robbed again. This time the thief, who saw her as nothing more than some little old lady, "bound and gagged" her before making off with a wristwatch, a manicure set, and two sets of earrings. He was caught and held for trial, but the robbery was Helen's complete undoing. The *Salt Lake Tribune* would later say Helen "had been in a nervous condition" ever since the robbery. The small amount of goods Jensen stole spoke for what little the former madam had left aside from her cash in the bank. And, being tied up and gagged must have made Helen realize that she was officially no longer the nightlife queen who once held so many under her power. Six months afterward, on June 23, Harriet Hoff walked into an eerily quiet house. She finally found Helen dead on the bathroom floor. The woman had shot herself through the heart, leaving a note reading, "I am through with life." She was buried at Wasatch Lawn Memorial Park, where today the grass crowds around her small grave marker.[22]

CHAPTER 17

Good Time Girls of Ogden

Ogden was first known as Fort Buenaventura when it was settled by Miles Goodyear back in 1846. Fast-forward to 1869, when the Transcontinental Railroad made it to Ogden, and the good time girls "came in droves" to the new town.[1] Just up the block from the train depot, a budding red-light district flourished among gambling dens and saloons on today's lower 25th Street, aka "Two Bit Street," and lower 24th Street. The depot soon became the center of much vice and violence, to the extent that two police officers were assigned to daily patrols and were not allowed to clock out until they made sure no one lingered on the streets.

By 1871, 25th Street's raucous reputation was well known throughout the West. Madams like "Gentile Kate" Flint were ruling over the demimonde with vigor. Indeed, Ogden was now "a wide-open western town with a variety of unsavory activities."[2] One of the most notable clients at Ogden's varied houses of prostitution was Frank Cannon, the son of a leading Latter-Day Saints apostle. Cannon eventually became a writer and editor for the *Ogden Herald*. As he pursued his career, however, Cannon became noted for his heavy drinking, and because he continued patronizing brothels owned by Kate Flint and others. Cannon wasn't the only one enjoying what 25th Street had to offer. By 1889, in the battle between the Mormons and a new "Liberal Party," the street's notorious vices became a pawn in the fight for power. The Liberal Party won, making Ogden "the first major city in Utah to have a non-Mormon government."[3]

It is interesting to note that as far as official documentation went, prostitution went largely unnoticed in newspaper articles about Ogden. Even the Sanborn Fire Insurance map of 1890 failed to note the usual "female boarding," or sometimes simply "f.b." that indicated a house of prostitution in Block 24, where the industry flourished. By the time of the 1900 census, an area in the middle of the block was designated as Electric Alley (so-named for the string of electric lights running down the alley and sometimes called Electric Avenue), which ran east to west between Grant and Lincoln Avenues. This was the center of Ogden's demimonde, and only a sprinkling of good time girls were enumerated. They were Madam Dora Topham with six boarders, and Mary Brooks, Imogene Scarborough, and Amelia Fontelli, who each worked alone. Leona Jionier and Josie Cunningham shared their quarters, as did Margaret Saville and Ollie Mickeby. At the latter house a man named Guy Dufloth was documented by the census taker, and it is anyone's guess whether he was a client of the girls. All of the women were listed as keepers of a "lodging house," with no clue that they really were working girls.

Not until about 1904 did city authorities finally address Ogden's red-light ladies on Electric Avenue, as well as another area on Hudson Avenue. Somehow, the Electric Avenue demimonde had grown to an amazing thirty-three houses of prostitution, according to the *Ogden Standard Examiner*, which reported that revenue officers wanted to make sure the inhabitants would at least pay for their liquor licenses, which they did. The paper surely exaggerated the number of brothels, however, for two years later, the 1906 Sanborn Fire Insurance map showed Electric Alley as being home to three two-story parlor houses, various sets of cribs ranging from two to eleven rooms, and some cribs

Electric Alley's numerous cribs and brothels are identified as "F.B.," meaning "Female Boarding" in this 1906 Sanborn map.
Courtesy Library of Congress Prints and Photographs Division

attached directly to the European Hotel at 242-244 25th Street. Most of the brothels were accessible directly via Grant Avenue to the east, or through saloons and even more respectable businesses.

Although the 1910 census taker identified the ladies of Electric Avenue, missing are such important facts as birthplaces, marital status, occupations, and other information. Was the census taker shy and so just hurried through the red-light area? Or just simply lazy? Perhaps both, for most of the census does not even record the date it was taken, much less the name of the person who conducted it. Also, although a number of respectable-seeming residents and numerous Chinese appear in the census, they too are missing such vital information.

The census aside, there were others keeping a closer eye on Ogden's demimonde. In January of 1912, reformers against Ogden's red-light district decreed that no more liquor would be sold in the district. Some of the women gave up and left town. One of them, twenty-two-year-old Edith Brooks, appeared in Cripple Creek, Colorado, in 1912.[4] Others stayed on, if only because it was now obvious that the authorities tolerated vice, including their naughty ladies, "as long as they did not get out of hand." It is easy enough to assume that officials, including the police, allowed the prostitution industry to flourish as long as the authorities received money from the ladies and, most likely, bribes.[5] It is highly likely that the ladies were quietly selling liquor anyway when Utah became the twenty-fourth state in the union to enact its own prohibition law in 1917. And when nationwide prohibition became official in 1919, the state jumped on board to prohibit "the manufacture, sale, or transportation of intoxicating liquors . . . for beverage purposes."[6]

Despite prohibition, it generally remained known that alcohol, gambling, and pleasures of the flesh could still be found on 25th Street. As the 1920s loomed on the horizon, a number of Asians populated the area too, selling opium and offering additional games of chance. Anglo women continued moving in too: In 1922, Sarah J. Wheelwright purchased 268-270 25th Street and continued the tradition of leasing the upper floors to various women who were likely prostitutes. But 25th Street was getting rough; even gangster Al Capone declined to infiltrate the town, claiming that Ogden was too wild, even for him.

Electric Alley and its wayward women expanded as World War II loomed on the horizon. Thousands of soldiers visited their so-called "Victory Girls" along 25th Street before leaving on the train to go to war.[7] Aside from having one last date with a shady lady, the men also visited a certain barbershop and purchased hollowed-out watermelons in which to stash illegal hooch for the train ride. When Mayor Harman Peery came into office during 1942-43, there were still eleven houses of prostitution operating. Four of them were owned by Rossette "Rose" Duccinni Davie and Bill Davie: the Rose Rooms at 205 25th Street, the Denver Hotel, the Wilcox Hotel, and the La Siesta Hotel at 277 25th Street. Rose was particularly flamboyant, publicly expressing her opinions about prostitution in general while walking her pet ocelot (a small leopard) or driving her rose-colored Cadillac convertible along the city streets. She also was remembered as "a very beautiful woman, she was smart, and she was a good manager of business." It was no secret to police that the Rose Rooms offered sex for sale, but Rose and her husband were also known as "valuable police informants."

The Davies unfortunately came into the public eye in 1948 following a "Jollification" party that was held at the same time the Weber Wildlife Federation was throwing a convention at the Ogden Livestock Show Coliseum. Everybody knew that the event traditionally ended with a striptease show. On this occasion, however, the convention organizers decided to offer "legitimate entertainment" provided by Weber State University first, with such respectable acts as a barbershop quartet. Those in the know knew that strippers would indeed appear afterward, but the male audience became impatient and began "hurling bottles on stage, and yelling 'Bring on the girls.'" Unbeknownst to officials, Rose's girls had been quietly giving out matchbooks from the Rose Rooms with their names penned inside the covers, and explaining they would indeed perform after the more respectable entertainment.[8]

Mayor Peery, in the meantime, maintained his belief that it was better to let the prostitution industry alone as a way for the city to make money off of it. In recent years, rumors have floated around that Peery "got rich from allowing these kinds of establishments to exist on 25th Street, but the truth is he did not. The funds went into the city treasury, not into Harman Peery's pockets."[9] In addition to prostitution, Peery also turned a blind eye to the sixty-five or so gambling joints around 25th Street. Nobody seemed to disagree with him, and he was elected again in

1934, 1942, and 1948. During that time, the ladies of Electric Alley were free to conduct business. One of them, Lettie Mahan, purchased Dora Topham's former brothel at 268-270 25th Street and leased the upper floors to other women. Peery, meanwhile, defended the denizens of 25th Street as certain citizens began lobbying to clean up the city. There was talk of moving the whole district "out of Ogden and the county," but that failed to happen. Peery remained in office through 1949.[10]

With a new election coming up, the ladies of Electric Alley surely knew that the end of their demimonde days were coming to a close. In 1949, when Lettie Mahan leased her building to Otto Waldron and E.J. Doherty, the contract included a clause that the property was to be used strictly as a rooming house "to conduct only legitimate and lawful business."[11] Sure enough, W. Rulon White was elected mayor in 1950 and successfully set about efforts to shut down the illegal activities along 25th Street. Of particular interest to the public was the arrest and conviction of Rose and Bill Davie, who were sentenced to two and half years and five years, respectively, for running a house of prostitution. Another notable bust was that of Eddie Doherty, tagged as "a big-time gambler, pimp, dope peddler and junkey [sic]." Several brothels, including the Marlene Rooms, the Hyland Hotel, the Parkway Hotel, the Reed Colorado Hotel, the Rose Rooms, the Wilcox Rooms, the Wilson Rooms, and the Wyoming Rooms were closed down.[12]

With its brothels closed, 25th Street was soon filled with empty buildings, vagrants, drunks, and vandals. Lee Witten of the Union Station archives recalled that as a teenager, "We would drive through town, and 25th Street was just kind of a thrill ride with your windows rolled up. We'd see drunks, and there was an alley [Electric Avenue] between 24th and 25th streets where we could drive behind the buildings—we'd go see if you could see red lights in the windows in the tenements."[13] For the most part, Odgen was indeed swept clean of its soiled doves. Most of the good time girls and their gambling cohorts discreetly relocated to remote places out in the county, but Captain F. Roberts Carver of the Ogden Police City Department expressed his relief that at least vice was no longer present on 25th Street.[14] Today Ogden's shady ladies are just a memory; in a 2003 interview resident Tom Reese remembered that his grandmother was once a 25th Street madam. "But I was so young I didn't know," he said. "All these women around, I just thought she was popular. We used to watch people coming out of the bus station, drunk. It was a wonderful childhood."[15]

CHAPTER 18

———•◦•———

Dora Topham, the Genteel Madam

D ora Belle (sometimes Bella) Topham was one of the most unique madams the West would ever see. It is true she was a madam in Ogden, sometimes employing several women in the illicit prostitution industry. But Dora was actually much more than that: She was a wife, a mother, a concerned citizen who realized that by taking in wayward women she could often help them to eventually better their lives. She certainly did not dress or act like a madam, but as a businesswoman. And she wasn't afraid of the authorities, or the Mormon church. Rather, Dora exhibited an unusual willingness to work with city officials to see that the red-light districts within her realm ran smoothly and within the limits of the law. Most interesting is that she was one of the very few women in the industry who was eventually employed by a municipal government to select, build, and run a red-light district.

Dora was Dora Long when she was born in 1867 in Illinois to a young farming couple, William and Elizabeth Long. By the time of the 1870 census, the family was living in Goose Creek and Elizabeth had given birth to another daughter, Lucretia "Delia." The family had migrated to Nebraska by the time Elizabeth died in 1876. Two years later, William remarried to Marie Fritsch. Marie already had four children from

Madam Dora Topham, looking quite proper for the madam she was.
Courtesy University of Utah, #17253

a previous relationship, and gave birth to another daughter by Long named Rose. When the 1880 census caught up with the family, William worked as a grocer. At home Dora, the oldest of the seven children, attended school, but also likely helped her stepmother raise her siblings.

Doing so perhaps ingrained in Dora the motherly instinct she would later apply to the women of the demimonde.

In 1885 Dora married for the first time, to James Hughes. But Hughes died just about a year later. Where did Dora go from there? Nobody knows; for four years, Dora wandered the West, apparently declining to go home to her family while she found the means to make her own way. Then, in 1889, the tiniest of blurbs appeared on a back page of the *Salt Lake Herald* in the column dedicated to Ogden news: "Belle London, proprietor of a *maison de joie*, and her two 'girls' were examined yesterday before Commissioner Perrin and the case against them dismissed for want of evidence."[1] Belle London was Dora's new moniker, and for the next two decades the two names became interchangeable. There was Belle London, budding madam, and Dora Topham, the once respectable lady who furthered her good reputation in the community by marrying Thomas Topham on May 1, 1890. Two years later, Belle London appeared in the Ogden City Directory on the north side of Stephen's Alley west of Grant Avenue. And the following year, she purchased Lot 3 in Block 24, in what would become Ogden's unofficial demimonde, Electric Alley, aka Electric Avenue.

Having begun her red-light career at the age of just twenty-six years, it is probably unlikely that Dora knew what the red-light life was really like. She soon found out; in 1894, one Nellie Ogden was found hiding out at Dora's brothel after fatally stabbing her lover, Kid Mason, in a Salt Lake City bagnio. Interestingly, when found Nellie "was dressed in deep mourning." In reporting the incident, the *Salt Lake Herald* noted that Nellie had a mother and four siblings, plus a child of her own. She also told officers that she had acted in self-defense. The paper did not expect Nellie to be arrested, but the authorities did take her back to Salt Lake City to sort out the details.[2] Nellie probably knew Dora from the madam's fledgling days in Salt Lake City. And, her assistance to Nellie would not be the last time Dora reached out to a woman in need.

Men were another matter. Thomas Topham is not listed in directories as living with his wife at 44 Electric Avenue until 1895. Notably, he was working a respectable job as a clerk for businessman Arthur Bailey. Dora appeared to be very much on her own, with little or no assistance from her husband. When a man named Stewart forged Belle London's name on an order for a new suit in July 1896, the lady herself complained. Chief Davenport wrangled Stewart in Salt Lake City and brought him back to Ogden. But in spite of having to fend for herself, Dora's relationship with her husband seemed solid enough. The couple was on a visit to Nebraska when Dora gave birth to, or possibly adopted, a daughter named Ethel in October.

Back in Ogden, Dora's attempts to help troubled women continued. In April 1897 the *Salt Lake Herald* reported on the shooting death of Glenna Carter, aka "Mamie Evans," who was killed by her lover on the Union Station platform. Mamie had recently been in a relationship with John Ross, which went south. The two apparently separated, during which time Mamie was wrought with heartbreak when she received no letters from the man. He felt the same way, although a letter from Mamie that did make it into his hands confirmed that there was "something wrong with the mail." Mamie was departing next for Butte, Montana, and Dora walked her to the train station. When Ross showed up, Dora left. Little did she know that the man had already penned a letter reading, in part, "I wish to ask the public to pardon me for the act I am about to commit." The "act" was that of shooting at Mamie, four times. Only one of the shots hit her, and as she collapsed on the ground, Ross shot himself in the head.[3]

Mamie's murder might have been the end of the story but for John D. Williams, an Ogden "crime boss" who was seeing Mamie in Ross's absence. With Mamie gone Williams turned his attentions to Dora. The *Herald* would claim the man "never made love to Belle [London] until after he recovered from the death of Mamie." That took about a month, or so, when Williams developed an infatuation with Dora and threatened to shoot her. He had, Officer Tom Hilton claimed, "been practicing at a target . . . so that his aim might be true when the moment came for sending Belle London to join her friend." A terrified Dora was able to notify the authorities, and Williams was arrested. On the day of his trial, however, the frightened woman did not appear in court, nor was she to be found in the red-light district. Nobody could blame her. Williams was sentenced to jail.

In its article about Williams, the *Herald* described where Dora lived. Her brothel was called the Red Light, "a house of a very unsavory reputation in a dingy alley back of the city jail. A blood red lantern shines down the alley after dark, and beckons the unwary with its evil eye."[4] It is notable that Dora had enough sense to set up shop behind the jail, where she probably felt she would be safer. But the men in her life were clearly unstable at times, including her own husband. In September of 1899, Thomas Topham was now the proprietor of the Mint Saloon. One night, according to a witness, Charles Wessler came in, drunk, and successfully borrowed money from Topham. After gambling it away Wessler came back in, asked for more money, and was refused. When Wessler struck Topham on the face, both men slipped and fell to the floor before Topham leaped up and began kicking his adversary. Wessler went to the police station, where he threatened to kill Topham but was successfully induced to go home instead. A short time later, Wessler died from internal injuries. Topham was arrested.

Of Thomas Topham, the *Salt Lake Herald* noted that "in build he is a giant and well-known among sporting men . . . he is of pleasant disposition when sober, but is extremely quarrelsome when drunk."[5] Topham's trial would drag on for over two months as he sat in jail. He was finally acquitted in December. As for Dora, she still lived alone when the census taker came by 10 Electric Avenue on June 8, 1900. Her employees included Dawn Frost, Leslie St. Elmo, May Rich, Pearl Mack, Annie

Borg, and Jennie Anderson. Only Jennie's occupation as a housemaid was likely truthful. Dawn Frost said she was a music teacher, and Leslie St. Elmo said she was a dressmaker. The other three girls put their occupation as "sewing." Also living in the house was three-year-old Ethel.

With five girls working with her, Dora was raking in a lot of money. Her married life, however, had indeed turned sour. In 1902 Dora filed for divorce and, as usual, the *Salt Lake Herald* delighted in revealing that she was "otherwise known as Belle London" who owned lots of property along lower 25th Street. The paper also noted that the "allegations of the complaint could not be definitely learned as the papers are withheld by the clerks office."[6] Alternatively, the *Ogden Standard Examiner* had no problem giving such juicy details as Dora's reason for the divorce: "willful neglect." Furthermore, the woman wanted her previous name, Dora Bella Hughes, restored. She also requested $75 to $100 per month in alimony. But the *Examiner* seemed not to know about little Ethel, stating instead that the Tophams had no children. The paper also claimed that Dora recently inherited a large sum of money from relatives back East.[7]

There might have been something to the inheritance claim, for beginning in 1901 Dora took over an impressive expanse of property along 25th Street. The first of these was the Davenport Saloon at 246 on the north side of the street, a two-story building with the saloon and a restaurant on the ground floor and a number of cribs behind it. Later, when the London Ice Cream Parlor opened next door, Dora convinced the business to build a small corridor giving access to Electric Alley. Three years later, Dora also acquired the building at 268-270. This building was three stories high, with Paul Gysin's barbershop on the ground floor. Dora used the second floor as her new parlor house, the Fashion Rooms. The top floor served as her private home with Ethel. Dora's last purchase was in 1906, when she bought the buildings at 272, 274, and 278 25th Street. These too would contain "nicely furnished rooms," but most suspect they were utilized by Dora's girls.[8]

Ethel was not the only child Dora cared for. The lady indeed had a soft spot for children. In 1905, she had adopted another child identified as Walter Earl Topham. The baby had been born in Idaho in July but only lived three months, succumbing to enteritis (a bowel inflammation) in October. Dora and Thomas Topham appear as the child's parents on his death certificate; his real birth parents (if they were not the Tophams) remaining unidentified.[9] The child was interred in Ogden, and it is notable that after Thomas Topham died in 1906, two other children— "Baby Sears" and "Infant Lois Guilky" were noted on the reverse side of his tombstone. Topham's untimely death, from paralysis at the young age of forty-five years, also illustrates Dora's compassion, after a fashion. It was she who signed off on her ex-husband's death certificate. Also, she likely paid for his sizable tombstone, and made sure to emblazon the names of her adopted charges on it.[10]

With Thomas Topham out of her life, it was more important than ever for Dora to use caution in her business dealings. Beginning in 1907 her name appeared twice in city directories, once as Dora Topham who lived a respectable existence at 250 and 268 25th Street, and again as Belle London, the notorious madam at 10 Electric Avenue. Newspapers would later identify her under both names whenever they wrote about her. Initially, in the years after Thomas Topham's death news on Dora remained largely out of the papers. She was, after all, an astute business-woman and devoted mother, quietly running her houses of joy and rais-ing Ethel in the palatial surroundings of her private home. Little did the madam know that the authorities in Salt Lake City would soon be look-ing at her closely, and for a most unusual reason: They wanted her to help to create one of the only city-owned brothel districts in America. It was called the Stockade.

CHAPTER 19

---•◦•---

Dora and the Salt Lake City Stockade

The plan to build the Stockade, a city-run demimonde, began back in 1907 with non-Mormon mayor John Bransford. At the top of Bransford's agenda was the prostitution industry, which was running rampant throughout Salt Lake City. One particular report on the problem, generated by Thomas Pitt of the American party, caught Bransford's eye: "Let the city set aside a piece of ground of sufficient size to accommodate several hundred of these prostitutes," Pitt proposed. "Enclose same carefully with high fences; build cottages or houses to accommodate these inmates; charge them rent; license them and place them under control of the Police Department as to their safety and confinement, and to the Board of Health as to their cleanliness and sanitary conditions." Any prostitutes refusing to comply could be "run out of town or sent to the place where she belonged."[1]

Bransford mulled the idea over for nearly a year before deciding to act on it. Already in place was Salt Lake City's fining system wherein madams turned in a list of their girls with a $10 fine for each one each month. In a carefully written announcement, Bransford submitted his intention "to take these women from the business section of the city, and put them in a district which will be one of the best, if not the very best, regulated districts in the country." Dora Topham, the powerful queen of Ogden's underworld, seemed like the excellent choice to run such a place. According to Bransford, "I told her that if she did as I wished, and followed out the directions . . . I would see to it that the women of the downtown district were removed to the new location."[2]

Mayor Bransford and three city councilmen did their homework by visiting eastern cities to see how their prostitution industries were regulated. The mayor also kept the public abreast of his plans. "I would prefer to see the city in a condition where there would be no such houses at all," Bransford explained. "That is, of course, the ideal which, I am sorry to say, is at present unattainable." At least some citizens agreed, and even submitted a petition supporting the Stockade to city council. A much larger bunch, however, launched a series of protest petitions and mass meetings. Their West Side Citizens League would harass the Stockade up until the day it closed for good.[3]

By the time Bransford announced his plan, Thomas Pitt had changed his mind about the idea of a city-run demimonde. Even as Dora agreed to the deal and city officials moved forward, Pitt refused to follow up on his own plan and was subsequently fired. He never publicly made the reason behind his reverse decision known, but it should be noted that his wife was heavily involved with the Women's Christian Temperance Union, an organization bent on shutting down saloons, gambling dens, and bordellos across the nation. Others shared Pitt's opposition to the Stockade. By June of 1908, upward of a thousand people signed a petition objecting to the plan as Salt Lake's city council brazenly forged ahead. The *Salt Lake Tribune* reported on June 27 that in spite of the petition the city, as the "Citizens' Investment Company," had filed a Deed of Trust for $200,000 comprising nearly an entire city block in Block 64 on the edge of the city, and took out a loan for an additional $200,000. And, Dora had purchased five additional pieces of property for $120,000.

Subsequent news articles reported that a number of discreet investors were in on the Stockade project, and that even a nearby Greek neighborhood seemed apathetic over the plans. Property owner A.R. Carter had willingly sold his property to the Citizens' Investment Company since the Western Pacific Railroad tracks would soon surround the parcel anyway, rendering it useless for any other purpose. Other properties within the block around the Stockade would be relegated as warehouses and other industrial or commercial buildings. The Stockade indeed seemed like a good idea; even the bishop of the Mormon church gave a nod of approval once the plan was "fully explained to him." But neither certain citizens, nor the press, were impressed. Meetings, proposed lawsuits, and caustic public comments continued as the Stockade plan moved forward. Judge Joseph Myer said he had talked to one madam already who said "she would not move; she would go out of business first." On the other end of the spectrum was Myers's interview with Dora, who explained that there would be "200 cribs at $2 the night, or $12,000 the month, and then seven big houses will make another $1,400 more, about $14,000 a month. This does not include the liquor."[4] It truly was a sweet deal for the city.

Dora approached the building of the Stockade with vigor. In July, she donated one of her properties near Jackson Avenue to the Salvation Army. She also offered to oversee a funding list for construction of the Stockade starting with her own sizable donation. Was Dora trying to ply the city with her kindness? Knowing Dora—savior of children who coddled her own good time girls like they were family—her heart was likely in the right place. Yet her kindness meant little to those opposing the Stockade. For the next several months, injunctions were filed as plans were drawn up, permits were issued, and editorials were written. The matter was put to Governor John Cutler and Attorney General Breeden for consideration in September, but neither man had responded as of October. Construction commenced, and was completed by early December.

The Stockade was indeed impressive. The architect, a city councilman named L.D. Martin, promised that "from the outside of the

Salt Lake City's notorious Stockade, shortly after construction began.
Courtesy University of Utah, #Shipler #08629

stockade nothing can be seen of the movements within, and the offensive sights which have greeted passers-by in the neighborhood of Commercial Street will be absent. There will be but two entrances to the stockade and there will be a policeman on duty day or night at both gates." True to the plan, a twelve-foot-high wall surrounded the whole project. The main entrance was on 1st Street South, right beside Dora's office just inside. Next door to the office was one of many brothels, perhaps used by Dora to train the girls hired to work at the Stockade. A second entrance was on 2nd Street South with two separate gates. The area in between the walls was inexplicably called Boyd Avenue. Dozens of one-room cribs, fancier duplexes, and actual parlor houses ranging from one to two stories to appease every type of customer ran down either side of the street.

Aside from sexual services, other entertainment at the Stockade included a billiard hall and/or dance hall, some saloons, and a cigar store. There was even a small jail cell for anyone who got out of hand. With its construction complete, Dora next began ordering furniture for the Stockade's buildings. On December 3, "furnishings by the van load" were brought in and placed on the new, clean linoleum floors of each place. The *Deseret Evening News* estimated that "every house will probably be completely furnished by nightfall."[5] It was guessed that in all, between one hundred and one hundred fifty women could work in the Stockade at any one time.

Dora was next tasked with rooting up the red-light ladies of Salt Lake and persuading them to move to the Stockade. She began by offering the women free room and board for a week if they would give it a try. "There is no danger," Dora assured them. "I will protect you with my life, if need be. I know what I am talking about and want you women to show the others in Salt Lake that this place will not be molested." Madams Cleo Starr, Madge Daniels, Irene McDonald, and Rose Bartlett accepted Dora's offer. Madams Lou Sheppard, Edna Prescott, and Bee Bartlett, however, did not. Other independent operators refused to vacate their old premises too. "I own property here," declared one woman, "and neither the chief of police, the mayor, nor anyone else will drive me away. I'll not go into any district or stockade and any woman who does, that is one who owns a house, is a fool. They can't bluff me. I'll stay where I am."[6] Dora allegedly resorted to advertising for women from other towns to make sure the Stockade was full. She also made sure to welcome women of all races and ethnic backgrounds.

In the end it is estimated that roughly one hundred women willfully relocated to the Stockade. Dora rented cribs to individual girls, procured madams for each of the parlor houses, and laid down the rules. Cribs rented for between $1 and $4 per day. Parlor houses rented for $175 per month. The women of each house would receive 50 percent of what they made, with the madams splitting the other half with Dora, who also received the monthly rent. All employees of the Stockade were to wear short red dresses and were subjected to regular health exams, for which they paid between $1 and $3.

Councilman Mulvey next made it clear that the "women of the town will not be told that they must reside within the shelter, but they will be given to understand that if they do not, things will be made unpleasant for them," also that "they will be allowed to live undisturbed within the stockade."[7] Those who did not actually live at the resort, including crib girls, could live in Dora's Washington Rooming House just outside the south entrance to the Stockade, or Mayor Bransford's own boarding-house, the Plumas, for $5 per week. No matter where they lived, police began keeping a register listing each madam, who was in turn expected to supply an up-to-date list of her employees. All girls were to pay a monthly $10 fine to the city. Furthermore, customers entering the Stock-ade were advised that an elaborate alarm system would periodically let them know that the police were patrolling the place and staging required raids to keep the general public satisfied. And, as promised, policemen were posted at each entrance.

With everything in place, Dora announced the grand opening for December 15, even as a new lawsuit was filed against the Citizens' Investment Company. Five days later, city police made the rounds on Commercial Street and Victoria Alley, informing the good time girls that they must vacate the neighborhood by four o'clock the next morning. The *Deseret News*, meanwhile, criticized the cribs, which measured only "ten-feet square, with a door and window in the front." In the windows "sits the painted denizen of the underworld calling to passers between puffs on her cigarette [sic]." The windows had curtains, and each crib was furnished with a chair or two and a washstand in front and "a white enameled iron bed."[8] What the *Deseret News* neglected to say was that all window shopping was conducted well inside the safe confines of the

Stockade, away from the public eye. But there also was another problem: Customers wishing to avoid being seen entering the Stockade soon began knocking clandestine holes in the cement wall surrounding the place. The police acquiesced by installing a second secret alarm system to give customers extra time to vacate the premises.

It is no wonder that between her hard work to get the Stockade open and the loud voices of those opposing her, Dora came down with a serious rash, classified as erysipelas, in late December 1908. The madam was in an Ogden hospital when the first of many lawsuits came to court, and proceedings were delayed as she recovered. Dora's private home on 25th Street was indeed a needed retreat for the lady when the onslaught of charges against her, both in the public eye and the courts, got to be too much for her. But the minute she disembarked from a train after leaving the hospital on January 6, Deputy Sheriff Booth served her with papers to appear in court. Meanwhile the *Deseret Evening News*, in reporting the incident, posed doubts that Dora was really even sick.

In court, a restraining order was requested to prevent any prostitutes from entering or working at the Stockade. There were witnesses: L.D. Martin professed his ignorance when Dora asked him to design the cribs for the Stockade, saying he had no idea what a crib was, and that he had no idea his plans would be used for a place of prostitution. Other witnesses, including other prostitutes and madams, were summoned in an effort to expose and shame Dora. On the third day, Dora failed to show up for court. Her doctor sent a note explaining that she was "necessarily confined to her room." The day after that, it was noted that Dora had also sent a message that "she would come in right away if wanted, but pleaded not to be made to come to court."

The press listened eagerly as it became clear that Dora was afraid to face the court, and jail. Back when she was served at the train station, the woman had "pleaded not to be taken to jail and fervently promised that if she was allowed to go she would voluntarily appear in court." Rather than embarrass her further with a bench warrant for her arrest, Judge Morse ordered a temporary order preventing women from entering the Stockade until the case could resume. Reverend Noble Strong Elderkin, meanwhile, actually stood up for Dora. In a sermon on January 17, 1909, Elderkin demanded "the repeal of the laws against vice and lawbreaking to save citizens from hypocrisy." He also "denounced Salt Lake for its discourteous treatment of Belle London."[9]

As the court case droned on, four women and night watchman J.D. Whitmore were arrested at the Stockade on February 19 by Sheriff Sharp and his deputies for vagrancy during the first of many raids. The officers were initially ordered to leave by Whitmore, who was told he "was under orders to throw out any officer who came into the Stockade except police."[10] Dora, along with A.G. Falkenstein, bailed the group out and was immediately held in contempt of court for ignoring Judge Morse's orders. A second raid was staged in April, netting seven more women. Because Dora was in Ogden for the evening, the ladies had to spend the night in jail before being bonded out. Then, quite by chance, Dora did something that earned her much respect: She saved a baby.

In late April, Dora heard about a four-week-old baby girl on West Second South Street who was born with "disease, a legacy of her parents." The infant was taken to the juvenile court. A few days later a woman called Officer Brown on the telephone and said, "I understand from the newspapers that you have a 4-weeks-old baby girl that needs a home and medical attention. Have you found a home for it yet?" When Brown said no, the woman offered, "If you will let me have the child I will place it in a good home and provide it with the best medical attention obtainable." Brown asked who was calling, and when he heard Dora's name "almost dropped the telephone." Ever determined, however, Dora willingly gave the name of the family she wanted to give the child to, "and gave such assurances that her request was acceded to, after the court authorities had satisfied themselves as to the respectability of the family." The *Salt*

Lake Tribune could hardly disguise shock and surprise as Dora "made her appearance in an entirely new light." The *Deseret Evening News* provided more gritty details. The baby with the "loathsome disease" had been abandoned by her mother in a rooming house directly across the street from the Stockade. True to her word, Dora had "found a home for the child and promised to pay all expenses and give it the best medical attention."[11] Neither newspaper expressed thanks, or even relief, for Dora's act of kindness. But the madam had clearly won a round, for a moment.

Raids and tirades continued against the Stockade. Ten women were arrested in May as the *Salt Lake Tribune* accused Dora of buying favorable reports from a publication referred to as the "'Smoot' Mouth." Dora also suffered another arrest that month, but immediately paid bail to avoid spending any time in the jail she detested so much. Following another raid on the Stockade that netted thirty-one arrests on June 19, the *Salt Lake Herald* told how Dora let the women sit in jail overnight and refused to pay their bail—because she was again in Ogden, and didn't have the required cash on hand. A bigger raid was staged two weeks later, with the intent of forcing the Stockade out of business. Fed up at last, Dora sold the Stockade in its entirety to H.J. Mundt on June 30 and willingly spoke with the *Ogden Standard* about it. When asked the purchase price she replied demurely, "Oh say it was $200,000. That wasn't it but it's close enough. It was in that neighborhood." Mundt, Dora claimed, "says he is going to build some warehouses in there and will try to get a franchise from the city to run in a spur track. I don't care what he does. My fight is over. He's commenced to tear down the walls already."

The *Standard* also made commentary on the one-hundred-fifty women from the Stockade, some of whom had clothing and personal belongings left behind but were not allowed to retrieve them and had no place else to go. As a result, they were "scattered all over the town." For once, Dora turned a blind eye to the women's plight. "I want you to understand that I am through, as far as I'm personally concerned, with this business in Salt Lake City," she told the *Standard*. "But the women—well you wait. There's going to be lots of trouble in Salt Lake yet. I gave Salt Lake the stockade, the only possible solution of the social evil, and the city threw me down. Now the city can try and solve its own problem and mark my word, it's got a hard one to solve right now."[12]

As long as she had the floor, the frustrated Dora decided to grant an even longer interview to the *Salt Lake Herald* on July 1. The Stockade was now empty, the ladies having been granted access long enough to gather their things. Dora retained the furniture she had purchased, vowing that she would not leave Salt Lake City until it had been sold and her business matters had been settled. But she made it clear that building the Stockade was the idea of the businessmen who approached her about how bad prostitution was in Salt Lake City and asked her to run the place. "There were two reasons why the plan appealed to me," she explained. "The first was a business reason. I saw there would be money in such an investment. I'm a business woman. I'm a good manager." The second reason was given with the caveat that "it is usually hard for the general public to see things as we—women of my class—see them." Dora opined that she had been in business for so long that "I have no ambition to try anything else. I don't like it. I abhor it. My conscience—yes, I have a conscience—has troubled me about it a good many times and I have sometimes thought about it all a great deal and this is the way I have figured it out: My reputation as a pure woman is gone. If I give this up, there is nothing left for me to do. Nobody would believe in me. Nobody would help me. I've got to stick to this, but I can do this much, I can make this business as clean as it is possible for such a business as this to be, and I can persuade a great many girls who are just starting in to lead a life of shame to travel other paths."

Dora furthered her statement by talking of how many girls she had tried to save from becoming prostitutes. "No girl has ever fallen through any influence of mine," she claimed. "Many girls who have come to me I have dissuaded from going wrong. I have advised them against it and in not a few cases I have helped them to keep away from it." The only arrests at the Stockade, she said, had been during the raids. "Not a single call has gone to police headquarters from here," she verified. "There have been no drunks, no quarrels, no fighting, no robberies. From the time this place was opened, it has been the rule that every woman entering the stockade must have a medical examination before she enters and must have a physician's certificate of health every ten days. You would be surprised if I were to tell you how many women have come here and have refused to be examined and how many were found who could not pass the examination." The madam ended her interview by explaining she also had planned to build a hospital here for women who were sick, "for I wanted this to be an ideal place of its kind." Instead, she said, some one-hundred-seventy women were now scattered all over the city "in rooming houses, in hotels, in the residence parts of the city."[13]

Dora's speech worked like magic. The charges against her and the Citizens' Investment Company were dropped. But in a letter to the editor of the *Ogden Standard*, A.W. Agee took umbrage when the madam apparently advised fifteen women to leave Salt Lake City, claiming that she could easily replace them with fifteen more prostitutes. And in September, Dora was inexplicably again charged with running houses of prostitution in Salt Lake City. She did not appear in court. The rumor-mongers finally had something to really talk about in November, when the *Salt Lake Herald-Republican* announced that Dora was indeed back at the Stockade making needed repairs, in preparation for reopening the resort.

This time, Dora made several attempts to garner the trust of those against her. In March 1910, she boldly extended a heartfelt invitation to some prominent ladies of Salt Lake City, including a minister's wife, to visit her lavish home in Ogden, which they actually accepted. "I am the greatest woman reformer in the world," Dora told them as they arrived. "I want you ladies to feel that you are most heartily welcomed to receive my most cordial hospitality while you are with me today, and any other time that you give me the pleasure of your company." The ladies toured Dora's home, noting one picture hanging on the wall declaring "Christ is All"—but also a "life-size painting of a nude female" on the other. Yet another read, "A true friend is one who knows all about you and yet cares for you." The ladies also observed the "handsomely and luxuriously furnished reception room." Dora assured her visitors, "When you know me and the grand work of reform that I am doing, you will hold me high in your esteem." The lady held nothing back, willingly answering the women's questions as she led them through "her entire mansion from garret to wine cellar." She even introduced them to her callers as they came by, and gave them a tour of her cribs and parlor houses.[14]

Later that same week, Dora also arranged a visit with "another prominent club woman" who was concerned about "the white slave traffic" in Salt Lake City. "I want you to think of me as a philanthropist," she told the woman, and further explained how she always did her level best to talk women out of entering the prostitution industry by telling them of "the awful shame, degradation, and misery that is invariably the final result of seamy life in the underworld. But if, in spite of my persuading efforts toward conversion, a woman willfully insists upon throwing her life away, then I receive her into my district." Dora was speaking in earnest, but the *Deseret Evening News* in particular dismissed her as "the devil's right hand mistress on earth."[15]

Once the Stockade reopened, Dora updated the house rules. Women wishing to change houses or move to a crib had to procure permission first. They also were "forced to patronize Stockade businesses." The ladies in general objected to these and other rules, including regular requests for donations "for a fund to buy off the police." And when a cook named John Halner claimed that a parlor house girl had stolen $11

from him, he was beaten unmercifully by a Stockade watchman identified as R. Reuting. Halner claimed that "he made his complaint to the
watchman in a peaceable manner when the latter screamed, 'How dare
you?'" and beat the man with his baton. Reuting was dragging Halner to
jail when the latter talked him into stopping at the Germania Saloon for
a beer. There, Halner "got hold of the heaviest beer mug in the saloon
and smashed it" in Reuter's face. The man required four stitches as
Halner was hauled off to jail anyway. In reporting the incident, the *Salt
Lake Herald-Republican* said that Chief of Police S.M. Barlow would be
investigating the matter further.[16]

Things only got worse from there. In May, prostitute Grace Gilmore
claimed she was forced to return to the Stockade against her wishes. The
incident depressed her to the point of attempting suicide, twice. "My
experience there was not only one of enduring almost unbearable filth
but Belle London made demands on me that took every penny I earned
and it seemed to be her desire to keep me in debt and in slavery," Grace
declared. But the lady had exhibited questionable behavior several days
before, when she left the Stockade with a soldier who took her to Fort
Douglas and got her incredibly inebriated. Police found her wandering
around Salt Lake's parade grounds. It was while they were taking her
and the unnamed soldier to the headquarters that Grace, still drunk,
tried to jump from the carriage. The soldier was trying to keep her from
jumping again when she snatched a knife from his pocket and tried to
stab herself. The *Herald-Republican* claimed that city officials and Dora
herself threatened to keep Grace in jail until she agreed to return to the
Stockade.[17]

Naturally, Grace's claims generated a huge article on the front page
of the *Deseret Evening News* on May 25. "'White Slaves' of Mrs. Dora
Topham," blared the headline. The article talked of how Dora was
"snooping about rooming houses, tracing out women of the underworld
and ordering them to go 'where you belong.'"[18] There was an opium den

next to the Stockade, said the paper. Grace was just one of many "white slaves" being held against their will and being forced to give Dora their money. None of the ladies, the paper said, could gather enough money to leave town. Beer was being sold on the premises. Women who dared to leave were ordered to return to the Stockade by police. There had been a knife fight and a man had been robbed just outside of the resort. The accusations went on and on. Next, the Stockade's own physician, Dr. Edward Manz, was jailed as a warrant also was issued for Dora's arrest. But when acting Police Chief John Hempel went to the Stockade to arrest her, the lady was nowhere to be found. She did eventually pay her bail, a hefty $2,700, and went to court as the Stockade closed again. Fed up again, Dora once more promised to vacate the resort.

In time, the authorities finally concluded that the only way to get their wayward women off the streets was to reopen the Stockade. Sure enough, the resort was back in business by March as the cat-and-mouse games between authorities, the press, and Dora continued. Finally, in July, the case of sixteen-year-old Dogney Lofstrom Gray proved to be the Stockade's ultimate undoing. Dogney had only recently married a soldier named Gray, but he suddenly and inexplicably deserted her. In court, she said a woman named Moore had then invited her to supper, drugged her coffee, and dragged her to the Stockade. Dogney also claimed that back in Ogden, Belle London had broken up her parents' marriage. She also had run away before, but her mother had found her and taken her home. At the Stockade, she said, she asked Dora to telephone her mother. Helen Lofstrom, Dogney's mother, was in Ogden at the time but retrieved Dogney when she returned to Salt Lake City. It was the following day, said Dogney, that she had married Gray, living at the Rex Hotel after he abandoned her. There, she was arrested for vagrancy and had spent the last two months in jail.

The holes in Dogney's story were incredibly obvious, but proceedings began against Dora anyway. Her case was delayed twice because she once again fell ill. In the coming weeks, both Helen Lofstrom and Dogney would claim that when the girl awoke at the Stockade, she found her dress was that of the Stockade uniform and that her face had been painted. Dora had at first refused to call the girl's mother. When she finally did, Helen Lofstrom was so leery that she arrived at the Stockade with a loaded revolver and the soldier who married Dogney.

Helen Lofstrom's credibility slipped considerably when it was discovered that back in 1906, she did indeed know Dora: Mr. Lofstrom was a tailor who made clothing for Dora's girls. Helen backed up Dogney's claim that Dora had broken up her marriage. She also testified that when Dora called her to tell her Dogney was there, the madam had inexplicably told her, "I am getting even with you. I have got your daughter in a house of ill fame." Further testimony, however, revealed that Dogney was at the Stockade a whole day before Dora even knew she was there, and had engaged in sex with at least one customer—thus violating the rule about getting a physical exam before going to work. The papers, of course, ate up only the damming testimony against Dora with a spoon, and she was found guilty in September of pandering. A few days later, the *Ogden Evening Standard* published a final announcement from Dora herself: "The Stockade will be closed on Thursday and the same will not be opened again. So soon as I can arrange my business, I shall advertise the property for sale." The madam followed her decree with a lot of other commentary regarding her innocence, what she had tried to achieve, and even a letter from a girl she had saved from prostitution who expressed her gratitude.[19]

Unfortunately, neither the courts nor the newspapers were done with Dora. On October 20, the *Ogden Evening Standard* announced that Dora was sentenced to eighteen years in prison for "enticing Dogney Gray, a young Salt Lake girl, to the 'stockade.'" This shocking news was received with much interest by Salt Lake's citizens, especially those who could see Dora had not received a fair trial. *Goodwin's Weekly*, Salt

Lake City's "thinking paper for thinking people," pointed out how Dora had obviously been railroaded. As for the *Ogden Evening Standard*, the paper reprinted an article from the *Weber County Citizen* wherein the editor, Wilson, had called the crusade with the Stockade an assault on Mayor Bransford and the American party due to "politics, cheap politics, dirty politics." Meanwhile, the Stockade was sold again as Dora took her case to the Supreme Court. At long last, in May of 1912, her case was overturned.[20]

In the wake of Dora's departure from Salt Lake City, the Stockade was demolished as the Women's League quickly organized a rescue mission for the city's now unemployed prostitutes. The effort was a very limited success. Rather than work menial, low-paying jobs, most of the women either left town or resumed their profession elsewhere in the city. It is guessed that only a dozen or so of them accepted the services of the Women's League. Within a few years, Salt Lake's good time girls were once again a public nuisance. As for Dora, the woman had virtually been kicked in the teeth for doing a job that city officials hired her to do. And her parting words before leaving Salt Lake rang true. "I know, and you know, that prostitution has existed since the earliest ages," she said, "and if you are honest with yourselves, you will admit that it will continue to exist, no matter what may be said or done from the pulpit or through the exertions of women's clubs."[21] Yet Salt Lake City just didn't get it, and debates about the prostitution industry continued for many more years.

Dora was a free woman now, but even the *Ogden Evening Standard* in her hometown turned on her. She remained in Ogden long enough to finish up her business until about 1914. By 1917, she had invested in over six hundred acres of property outside of the town of Beryl with Thomas Matthews, a police lieutenant who worked with her during the Stockade days. The couple eventually left Utah altogether and were in San Francisco by 1920. The census found Dora living under the name Maxine Rose at 317 Lyon Street. Also in the house were her daughter

Ethel, another eighteen-year-old adopted daughter named Charlotte Hill, and several boarders. Notably, Dora had previously paid for both Ethel's and Charlotte's educations at Berkeley University, but had lost much of her money in the Stockade before leaving Utah. Dora had told others she "wanted to forget the past and live a new life among people." Her plan worked, and she became "well-liked and respected by all who knew her."[22]

Around the time the census was taken, Dora pawned her diamonds and jewelry to purchase a nice, respectable hotel in San Francisco and made other investments as well. Eventually she was able to purchase a small ranch outside of the city to grow fruits and vegetables. Unfortunately, tragedy struck in December of 1924. Dora's Chinese employee was having car trouble, and Dora obligingly towed the vehicle from her ranch up to the road. She was untying the tow rope when the Chinese man's car "accidentally started up" and crushed her between the two automobiles. Dora suffered a broken leg and collarbone, plus serious internal injuries. She died five days later. Word eventually got back to Ogden, where the *Standard Examiner* simply reported that Dora B. Topham, once known as the notorious Belle London, died, but did not have more details. Weeks later Dora's good friend in Ogden, D.W. Brown, had the last word in a letter to the editor. The lengthy note defended such kind acts as Dora's willingness to feed, clothe, and warm the poor, how much she was liked in San Francisco, and how successful Ethel and Charlotte had turned out. Brown ended the letter by saying that "you can rest assured that this account of her life is correct. If you wish to ask any questions concerning this account, drop me a card and I will call at your office."[23]

CHAPTER 20

Park City's Rachel Urban

Park City's best-known madam was Rachel Beulah Urban, aka Mother Urban. Many things have been said about the 200-pound woman, mostly kind. Aside from running a series of brothels, Rachel was known for hosting or donating to regular parties to which everyone was invited. Like other madams, she willingly gave money to various causes. She was friendly with people of all walks of life. From her humble beginnings as the daughter of a menial street laborer, Rachel worked her way through at least three marriages, several children, and the loss of one leg to make it as the best remembered good time girl of Park City.

Rachel Beulah Gillespie was born in about 1863 in Cleveland, Ohio, to Irish immigrants William and Jane Gillespie. By 1876 Rachel's father had died, leaving her mother to toil as a seamstress while supporting her children. Three years later, Rachel left her mother's house to marry Joseph C. Bowman. After that, tracing Rachel's life becomes a bit muddy; she would later verify that she had given birth to a total of six children, but only one still lived. By the time she arrived in Park City in about 1888 she was alone, and missing one of her legs.

Park City, one of Utah's early mining towns, had good time girls fluttering about town as early as the 1870s and had only incorporated in 1884. By the time Rachel got there, the population was already over five thousand people. Within a year of her arrival, Rachel would give birth to her daughter, Florence. Who was Florence's father? It is hard to say, since Rachel was presumably still married to Joseph Bowman when she arrived in Utah. They say she walked with a cane due to her weight and limited walking ability.

By the early 1890s, Park City's red-light district was located near the train station in the vicinity of Heber Avenue as it led into Deer Valley. There is nothing to verify that Rachel was working in the red-light district, which appears on the 1889 Sanborn Fire Insurance map but for which no details are given. In 1896 Rachel married again, to Charles G. Westcott in Heber, some sixteen miles south of Park City. The union did not last. Rachel would later say of her husband that she "had supposed he was killed in Arizona a few years later. She said she had not heard from him again."[1] After waiting for two years Rachel married a third time, which was indeed a charm. Her chosen mate was a Danish mining speculator named George Charles Urban. The couple wed in Park City on October 13, 1898. By the time of the 1900 census, they were living on Heber Avenue with eleven-year-old Florence, who was given the last name of Urban and was attending school. Next door to the Urbans were two houses that were most likely brothels. One was occupied by Goldie Ludlow, who had two young ladies living with her. Next to Goldie was Maud Rogers, who kept three girls. The occupations of the women, including Rachel, were left blank by the census taker.

There is little doubt that Rachel lived on Heber Avenue because she was in the prostitution profession. Stories abound about her business acumen as a madam. For one thing, Rachel did not allow her employees to walk the streets for fear they would solicit customers and cause problems with the authorities. To make sure the girls behaved, Rachel paid a crippled neighbor named Mr. Reynolds (possibly William Reynolds, as identified in the 1900 census) to run their errands. Any girl caught breaking the rules received a one-way train ticket out of town.

Rachel's girls also were expected to be on hand for the annual Christmas party the madam threw for the single miners in town. Rachel had a soft spot in her heart for the men, offering them "a respectable place where they could gather. It was also a place where they could go and have a letter written home as many of them did not know how to write." Rachel's efforts were much appreciated by the mine owners. They knew that if their employees could not find sex for sale in Park City they might travel to other places, resulting in absences and delays in getting to work. At the same time, Park City's streets were made safer for respectable women while Rachel herself earned respect as a generous businesswoman. One old-timer recalled that if there was a death in the family, Mother Urban would discreetly visit in the night and give money to the family.[2]

Aside from her good deeds Rachel tended to keep to herself for the most part, but there were exceptions. She had a parrot, for instance, which usually occupied a perch on Rachel's front porch and delighted in squawking cusswords as people passed by. On at least one occasion, however, Rachel attempted to ingratiate herself to two of Park City's respectable ladies who happened to be strolling past her brothel. Rachel recognized one of the women, Blanche Fletcher, as a local piano player. She hospitably invited the ladies in for tea, with the promise that she was the only one home. Amazingly, the women accepted. After an enjoyable hour or so the women made their leave and Rachel asked the one woman, who was a stranger to her, what her name was. When the woman told her, Rachel smiled and said, "Oh yes, I know your husband well." Whether her comment was a slip of the tongue or a tongue-in-cheek joke is unknown.[3]

Rachel was able to operate unmolested until about 1907, when talk came of closing Park City's red-light district. Rachel knew just what to do, and had a chat with a local mine superintendent who happened to be single. The man followed up by addressing Park City's council, and the matter was resolved by changing the official occupations of Deer Valley's twenty-five naughty girls to "seamstresses." It was also agreed that the district should move farther east. Local legend speculates that George Urban, who alternated his time as a mining investor by performing carpentry work, built upward of sixteen houses along Heber Street expressly for use as brothels—although an updated 1907 Sanborn Fire Insurance map shows only five small bordellos and three larger parlor houses. Rachel's was one of the latter. Her place, identified as 346 Heber Avenue (or 345 Heber Avenue on the Sanborn map) became known as the "Purple Palace" or the "Purple Parlor." The outside of the building was, of course, painted purple. Rachel furnished the interior with lace curtains and fancy furniture. One source claims she may have also been running the smaller houses. Park City now had a monthly fine or business license policy of $40 per madam and $20 per prostitute. Rachel dutifully paid them on time, for herself and her girls. The endeavor paid off, and she was making good money. When she eventually purchased a real automobile, she hired a Black uniformed chauffeur to drive her around town.

Rachel and other women like her did weather occasional trouble with the law. On one of the very few occasions she appeared in the newspapers, it was because of a prostitute named Rose Fox, who was alternately identified by the *Salt Lake Herald* as Mrs. Walter Sweatman. In May of 1908, according to one George Morse, Rachel "allowed Walter Sweatman and his wife to drink, quarrel and fight," after which Rose died from the amount of alcohol she had consumed. Rachel was arrested in the incident, and Judge Waters told her that "the present condition of affairs in the district where she resided would no longer be tolerated." He also opined that Rachel "was guilty of shielding the party at the Inquest whom it is believed was directly responsible for the death of the woman." Rachel was fined $25.[4] The madam paid it and went on with her life.

The 1910 census found the Urbans still living at 345 Heber Avenue. Florence no longer lived with them, and unfortunately what became of her remains unknown. George now worked full-time as a carpenter and Rachel's occupation, as usual, was undocumented. Their neighbors included Madam April Crawford, who employed six women, Madam Julia DeGarmo with three women, and Daisy Hubbard and Frankie Miller, who were the sole occupants of their houses. Notably, there were no other occupants listed at the Urban house, supporting the idea that Rachel's employees lived elsewhere or lived and worked in other properties she owned. In 1912 it is known she sold four properties on Heber Avenue, identified as being "known as the Red Light [district]," and including the houses at 321, 339, 345, 555, and 777 Heber Avenue. Alternatively, however, the 1910 census records miner George Hanks and his family at the small house at 555 Heber Avenue. Because the house numbers along Heber Avenue have changed over time, it is difficult to ascertain whether all of the buildings Rachel sold were brothels and also leads to speculation that she rented some of them to respectable residents.[5]

Rachel's efforts to be a part of her community are further evidenced by an editorial she wrote to the *Park Record* in 1913, in defense of Dr. E.P. LeCompte. Why she was compelled to do so is unclear, but Rachel was obviously a bit hot under the collar when she wrote, "Never in the history of the camp has a doctor been more attentive than Dr. E.P. LeCompte, and if he had just one-fourth of what is owed him he could undoubtedly move into Salt Lake with his family and live on Easy Street. I have called him hundreds of times to come over and see some unfortunate woman of the underworld and, unlike some of the other doctors, he did not ask me who was going to pay him . . . but he would come immediately and render all assistance possible."[6] Later that year, on New Year's Eve, Rachel appeared at the Volunteer Fire Department's meeting where "refreshments were spread in abundance, the liquid portion thereof and many delicious turkey sandwiches being furnished by Mrs. Rachel Urban, with happy new year greetings for the entire 'bunch.' Mrs. Urban never forgets the fire laddies at their monthly meetings, contributing always to the enjoyment of the gatherings and always with words of cheer and encouragement for the department, which is much appreciated by the recipients."[7]

Whether Rachel's family back East knew what she did for a living is unknown, but she did stay in touch with one sister, Annie, who was married to Andrew S. McIntosh in 1914. When Andrew, "a very wealthy and prominent man of Cleveland" died that year, Rachel left Park City to be at her sister's side.[8] The *Park Record* announced her departure, saying she was expected to be gone for some time. Rachel did return to Park City, where her benevolent contributions continued. In 1917 for instance, the madam donated a large flag for the city, "to be flown continually from the big city flagpole."[9]

In 1919, Rachel appeared in the *Park Record* again—in a different light, and through no fault of her own. In the early morning hours of November 3, the madam heard "a big automobile turn around in front of her house and drive rapidly away." The madam thought little of it until she realized she had not seen one of her crib girls, Clara Maybell Huey, in a few days. Rachel knocked on the front door of Clara's crib, which was locked. Suspicious, Rachel called the police. When officers arrived, they found the back door to the crib open. Inside Clara's room, the twenty-four-year-old harlot lay dead on her bed, wearing only her "stockings, a low-pair of slippers, and a kimono. Her nightgown was carefully folded under her head . . . the pillow had been taken from the head of the bed, and was over the woman's face, but in a perfectly smooth condition, not the least sign to indicate that it had been used to smother" her. But Clara's revolver and her money were missing.[10] Clara was buried in Salt Lake City's Mt. Olivet Cemetery as police immediately began investigating the mysterious case.

Clara had been living in Park City for the past year and a half. Her husband, James "Cupid" Huey, drove a taxi in Salt Lake City. The couple had recently quarreled, but Huey claimed he was in Salt Lake the previous night when he got a call around 11 p.m. to go to Kamas. He said that he got stuck in the mud and snow near Wanship, and because of that did not return to Salt Lake until 6 a.m. the following morning. Huey also said that Clara "was subject to spells during which she found breathing extremely difficult." The authorities kept this in mind as they searched for others who might have seen Clara before her death. They found Lawrence Buys, a Salt Lake City wrestler who confirmed he was with Clara the night before she died. Buys said he and his brother Frank went out for a bite to eat, returned to Clara's room, and left early the following morning. What concerned police, however, were the three bloody handkerchiefs and a bloody collar in Buys's suitcase. The man could not explain how they got that way. Certain they had their men, the police arrested Buys and his brother. Unfortunately, nothing else came of the case, and the men were "released due to lack of evidence."[11]

By 1920, Rachel might have been retired. Few, if any, good time girls appeared in the census on Heber Avenue that year. All remained quiet in the Urbans' lives until George succumbed to pneumonia on September 24, 1924. Rachel naturally bought a fancy casket costing $365, and Urban was buried in Park City's cemetery. The *Park Record* published a nice, if short, obituary for him on September 24: "Wednesday of this week was the sudden passing on of George Urban, one of Park City's best-known carpenters, miner and prospector. Deceased was born in Copenhagen, Denmark, on October 13, 1860. On October 13, 1898, he married Rachel B. Hayden of this city, who survives him. It was he who found the Valeo [mine], and brought it into prominence in the early days, making considerable money from the sale thereof later on. Funeral Services were held at the undertaking parlors of Wildermuth and Archer."[12]

Here lies another mystery about Rachel. George Urban's obituary, and death certificate, identify Rachel as once having the last name of Hayden. Yet no record of a Rachel Hayden is identifiable in census or marriage records, or any other official documents. Although her husband left behind only $84 in cash and about $100 worth of carpenter's tools, Rachel duly filed for probate on his estate and even deposited a $500 bond to do so. Notably, the papers said that Urban had no children of his own, clarifying once and for all that he was not the father of Rachel's daughter, Florence.

About a year after Urban's death, Rachel filed a patent on the Marcella mining claim south of Park City, with which her deceased husband might have been involved. Next, she filed a public notice against H.M. Swan and Ole Jorgenson, notifying the men that she had been paying for assessments on the claim since 1916. If they did not pay their share of the costs, the claim would be forfeited over to Rachel. Whatever became of Rachel's claim, however, was superseded by a most interesting event in 1926: Charles G. Westcott, her husband whom she presumed was dead years ago, surfaced in Los Angeles—as the victim of a murder by his own son.

On October 20, Westcott had heard the doorbell ring at his stylish Wilshire home in Los Angeles. When he answered, he was shot by an unknown assailant hiding in some nearby shrubbery. As he lay dying, however, Westcott identified the shooter as his son, Carl. Police found Carl, and discovered pieces of the same shrubbery in the cuffs of his trousers. He was booked on murder charges. Carl Westcott used a variety of alibis, including that he was at a dance hall (which was verified by a couple of his bootlegger pals), or at a hotel. The man apparently had been bad news from the start, having spent time in a Colorado reform school, as well as prisons in Washington, Minnesota, and Arkansas. He also used several aliases.

As Westcott was held for trial, Rachel heard the news that her long-ago husband had been very much alive until recently. In March of 1927, the madam traveled to Los Angeles and filed a petition "for special letters of administration." California's *San Pedro News-Pilot* referred to her as "Mrs. Rachael B. Bowman-Westcott of Park City, Utah." What Rachel did not know was that a second "widow," Hazel Westcott, claimed she was the rightful heir to Charles Westcott's estate. In her petition, Rachel referred to Hazel as a "pretender wife." And, "according to Mrs. Emma Westcott, mother of the convicted man, the slain man had at least four wives to her knowledge and she expressed the belief that he had been legally married to the Utah woman."[13]

Carl Westcott had hoped to inherit some $120,000 from his father's estate. Rachel's sources told her that the estate was really only worth about $11,000, still enough worth fighting for. But it was a sticky situation, seeing as Hazel Westcott had already testified at Carl's trial as Charles' widow. Even so, Rachel finished the necessary paperwork. By March 25, she was back in Park City, where the *Park Record* reported on the Westcott case with much interest. The paper kindly referred to Rachel simply as "the proprietress of various rooming houses in Park City" over the past thirty years. A friend of hers, Mrs. I. Watson, had verified that Rachel once told her she had married Westcott back in the 1890s, and the newspaper had found the original marriage certificate to prove it. Upon her return, Rachel appeared victorious as the "legal widow." The article ended by stating that Rachel "proposes to fight for her rights—and get them."[14] But Rachel did not get her wish. In July, she inexplicably dropped her court action against Westcott's estate. Her reasons for doing so are unknown, but she likely watched the newspapers as Carl Westcott appealed his conviction three times, was ultimately found guilty, and was sentenced to life at Folsom Prison in California. In 1929, he was found insane and committed to an asylum in Norwalk.

Rachel was now sixty-five years old. In the 1930 census she was documented as a "real estate" manager. Next door to her were several houses, each occupied by single women ranging in age between twenty-three and forty years old. Rachel owned her home; the others rented theirs. Based on legends that she indeed controlled Park City's red-light district, the ladies likely paid rent to their landlord, Rachel. Three years later, unfortunately, Rachel contracted cancer of the stomach. Following a three-week stay at the Miner's Hospital, she died on March 23, 1933. Blanche Fletcher, the proper lady who had enjoyed tea in Rachel's parlor so many years ago, played piano at her funeral. She was buried in Park City's cemetery, next to George Urban.

Unfortunately, there was nobody left to claim Rachel's property. Her taxes remained unpaid for several years until 1938, when the properties were offered at a county tax sale. Some of Rachel's houses may have remained as cribs or brothels; the last one, known as "Bessie's House," was closed down in 1956 and burned in 1970.[15] As for Rachel, the endearing madam was only briefly mentioned in books and articles for many years, with no clue as to what became of her. Fast-forward to 2005, when history buff Gary Kimball spent eighteen months researching newspapers and other documents to find a list of burials at Park City's cemetery after discovering that many records were "erased or half entered." Among the one-thousand-twenty burials Kimball found, Rachel's was one of them. The researcher published his findings in a book, *Death & Dying in Old Park City*, telling the *Park Record* he suspected that "city officials asked for Urban's name to be taken off the books, because they didn't like the idea of having her name on the list." Rachel Urban, like so many other madams across Utah and the West, might have been forgotten. But she is certainly remembered now.[16]

CHAPTER 21

———— •❦• ————

No Nose Maggie

One of Utah's last notable prostitutes was Mrs. Mary Alice Ann Devitt Laird of the tiny mining town of Joy, located in the Detroit mining district some thirty miles northwest of Delta. Harry Joy and Charles Howard organized the Drum Mountain Mining District in 1879, and the tiny community was born. Harry Joy would later be a founding member of the Packard Motor Company, but his namesake town was so inconsequential that nobody is even sure when it became a ghost—except for Mary Laird. Mary's parents, James and Bridget Devitt, were Irish immigrants who already had two children when they came to America. More children would be born as the family moved through Illinois and Minnesota—ten in all, including Mary who was born circa 1858. In 1874, James and three of his sons packed nearly everything and headed for Fargo, North Dakota. Bridget remained behind, waiting until spring to bring the rest of the children by train. After farming for a time in Ransom County, the Devitts returned to Fargo where James and Bridget managed the Lake Hotel. By the time of the 1880 census, Mary was one of only three children still living at home. Three years later, she appears to have been alone when she was residing at a place on Front Street in Fargo as Maggie Devitt. She was employed as a domestic servant.

Family lore speculates that Maggie possibly married one Charlie Christianson during the 1880s, and bore a child by him. But Christianson traveled, perhaps due to his job with a railroad. At some point Maggie began receiving mysterious letters addressed to her husband. When at last she opened one, she found a drawing of a child's foot and a note reading, "Look how much your little boy has growed since you last saw him!"[1] That tore it for Maggie, who packed her bags and left for Seattle. The family story went that she entered a convent there, and quite possibly gave birth to twins. In the coming years, no matter where she was, Maggie sent money for the children's care. In Seattle, Maggie began using the name Mary Moran, her mother's maiden name. Later, she is believed to have moved to San Francisco and, later, Virginia City, Nevada. There, she found work as a barmaid and good time girl in the nicer saloons. From Virginia City, Maggie next traveled to Pioche, Nevada, and the mining camps around Eureka, Utah. Quite possibly, Maggie did not know that her father died in 1890, although she surely found out later.

By 1891 Maggie was in Fish Springs, a tiny settlement in the Utah desert. She was making good money as the only prostitute in town until another woman, Katie Kilkowski, arrived. Maggie naturally resented another woman plucking her pigeons, and tensions rose quickly between the two. One night, after exchanging insults, the ladies broke into a "no-holds-barred" catfight, rolling on the floor as they clawed and kicked at each other.[2] After several minutes, with much betting going on between the men who watched, the pair was separated. The women caught their breath as they glowered at one another, until Katie suddenly grabbed a whiskey bottle and hit Maggie in the head so hard that the bottom of it shattered as jagged glass worked its way down her face. A big, horizontal gash tore across the bridge of Maggie's nose and on either side of her face. Katie escaped out the back door and, most interestingly, eventually wound up dead at the bottom of a well.

Mrs. Mary Alice Ann Devitt Laird, better known as "No Nose Maggie" of Joy, Utah.
Courtesy Delta City Library, Utah

The scar on Maggie's face disfigured her for good. She was now around thirty-three years old, no longer attractive to men, and could not possibly face her family. When Bridget Devitt died the following year, her obituary acknowledged that "Marianne's" whereabouts were unknown. With no money, Maggie had no choice but to go back to work as a barmaid. Most everyone knew how she came to have that scar on her face, and they likely felt sympathy for her. But although she found acceptance among the people of Fish Springs, Maggie had trouble reckoning with her own past and where it had led to. As time went on she developed a drinking problem, allegedly imbibing around the clock.

Maggie's family later surmised that a local bartender, Anselem "Mac" Laird, felt especially bad for the woman. Laird was quite possibly present when Katie Kilkowski smashed in Maggie's nose, and perhaps even felt guilty for not intervening as the women fought. Clearly, the girl needed a fresh start. Thus Maggie woke up one morning in about 1893 with a fresh hangover, only to find herself laying in a moving wagon. The driver was Mac Laird, who laughed uproariously as Maggie became aware of her predicament. "Honey, you and me's gonna find Joy!" he told her. "You ain't taking me to that damned hole," Maggie retorted, "I'll walk back!" The furious harlot threw off the blanket over her, only to discover she wasn't wearing a stitch of clothing. After spewing forth epithets and insults, Maggie demanded to know where her clothes were. "Back at the mine," Laird answered, and laughed even harder. [3] Walking back to Fish Springs in the desert sun, naked, was not an option. Maggie had no choice but to accept her fate of the moment. And by the time the couple reached Joy some thirty-seven miles away Maggie was seated beside Laird, the blanket wrapped around her.

Surely the townspeople of Joy were shocked to see this half-naked, disheveled woman with a horrible scar on her face as Laird's wagon rolled into town. In time, however, Maggie's status as an odd newcomer would change as people got to know her. She was able to secure a job as a cook at a local cafe, next to a hotel. On the side, she also partnered with one of her coworkers, Charley Woodward, to manufacture and sell batches of "snake oil."[4] But she also maintained her romance with Laird, who became postmaster at the nearby town of Dru in 1893, and whom she married in Fillmore, Utah, in 1895. One source notes that there were discrepancies on the marriage certificate, namely that Mac Laird documented his name as Archibald, not Anselem, and both he and Maggie lied about their ages. Both also adopted the popular Mormon faith—or at least pretended to.

Admittedly, the Laird union was not always ideal. Joy resident Myrtle Mikesell Spor remembered the first time she met Maggie when the Mikesell wagon pulled up outside of Laird's Store. Inside, Myrtle could hear Maggie and her man, drunk and fighting. When Myrtle's father inquired about getting a meal, Maggie responded, "No, I'll not feed any [censored] today!!" A furious Mac Laird, hearing Maggie spewing cusswords, retorted, "Woman! Git some food on that table!" He also "snatched a whip from stock and hit her a smarting lash" across the shoulders.[5] The Mikesells presumably got their meal, and Myrtle remained friends with Maggie for the rest of her life. On another occasion, in 1898, Laird unaccountably left Maggie for a time. Evidence that Maggie did stay in touch with certain members of her family comes with her brother Andrew, who moved with his wife and numerous children to Utah for a couple of years after Laird left. The wandering husband had returned home, however, by the time of the 1900 census.

As much as they fought, the Lairds experienced much success in Joy. Laird's Store kept the locals supplied with food and other stock, some of which Maggie kept cool in a cave near a spring by the store. It cost a quarter for travelers wishing to water their animals at the spring. In time the couple also built rooms onto the store where travelers, or the local drunks, could stay the night. In the morning, Maggie fed her guests a simple breakfast of "'dough gobs,' hot coffee, and bacon or mutton."[6]

In 1899, Joy's post office was established inside the store. The business had to have been profitable, since the 1900 census shows the Lairds and their boarder, J.W. Adam, were three of just fourteen people living in the Detroit Mining District. Nearby, Mount Laird and Lady Laird Peak both were named in honor of Mac and Maggie.

Following the death of his wife in 1908 another of Maggie's brothers, Michael Devitt, moved to Joy with his fifteen-year-old daughter, Kate. Unfortunately, plenty of folks knew about Maggie's past as a good time girl, and some of them assumed Kate was brought to town with the purpose of opening a new brothel. Maggie used her pistol to get her point across that Kate was not available. Ironically, one of the men who came to have a look at young Kate, William McDonald, actually fell in love with her. Maggie approved, and, anxious to remove Kate from the raw life in Joy, Maggie allowed McDonald to run his sheep on her land so he could court the girl. In 1910, McDonald married Kate.

That same year, for reasons known only to themselves, the Lairds were back in Fish Springs. Sadly, Maggie told the census taker that she had given birth to three children in the past, but none of them lived. Laird was working in mining, and the occupation of Maggie's brother Michael was documented as a laborer. The endeavor must have been successful, for in 1916 Laird filed for a homestead just north of today's Little Sahara Recreation Area. Most unfortunately, however, he died the following year during the legendary influenza epidemic that gripped the nation. He was buried in Deseret City. Maggie was now in her sixties. This time, her brother Andrew came to Joy to help his sister. Maggie inherited the Laird homestead, as well as a half interest in several mining claims. The total estate was valued at $1,200—nearly $27,000 today.

Between her real estate and Laird's Store, Maggie was able to get along nicely even after Joy's post office closed in 1919. By the 1920 census, she was making money selling hay and grain, and had two boarders residing with her. Most unfortunately, however, certain of Maggie's male customers took advantage of her, refusing to pay for goods and services. Brother Andrew came to the rescue once again in 1921, setting her books straight and making sound investments in stock and other goods. Myrtle Mikesell Spor, meanwhile, sent her young daughter Alice to stay with Maggie on occasion. Alice would later remember that Maggie was an animal whisperer of sorts. She was able to approach wild horses, kept numerous cats, and made homemade meals for her dog, Man.

The animals were Maggie's comforts, for she still felt so terrible about the scar on her face that she refused to keep any mirrors out. Alice recalled a day when a mirror was accidentally left on the wall by the washstand. "She walked by and just caught a glimpse of herself in the mirror," Alice said, "and she started screaming, 'Sweetheart, sweetheart, come quick!' We ran in as fast as we could. She was just standing in front of the mirror and she said, 'No wonder people look at me. Look at that! I'm just real ugly.'" Alice assured her she was not, but it is doubtful that Maggie believed the girl. Alice also noted how handy Maggie was with her pistol. Once, when some mining speculators were staying with her, she idly watched them shooting cans before showing off her own marksmanship. Not only did she practically shoot the cans from under one man's hand, but she also "made a rock dance on the ground with the six-shooter. Then she reloaded and picked up a can and threw it in the air and just shot six times. She kept the can a twirling."[7]

Maggie also exuded warm greetings to all of her visitors. "My Gad, sweetheart, where yuh bin?" she would say. "Have yuh ett? Fixins ready, no trouble at all."[8] If someone fell ill, Maggie's mustard packs were known to cure them. When sheepherder Floyd Myers was caught in a bad snowstorm, his horse instinctively brought him to Maggie's place. Maggie snatched the hypothermic man from his saddle, rolled him in the snow to make sure he was alert, dragged him into the house, and warmed him by the fire as she fed him "bacon and dough gobs on an old tin plate and poured him a couple shots of whiskey." Floyd remained forever in her debt. Of Maggie's kindness, Alice Spor said, "She was one of the sweetest women; she never turned anyone away from her door. If they were down-and-out on their luck she would take whole families."[9] To wit, the 1930 census shows that Maggie once again had two male boarders at her house. Together they, along with Maggie's two brothers, constituted the entire population of Joy.

Sadly, Maggie's kindness cost her dearly toward the end of her life. In July of 1934, she took in a family whose car had broken down. According to Alice Spor, "they stayed until all the food was gone and then beat her almost to death and left her, just left her there." The poor woman lay on the floor, helpless, for two days before some passing sheepherders rode by Maggie's. It was nighttime, and normally Maggie left a kerosene lamp burning. One of the men, seeing the house was dark, went to investigate. There lay Maggie. "God bless you son," she gasped, "I needs help." Following a stay in the hospital, the Spors asked Maggie to move into their home in Delta.[10] Maggie's injuries from the beating likely contributed to her contracting pneumonia that winter. She died on December 18 at the Spor home.

In reporting Maggie's death, the *Millard County Chronicle* described her as "much worn with a vigorous and hard life . . . Mrs. Laird is known to all the old timers and her passing is regretted."[11] Maggie was buried at nearby Eureka. Later, Floyd Myers purchased Maggie's property. Today Joy is deserted, identifiable only by Laird Spring, Laird Peak, and, of course, Lady Laird Peak. There is also a memorial of sorts, in the form of a "grave" serving as a tribute to "No-Nose Maggie," the hard-living harlot with the heart of gold.[12]

ENDNOTES

———————•●•———————

CHAPTER 1: NAUGHTY NEVADA

1 Archer Butler Hulbert, *Forty-Niners* (Boston: Little, Brown and Company, 1931), 216.

2 Lambert Florin, *Ghost Towns of the West* (New York: Superior Publishing/ Promontory Press, 1971), 571–572.

3 Ibid., 548.

4 "Winnemucca Brothels," Wayback Machine, https://web.archive.org/ web/20030207184813/http://www.nvbrothels.net:80/win.htm, accessed September 25, 2019; "8 Famous Brothels That Have Closed Over the Years," October 2, 2018, RedLightVegas, https://redlightvegas.com/famous-closed-nevada-brothels/, accessed September 25, 2019.

5 Bob McCracken, "Hurdy houses, hurdy girls flourished in boom towns," *Pahrump Valley Times*, August 29, 2014, https://pvtimes.com/news/hurdy-houses-hurdy-girls -flourished-in-boom-towns/, accessed September 25, 2019.

6 Michael Rutter, *Upstairs Girls: Prostitution in the American West* (Helena, MT: Farcountry Press, 2005), 65.

7 Alexa Albert, *Brothel: Mustang Ranch and Its Women* (New York and Canada: Random House, 2001), 37–38.

8 Time-Life Books, *Gamblers of the Old West* (Alexandria, VA: Time-Life Books, 1996), 85; Florin, *Ghost Towns of the West*, 577–578.

9 Florin, *Ghost Towns of the West*, 578.

10 Albert, *Brothel: Mustang Ranch and Its Women*, 38-39; Alicia Barber, "Reno's Red Light District: The Colorful History of Brothels in Washoe County," KUNR, April 24, 2019, https://www.kunr.org/post/reno-s-red-light-district-colorful-history-brothels -washoe-county#stream/0, accessed September 26, 2019.

11 Albert, *Brothel: Mustang Ranch and Its Women*, 39.

CHAPTER 2: COQUETTES OF CARSON CITY

1 Willa Oldham, *Carson City: Nevada's Capital City* (Carson City: Nevada State Museum, 1991), 5.

2 George Williams III, *Rosa May: The Search for a Mining Camp Legend* (Riverside, CA: Tree by the River Publishing, 1982), 113.

3 Ibid, , 85, 157, 172.

4 *Carson Daily Appeal*, September 24, 1875, 3:3.

5 Carson City *Morning Appeal*, May 8, 1879, 3:2.

6 Ibid., June 27, 1879, 3:2.

7 Ibid., August 8, 1880, 3:1.

8 Ibid., February 9, 1881, 2:2 and March 2, 1881, 1:5.

9 "Quaint House Is State's Oldest Standing Brothel," *Las Vegas Sun*, November 12, 1998, https://lasvegassun.com/news/1998/nov/12/quaint-house-is-states-oldest-standing-brothel/, accessed September 30, 2019.

10 Ibid.

CHAPTER 3: ROSA MAY AND ERNI MARKS

1 George Williams III, *Rosa May: The Search for a Mining Camp Legend* (Riverside, CA: Tree by the River Publishing, 1982), 63, 84–85, 91–96, 113, 188, 194.

2 For reference, see stories in Jan MacKell Collins, *Good Time Girls of Colorado: A Red-Light History of the Centennial State* (Guilford, CT: Globe Pequot Press, 2019) and *Good Time Girls of California: A Red-Light History of the Golden State* (Guilford, CT: Globe Pequot Press, 2021).

3 Williams III, *Rosa May*, 103–112, 117–127, 129–130, 157–158.

4 MacKell Collins, *Good Time Girls of California: A Red-Light History of the Golden State*, 43.

CHAPTER 4: NOT SO VIRGINAL VIRGINIA CITY

1 George Williams III, *The Redlight Ladies of Virginia City Nevada* (Riverside, CA: Tree by the River Publishing, 1984), Author's Introduction.

2 Ronald M. James, "Women of the Mining West: Virginia City Revisited," *Nevada Historical Society Quarterly*, Fall 1993, Vol. 36, No. 3, 156.

3 "Virginia City and Gold Hill," Online Nevada Encyclopedia, http://www.online nevada.org/articles/virginia-city-and-gold-hill, accessed April 11, 2019.

4 Williams III, *The Redlight Ladies of Virginia City Nevada*, 5–6.

5 Virginia City *Territorial Enterprise*, August 6, 1875, 3:3.

6 James, "Women of the Mining West," 186.

7 Michael Rutter, *Upstairs Girls: Prostitution in the American West* (Helena, MT: Farcountry Press, 2005), 53, 65.

8 Williams III, *The Redlight Ladies of Virginia City Nevada*, 30.

9 Robin Flinchum, *Red Light Women of Death Valley* (Charleston, SC: The History Press, 2015), 37–39, 42–44.

10 Williams III, *The Redlight Ladies of Virginia City Nevada*, 24; Rutter, *Upstairs Girls*, 66.

11 Sharon Lowe, "Pipe Dreams and Reality: Opium in Comstock Society, 1860–1887," *Nevada Historical Society Quarterly*, Fall 1993, Vol. 36, No. 3, 186.

12 Williams III, *The Redlight Ladies of Virginia City Nevada*, 32; Rutter, *Upstairs Girls*, 10.

13 Ibid., 13, 32.

14 Lowe, "Pipe Dreams and Reality: Opium in Comstock Society, 1860–1887," 189.

15 Williams III, *The Redlight Ladies of Virginia City Nevada*, 32.

16 Carson City *Daily State Register*, August 29, 1871, 2:3.

17 Virginia City *Daily Territorial Enterprise*, October 28, 1875, reprinted in the *Reno Gazette Journal*, February 10, 2014, https://www.rgj.com/story/life/2014/02/11/from-1875-fire-sweeps-through-virginia-city/5365781/, accessed March 31, 2020.

18 Williams III, *The Redlight Ladies of Virginia City Nevada*, 5–6.

19 Virginia City *Territorial Enterprise*, August 6, 1875, 3:2

20 Sherry Monahan, *The Wicked West: Boozers, Cruisers, Gamblers and More* (Tucson, AZ: Rio Nuevo Publishers, 2005), 103–105.

21 Williams III, *The Redlight Ladies of Virginia City Nevada*, 5–6,13, 32; Anne Seagraves, *Soiled Doves: Prostitution in the Old West* (Hayden, ID: Wesanne Publications, 1994), 116.

22 Carson City *Morning Appeal*, June 3, 1881, 3:2 and June 4, 1881, 3:4.

23 Ibid, June 16, 1881, 3:1.

24 Williams III, *The Redlight Ladies of Virginia City Nevada*, 6-8.

25 Marion Goldman, "Sexual Commerce on the Comstock Lode," *Nevada Historical Society Quarterly*, Summer 1978, Volume XXI, Number 2, 109.

CHAPTER 5: CAD THOMPSON, THE "GOOD SPORT"

1 George Williams III, *The Redlight Ladies of Virginia City Nevada* (Riverside, CA: Tree by the River Publishing, 1984), 28.

2 Alexandra L. Simmons-Rogers, "RED LIGHT LADIES: Settlement Patterns and Material Culture on the Frontier," thesis submitted to Oregon State University, October 28, 1983, 68; Marion S. Goldman, *Gold Diggers & Silver Miners: Prostitution and Social Life on the Comstock Lode* (Ann Arbor: University of Michigan Press, 1981), 79.

3 Simmons-Rogers, "RED LIGHT LADIES," 234–235.

4 George Williams III, *Rosa May: The Search for a Mining Camp Legend* (Riverside, CA: Tree by the River Publishing, 1982), 132.

5 Marion Goldman, "Sexual Commerce on the Comstock Lode," *Nevada Historical Society Quarterly*, Summer 1978, Volume XXI, Number 2, 121.

6 George M. Blackburn and Sherman L. Ricards, "The Prostitutes and Gamblers of Virginia City, Nevada: 1870," *Pacific Historical Review*, Vol. 48, No. 2, May 1979, by University of California Press, 241–242.

7 *Gold Hill Daily News*, July 6, 1867, 3:2.

8 *Elko Independent*, July 27, 1870, 3:3.

9 Williams III, *Rosa May*, 132–133.

10 *Virginia Evening Chronicle*, February 18, 1875, 3:3.

11 *Sacramento Daily Union*, August 16, 1878, 3:4.

12 *Pioche Weekly Record*, August 24, 1878, 2:2.

13 *Daily Alta California*, October 20, 1878, 1:4.

14 Williams III, *Rosa May*, 84, 130.

15 *Virginia Evening Chronicle*, September 30, 1882, 3:3.

16 Ibid., June 6, 1883, 3:3.

17 Ibid., June 6, 1885, miscellaneous file, author's collection.

18 Carson City *Morning Appeal*, March 24, 1897, 3:1.

19 *Elko Daily Independent*, March 24, 1897, 3:1.

20 Virginia City *Daily Territorial Enterprise*, April 21, 1897, 1:3.

CHAPTER 6: THE MURDER OF JULIA "JULE" BULETTE

1 Jeremy Agnew, *Brides of the Multitude: Prostitution in the Old West* (Lake City, CO: Western Reflections Publishing Co., 2008), 178.

2 Hillyer Best, *Julia Bulette and Other Red Light Ladies: An Altogether Stimulating Treatise on the Madams of the Far West* (Sparks, NV: Western Printing & Publishing Co., 1959), 23.

3 Charles E. DeLong, *Life and Confession of John Millian: (properly, Jean Marie A. Villain) Convicted as the Murderer of Julia Bulett, as Given by Him to His Attorney* (Virginia City, NV: Lammon, Gregory & Palmer, 1868), 4.

4 Best, *Julia Bulette and Other Red Light Ladies*, 23.

5 Francis P. Weisenberger, "God and Man in a Secular City: The Church in Virginia City, Nevada," *Nevada Historical Society Quarterly*, Summer 1971, 5.

6 George Williams III, *The Redlight Ladies of Virginia City* Nevada (Riverside, CA: Tree by the River Publishing, 1984), 35.

7 Alexandra L. Simmons-Rogers, "RED LIGHT LADIES: Settlement Patterns and Material Culture on the Frontier," thesis submitted to Oregon State University, October 28, 1983, 62.

8 Williams III, *The Redlight Ladies of Virginia City Nevada*, 43–44.

9 Best, *Julia Bulette and Other Red Light Ladies*, 24.

10 Weisenberger, "God and Man in a Secular City," 5.

11 Best, *Julia Bulette and Other Red Light Ladies*, 24, 26.

12 Michael Rutter, *Upstairs Girls: Prostitution in the American West* (Helena, MT: Farcountry Press, 2005), 115.

13 Douglas MacDonald, "From Our Library Collection: A Rare Photograph," *Nevada Historical Society Quarterly*, Spring 1972, 45.

14 Best, *Julia Bulette and Other Red Light Ladies*, 27, 29.

15 Ibid., 28.

16 Rutter, *Upstairs Girls*, 111; Best, *Julia Bulette and Other Red Light Ladies*, 28.

17 Virginia City *Territorial Enterprise*, June 27, 1867, 3:1.

18 Williams III, *The Redlight Ladies of Virginia City Nevada*, 37–38.

19 Best, *Julia Bulette and Other Red Light Ladies*, 31.

20 DeLong, *Life and Confession of John Millian*, 3–4.

21 Williams III, *The Redlight Ladies of Virginia City Nevada*, 35.

22 Charles Jeffrey Garrison, "Notes and Documents of Humor, Death and Ministers: The Comstock of Mark Twain," *Nevada Historical Society Quarterly*, Summer 2008, 101; Rutter, *Upstairs Girls*, 118; Williams III, *The Redlight Ladies of Virginia City Nevada*, 40; Best, *Julia Bulette and Other Red Light Ladies*), 32.

23 Simmons-Rogers, "RED LIGHT LADIES," 50–51, 75–76.

24 Williams III, *The Redlight Ladies of Virginia City Nevada*, 43–44.

25 Virginia City *Territorial Enterprise*, June 27, 1867, 3:1.

26 DeLong, *Life and Confession of John Millian*, 4–5, 11, 13–15.

27 Best, *Julia Bulette and Other Red Light Ladies*, 35–39.

28 Mary Ellen Grass, "Rails in the Mud: Last Years of the V & T," *Nevada Historical Society Quarterly*, Summer 1972, 39.

CHAPTER 7: THE ELUSIVE LADIES OF ELY

1 Nevada Adventures, http://www.nevadadventures.com/ghost%20towns/whitepine co/elymurrycreek/elymurraycreek.html, accessed April 3, 2020.

2 *Eureka Sentinel*, March 14, 1914, 3:6.

3 "The Big Four," Ely, Nevada, http://www.bigfourranch.com/ABOUT/index.htm, accessed September 19, 2019; Ely, Nevada, http://www.bigfourranch.com/ABOUT/ index.htm, accessed September 19, 2019; "Big 4 Ranch and Brothel," https://big-4 -ranch-brothel-and-vip-spa-business.site/, accessed April 12, 2020.

4 "The Big Four"; "Bronc Alley—Red light District at the west end of High Street, Ely, Nevada," US Genweb, http://theusgenweb.org/nv/whitepine/Towns/Ely_walking _tour/westendhighst.htm, accessed September 10, 2019.

5 "Bronc Alley—Red light District."

6 "Corner of 13th & B Streets 1908, CRIB ROW," http://theusgenweb.org/nv/white pine/Towns/Ely_walking_tour/13thstcribrow.htm, accessed June 7, 2020; "Bronc Alley—Red light District."

CHAPTER 8: THE TARTS OF TONOPAH

1 Bob McCracken, *A History of Tonopah, Nevada* (Tonopah, NV: Nye County Press, 1990), n.p., Nye County History, http://nyecountyhistory.com/tonopahbook2/ tonopahhard.pdf, accessed April 4, 2020.

2 Herbert Gold, "Tonopah—Survivor of Mining Days," *New York Times*, June 27, 1982, Section 10, p. 20.

3 *Tonopah Bonanza*, June 14, 1902, 2:2.

4 Ibid., July 12, 1902, 5:4.

5 Ibid., June 6, 1903, 5:4 and July 25, 1903, 3:2.

6 Mrs. Hugh Brown, *Lady in Boomtown: Miners and Manners on the Nevada Frontier* (Reno and Las Vegas: University of Nevada Press, 1968), 42–43.

7 *Tonopah Bonanza*, May 14, 1904, 4:2.

8 McCracken, *A History of Tonopah, Nevada*.

9 *Oakland Tribune* (California), January 13, 1907, 18:4; Tonopah Nevada Cemetery Brochure, https://www.tonopahnevada.com/CemeteryBrochureOnline.pdf, accessed April 7, 2020.

10 *Trenton Evening Times* (New Jersey), May 7, 1908, 1:5.

11 *New Castle News* (Pennsylvania), August 15, 1906, 1:6.

12 *Oakland Tribune* (California), January 13, 1907, 18:4.

13 *Trenton Evening Times* (New Jersey), May 7, 1908, 1:5.

14 "Bina Verrault," Findagrave.com.

15 McCracken, *A History of Tonopah, Nevada*.

16 Harold T. Smith, "Prohibition in Nevada," *Nevada Historical Society Quarterly*, Vol. XIX, No. 4, Winter, 1976, 239.

17 McCracken, *A History of Tonopah, Nevada*.

18 *Nevada, Death Certificates, 1911–1965*, Ancestry.com.

19 *Nevada State Journal*, December 28, 1951, 2:1 and December 29, 1951, 12:2.

20 Ibid., January 20, 1952, 20:1; *Nevada, Death Certificates, 1911–1965*.

21 *Nevada, Death Certificates, 1911–1965*.

22 McCracken, *A History of Tonopah, Nevada*.

CHAPTER 9: GOOD TIME GIRLS OF GOLDFIELD

1 Jan MacKell, *Cripple Creek District: Last of Colorado's Gold Booms* (Charleston, SC: Arcadia Publishing, 2003), 8–10, 28, 144; Jan MacKell Collins, *Wild Women of Prescott, Arizona* (Charleston, SC: The History Press, 2015), 95.

2 *Goldfield News*, September 15, 1905, 2:4.

3 Ibid., September 22, 1905, 4:4; *Tonopah Bonanza*, October 7, 1905, 8:2.

4 *Tonopah Bonanza*, October 20, 1905, 12:6 and December 29, 1905, 6:2.

5 Ibid., December 29, 1905, 6:6.

6 Laura Elizabeth Scharding, "Fat Ann, Baths and Brothels: Sexual Economies of the Wild West," UCD School of Archaeology, https://www.academia.edu/16996775/Fat_Ann_baths_and_brothels_sexual_economies_of_the_Wild_West, accessed March 2, 2020.

7 "Goldfield Cemetery Stories," Goldfield Historical Society, http://www.goldfield historicalsociety.com/featured-storyGoldfieldCemeteryStories.html, accessed March 2, 2020.

8 *Goldfield News*, July 15, 1916, 6:4.

9 Ibid., January 20, 1917, 3:2.

10 Ibid., January 20, 1917, 8:1.

11 Ibid., June 29, 1918, 2:2.

12 "Goldfield Historic District," National Register of History Places, https://npgallery .nps.gov/GetAsset/3a85979f-2f68-47b4-a13c-e32bce1c1c6f, accessed March 2, 2020.

CHAPTER 10: THE TRAGIC TALE OF MONA BELL

1 *Tonopah Daily Bonanza*, January 9, 1908, 2:4.

2 "Isabelle Sadie 'Mona Bell' Peterman Heskett," Findagrave.com.

3 "Grammas, Grandpas, Inlaws and Outlaws" family tree, Ancestry.com.

4 *Tonopah Daily Bonanza*, January 9, 1908, 2:4.

5 Ibid., November 12, 1907, 2:2.

6 Ibid., November 23, 1907, 2:1; Robin Flinchum, *Red Light Women of Death Valley* (Charleston, SC: The History Press, 2015), 84–88.

7 *Tonopah Daily Bonanza*, March 26, 1908, 2:3.

8 *Tonopah Daily Bonanza*, January 4, 1908, 1:3.

9 Ibid., March 27, 1908, 2:3.

10 Flinchum, *Red Light Women of Death Valley*, 89.

11 *Tonopah Daily Bonanza*, February 22, 1910, 2:1 and February 24, 1910, 2:1.

12 Ibid., February 23, 1910, 2:1

13 Ibid., February 22, 1910, 2:1 and February 24, 1910, 2:1.

14 Ibid., February 25, 1910, 2:1.

15 Flinchum, *Red Light Women of Death Valley*, 90.

16 *Tonopah Daily Bonanza*, March 24, 1908, 2:4.

17 *Elko Daily Independent* April 4, 1908, 3:1; *Tonopah Daily Bonanza*, October 14, 1909, 2;3.

18 *Tonopah Daily Bonanza*, February 26, 1910, 2:1.

19 Ibid., February 22, 1910, 2:1.

20 "Weird Tales," Internet Movie Database, https://www.imdb.com/title/ tt2137465/?ref_=fn_al_tt_5, accessed May 7, 2020.

CHAPTER 11: VIVA LAS VEGAS

1 Marie Katherine Rowley, "'So Much for Fond Five-Dollar Memories': Prostitution in Las Vegas, 1905-1955," University of Las Vegas Theses, Dissertations, Professional Papers, and Capstones, 2012, 1.

2 *Los Angeles Times*, May 16, 1905, 13.

3 *Las Vegas Age*, July 14, 1906, 1:2.

4 Ibid., June 23, 1906, 1:2.

5 Jan MacKell Collins, *Wild Women of Prescott, Arizona* (Charleston, SC: The History Press, 2015), 111.

6 *Las Vegas Age*, June 23, 1906, 1 and May 30, 1941, 1.

7 Rowley, "'So Much for Fond Five-Dollar Memories,'" 17.

8 Lynn Comella, "My Nevada 5: Prostitution in Las Vegas," University of Nevada, Las Vegas, September 11, 2014, https://www.unlv.edu/news/article/my-nevada-5 -prostitution-las-vegas, accessed May 3, 2020.

9 *Las Vegas Review-Journal*, January 17, 1946, 1:5 and January 17, 1947, 8:3.

10 *Goldfield News and Weekly Tribune*, July 18, 1914, 2:6.

11 Ibid., December 5, 1914, 6:4.

12 Walker R. Young, "Complaint as to conditions in Las Vegas, Nevada-Boulder Dam-Colorado River," August 25, 1930, Records of the Bureau of Reclamation, "General Administrative and Project Files, 1930-1945, Colorado River Project," National Archives and Records Administration, Rocky Mountain Region, Denver, Colorado, 12.

13 *Las Vegas Age*, March 21, 1929, 3:6.

14 Ibid, April 11, 1929, 3:6.

15 Ibid., May 28, 1929, 1:8.

16 Ibid., August 22, 1929, 1:8 and 2:2.

17 *New York Times*, July, 29, 1929, 1:1.

18 Young, "Complaint as to conditions in Las Vegas, Nevada-Boulder Dam-Colorado River."

19 *Las Vegas Age*, December 30, 1930, 2:1.

20 *Las Vegas Review-Journal*, April 27, 1934, 1:1.

21 Ibid., October 11, 1941, 3.

CHAPTER 12: THE GOOD TIME GIRLS OF UTAH

1 Harold B. Lee Library, Brigham Young University, *Encyclopedia of Mormonism* (New York: MacMillan Publishing Company, 1992), 1500–1501.

2 Jan MacKell, *Red Light Women of the Rocky Mountains* (Albuquerque: University of New Mexico Press, 2011), 295–296.

3 Thomas G. Alexander and Leonard J. Arrington, "Camp in the Sagebrush: Camp Floyd, Utah, 1858-1861," *Utah Historical Quarterly*, Winter 1966, Vol. 34 No. 1, 9–10.

4 Jeffrey Nichols, *Prostitution, Polygamy and Power: Salt Lake City, 1847–1918* (Urbana and Chicago: University of Illinois Press, 2002), 26.

5 Orson F. Whitney, *History of Utah, Volume 2*, 1870, Chapter XVII, Ancestry.com.

6 George A. Thompson, *Treasure Mountain Home: Park City Revisited* (Salt Lake City, UT: Dream Garden Press, 1993), 88.

7 Alta history display, Alta City Hall, Utah, visit by author, 2006.

8 Lambert Florin, *Colorado-Utah Ghost Towns* (Seattle: Superior Publishing Company, 1971), 98.

9 Archives West, "Women in Utah politics oral history project," http://archiveswest .orbiscascade.org/ark:/80444/xv37860, accessed November 12, 2019; Ronald G. Watt, *A History of Carbon County* (Salt Lake City: Utah State Historical Society, Carbon County Commission, 1997), 372.

10 Washington, D.C. *Evening Star*, May 31, 1937, 3:2.

CHAPTER 13: SIN IN SALT LAKE CITY

1 Jessie L. Embry and Lois Kelley, "Polygamous and Monogamous Mormon Women, A Comparison," in Patricia Lyn Scott and Linda Thatcher (eds.), *Women in Utah History Paradigm or Paradox?* (Logan: Utah State University Press, 2005), 7.

2 Jeffrey Nichols, *Prostitution, Polygamy and Power: Salt Lake City, 1847–1918* (Urbana and Chicago: University of Illinois Press, 2002), 25–27.

3 Ibid., 26.

4 Salt Lake City *Mountaineer*, February 4, 1860, 1:3.

5 Nichols, *Prostitution, Polygamy and Power*, 28.

6 Ibid.

7 Hal Schindler, "The Oldest Profession's Sordid Past in Utah," http://www.police prostitutionandpolitics.net/pdfs_all/Historical%20Prostitution%20Articles%20Info/ Mormons%20run%20brothels%20Utah%20History%20to%20Go.pdf, accessed May 5, 2020.

8 Nichols, *Prostitution, Polygamy and Power*, 54–58, 60–61, 68, 89.

9 Jan MacKell, *Red Light Women of the Rocky Mountains* (Albuquerque: University of New Mexico Press, 2011), 298.

10 Nichols, *Prostitution, Polygamy and Power*, 1.

11 John S. McCormick, "Red Lights in Zion: Salt Lake City's Stockade, 1908–11," *Utah Historical Quarterly*, Vol. 50, No. 2, Spring 1982, 173.

12 *Salt Lake Herald*, June 2, 1886, 4:1.

13 Schindler, "The Oldest Profession's Sordid Past in Utah."

14 Nichols, *Prostitution, Polygamy and Power*, 35.

15 Thomas G. Alexander and James B. Allen, "Mormons and Gentiles: A History of Salt Lake City," Vol. V, *The Western Urban History Series* (Boulder, CO: Pruett Publishing Company, 1984), 118, 148.

16 Nichols, *Prostitution, Polygamy and Power*, 57–58.

17 McCormick, "Red Lights in Zion," 171–172.

18 Nichols, *Prostitution, Polygamy and Power*, 59–62, 83.

19 McCormick, "Red Lights in Zion," 169, 171–174.

20 Ibid, 171.

21 Ibid, 171.

22 Nichols, *Prostitution, Polygamy and Power*, 66, 68.

CHAPTER 14: ADA CARROLL, INAUGURAL STRUMPET OF SALT LAKE CITY

1 *Chicago Weekly Times*, April 19, 1855, 1:5.

2 Ronald W. Walker, "'Proud as a Peacock and Ignorant as a Jackass': William W. Drummond's Unusual Career with the Mormons," *Journal of Mormon History* , Vol. 42, No. 3, July 2016, 3.

3 Dennis Lythgoe, "Utah's rogue judge: Infamous official coming back to life in family history," *Deseret News*, February 19, 1999, https://www.deseret.com/1999/2/19/19429756/utah-s-rogue-judge-br-infamous-official-coming-back-to-life-in-family-history, accessed May 15, 2020.

4 "Judge Drummond Used Up," *Latter-day Saints' Millennial Star*, June 27, 1857, 402.

5 Walker, "'Proud as a Peacock and Ignorant as a Jackass,'" 4, 6–7.

6 Ibid, 4, 6–8, 11–12.

7 Hal Schindler, "The Oldest Profession's Sordid Past in Utah," History to Go, http://www.policeprostitutionandpolitics.net/pdfs_all/Historical%20Prostitution%20Articles%20Info/Mormons%20run%20brothels%20Utah%20History%20to%20Go.pdf, accessed May 5, 2020.

8 "Judge Drummond Used Up."

9 Walker, "'Proud as a Peacock and Ignorant as a Jackass,'" 13.

10 "Judge Drummond Used Up."

11 Walker, "'Proud as a Peacock and Ignorant as a Jackass,'" 14.

12 "Judge Drummond Used Up."

13 James B. Allen and Glen M. Leonard, *The Story of the Latter-day Saints* (Salt Lake City, UT: Deseret Book Co., 1976), 298–299.

14 Lythgoe, "Utah's rogue judge."

15 Mount, John, "The Lost and Forgotten History of Johnstone's Army, the Utah War, and Camp Floyd 1857–1861," http://www.researchonline.net/pmwiki.php?n=Miscellaneous.Article48, accessed May 20, 2020.

16 Ibid.

17 *Latter-Day Saints Millennial Star*, August 15, 1857, 524.

18 *Turner County Herald* (South Dakota), December 20, 1888, 2:2.

CHAPTER 15: KATE FLINT, MAIDEN MADAM OF UTAH

1 National Park Service, "The Pony Express Stations in Utah in Historical Perspective," https://www.nps.gov/parkhistory/online_books/blm/ut/2/sec2.htm, accessed November 20, 2019.

2 Mark Devoto, "Ogden: The Underwriters of Salvation," January 1, 2016, http://mdevotomusic.org/?p=322, accessed May 7, 2020.

3 Jeffrey Nichols, *Prostitution, Polygamy and Power: Salt Lake City, 1847–1918* (Urbana and Chicago, University of Illinois Press, 2002), 28–30, 97, 213.

4 Hal Schindler, "The Oldest Profession's Sordid Past in Utah," History To Go, http://www.policeprostitutionandpolitics.net/pdfs_all/Historical%20Prostitution%20 Articles%20Info/Mormons%20run%20brothels%20Utah%20History%20to%20Go .pdf accessed November 25, 2006

5 *Salt Lake Herald*, March 16, 1880, 3:4.

6 *Ibid,* March 25, 1880, 3:5

7 Nichols, *Prostitution, Polygamy and Power*, 52, 53; *Salt Lake Herald*, April 15, 1880, 3:2.

8 "D. Frank Connelly," Findagrave.com; *Salt Lake Herald*, April 17, 1880, 3:4.

9 *Salt Lake Herald*, July 20, 1880, 3:7.

10 Ibid., January 30, 1881, 3:1.

11 Nichols, *Prostitution, Polygamy and Power*, 42–43 n.154, 52; *Salt Lake Herald*, July 21, 1882, 8:5 and July 22, 1882, 8:6.

12 *Salt Lake Herald*, October 20, 1882, 8:2.

13 *Ogden Herald*, October 28, 1882, 3:1; *Park Record*, November 11, 1882, 12:3.

14 *Salt Lake Herald*, November 18, 1882, 8:6.

15 *Ibid,* August 2, 1883, 8:3.

16 "D. Frank Connelly."

17 *Salt Lake Herald*, July 11, 1884, 8:1 and July 13, 1884, 12:5; "D. Frank Connelly"; *Utah, Wills and Probate Records, 1800–1985,* Ancestry.com.

18 *Salt Lake Herald*, January 25, 1887, 8:5.

19 Ibid, September 14, 1884, 12:6, October 7, 1884, 7:5, and October 25, 1884, 8:6.

20 Ibid., February 1, 1885, 8:1 and February 28, 1885, 8:3; Schindler, "The Oldest Profession's Sordid Past in Utah"; Nichols, *Prostitution, Polygamy and Power*, 65.

21 *Salt Lake Herald*, January 30, 1886, 8:5.

22 Ibid., June 9, 1886, 8:3.

23 Ibid., June 13, 1886, 8:4.

24 Ibid., June 19, 1886, 8:1 and June 23, 1886, 8:1.

25 Ibid., June 25, 1886, 8:5.

26 Ibid., October 5, 1886, 8:4.

27 Ibid., October 10, 1886, 1:2.

28 Ibid., October 13, 1886, 8:5.

29 Ibid, February 5, 1888, 5:4; *Deseret News*, September 13, 1890, 17; *US City Directories, 1822–1995*, Ancestry.com.

30 *Salt Lake Herald*, January 9, 1896, 8:3.

31 *Salt Lake Tribune*, October 16, 1898, 8:3.

CHAPTER 16: "HELL 'N BLAZES" AT HELEN BLAZES'S

1 "You're darn tootin'!," Grammarphobia, December 2, 2019, https://www.grammar
phobia.com/blog/2019/12/darn-tootin.html, accessed May 11, 2020; Charles McCoy
Snyder, *Comic History of Greece: From the Earliest Times to the Death of Alexander the
Great* (Philadelphia: J. B. Lippincott Company, 1898), 92.

2 *Olathe Gazette* (Kansas), November 30, 1882, 3:3.

3 "Salty Adventures into Cartooning History," https://gocomics.typepad.com/
rcharvey/2013/09/salty-adventures-into-cartooning-history.html, accessed May 20,
2020.

4 Jeffrey Nichols, *Prostitution, Polygamy and Power: Salt Lake City, 1847–1918*
(Urbana and Chicago: University of Illinois Press, 2002), 60–61, 68, 70, 93.

5 *Salt Lake Herald*, September 30, 1893, 8:5.

6 Nichols, *Prostitution, Polygamy and Power*, 113; *Salt Lake Herald*, February 1,
1895, 8:3.

7 *Salt Lake Herald*, February 10, 1895, 6:6; Nichols, *Prostitution, Polygamy and
Power*, 66.

8 *Salt Lake Herald*, February 2, 1895, 8:1 and February 19, 1895, 8:5.

9 Ibid, October 31, 1895, 8:6, and November 1, 1895, 8:6.

10 *Arizona Republican*, November 19, 1895, 1:5.

11 *Salt Lake Herald*, February 7, 1896, 1:1, March 27, 1896, 8:1, and September 3,
1896, 8:1.

12 *Salt Lake Herald*, April 23, 1899, 8:2 and September 26, 1899, 3:4.

13 Ibid., March 28, 1900, 8:3.

14 *Salt Lake Tribune*, May 31, 1900, 8:2.

15 *Salt Lake Herald.*, July 24, 1900, 3:4.

16 *Ibid*, December 15, 1902, 8:1.

17 *Ibid*, December 20, 1902, 3:3.

18 Ibid., December 22, 1902, 4:3.

19 *Salt Lake Herald*, February 7, 1908, 10, June 9, 1909, 12:12.

20 *Salt Lake Tribune*, September 21, 1913, 24:2.

21 Ibid., March 15, 1914, 21:2.

22 Ibid., February 19, 1932, 2:1 and June 25, 1932, 17:1.

CHAPTER 17: GOOD TIME GIRLS OF OGDEN

1 Hal Schindler, "The Oldest Profession's Sordid Past in Utah," History To Go,
http://www.policeprostitutionandpolitics.net/pdfs_all/Historical%20Prostitution%20
Articles%20Info/Mormons%20run%20brothels%20Utah%20History%20to%20Go
.pdf, accessed November 25, 2006.

2 Richard C. Roberts and Richard W. Sadler, *A History of Weber County* (Salt Lake
City: Utah State Historical Society, 1997), 138, 179, 182–183.

3 Becky Wright, "Historian says 25th Street's notorious reputation more about religion than prostitutes," *Ogden Standard Examiner*, Oct 13, 2013, https://www .standard.net/lifestyle/historian-says-25th-streets-notorious-reputation-more-about -religion-than-prostitutes/article_acab4390-7053-5915-9bae-97ed1684facd.html, accessed May 31, 2020.

4 Jan MacKell, *Brothels, Bordellos & Bad Girls: Prostitution in Colorado 1860–1930* (Albuquerque: University of New Mexico Press, 2003), 214.

5 Roberts and Sadler, *A History of Weber County*, 353.

6 Allen Kent Powell, "Prohibition," Utah History Encyclopedia, https://www.uen .org/utah_history_encyclopedia/p/PROHIBITION.shtml#:~:text=Utah%20did%20 not%20enact%20prohibition,the%20manufacture%20and%20consumption%20of, accessed May 25, 2020.

7 D. Launius, "World War II in Utah," Utah History Encyclopedia, https://www.uen .org/utah_history_encyclopedia/w/WWII.shtml, accessed June 11, 2020.

8 Wright, "Historian says 25th Street's notorious reputation more about religion than prostitutes." In 2020, Weber State University Special Collections in Utah discovered a real treasure trove: a 1951 interview with Rose Duccinni consisting of several pages. The trouble was, the entire interview was written in archaic shorthand and scholars were at a loss as to how to transcribe the notes. As of this writing, the interview remains a mystery but is being transcribed by volunteers. "Brothel owner's interview eludes historians," *Business Insider*, https://www.businessinsider.com/notorious-utah-brothel -owners-interview-eludes-historians-2020-2, accessed February 20, 2020; "University Piecing Together Old Shorthand Interview," *Arkansas Democrat Gazette*, February 29, 2020, https://www.arkansasonline.com/news/2020/feb/29/university-piecing-together -old-shorthand-intervie/, accessed June 7, 2020.

9 Wright, "Historian says 25th Street's notorious reputation more about religion than prostitutes."

10 Roberts and Sadler, *A History of Weber County*, 354–355.

11 Ogden City Register of Historic Resources, Ogden City Landmarks Commission, historic walking tour plaque, placed 1998.

12 Roberts and Sadler, *A History of Weber County*, 355–356.

13 Wright, "Historian says 25th Street's notorious reputation more about religion than prostitutes."

14 Roberts and Sadler, *A History of Weber County*, 355-356.

15 Jan MacKell, *Red Light Women of the Rocky Mountains* (Albuquerque: University of New Mexico Press, 2009), 322.

CHAPTER 18: DORA TOPHAM, THE GENTEEL MADAM

1 *Salt Lake Herald,* November 12, 1889, 5:4.

2 Ibid., January 4, 1894, 2:2.

3 Ibid., April 25, 1897, 1:7.

4 Ibid., May 18, 1897, 3:4.

5 Ibid., September 26, 1896, 1:4.

6 Ibid, March 11, 1902, 7:6.

7 *Ogden Standard Examiner*, March 11, 1902, 6:2.

8 Ogden City Register of Historic Resources, Ogden City Landmarks Commission, historic walking tour plaque, placed 1998.

9 *Utah, Death and Military Death Certificates, 1904-1961*, Ancestry.com.

10 "Walter Earl Topham" and "Thomas Topham," Findagrave.com.

CHAPTER 19: DORA AND THE SALT LAKE CITY STOCKADE

1 Jeffrey Nichols, *Prostitution, Polygamy and Power: Salt Lake City, 1847–1918* (Urbana and Chicago: University of Illinois Press, 2002), 139.

2 Jami Balls, "History of the Stockade and Salt Lake's Red Light District," Utah History to Go, https://historytogo.utah.gov/red-light-district/, accessed November 2006; John S. McCormick "Red Lights in Zion: Salt Lake City's Stockade, 1908–11," *Utah Historical Quarterly*, Vol 50, No. 2, Spring 1982, 176.

3 Nichols, *Prostitution, Polygamy and Power*, 141.

4 *Salt Lake Herald*, June 29, 1908, 1:7; *Salt Lake Tribune*, July 11, 1908, 1:6.

5 *Deseret Evening News*, December 3, 1908, 2:4.

6 Nichols, *Prostitution, Polygamy and Power*, 147–149.

7 *Salt Lake Herald*, December 10, 1908, 12:12.

8 Hal Schindler, "The Oldest Profession's Sordid Past in Utah, http://www.police prostitutionandpolitics.net/pdfs_all/Historical%20Prostitution%Articles%20Info/ Mormons%20run%brothels%20Utah%20History%20to%20Go.pdf, accessed November 2006.

9 *Deseret Evening News*, January 12, 1909, 2:4 and January 13, 1909, 1:3; *Salt Lake Tribune*, January 14, 1909, 12:5 and 14:1, *Salt Lake Herald*, January 18, 1909, 3:5.

10 *Ogden Standard*, February 20, 1909, 8:4; *Deseret Evening News*, February 26, 1909, 2:1.

11 *Salt Lake Tribune*, April 20, 1909, 14:1; *Deseret Evening News*, April 20, 1909, 2:3.

12 *Ogden Standard*, June 30, 1909, 5:5.

13 *Salt Lake Herald*, July 1, 1909, 11:2.

14 *Deseret Evening News*, March 19, 1910, 1:7.

15 Ibid.; Nichols, *Prostitution, Polygamy and Power*, 154.

16 Nichols, *Prostitution, Polygamy and Power*, 149; *Salt Lake Herald-Republican*, March 26, 1910, Sec. 2, 3:3.

17 *Salt Lake Herald-Republican*, March 26, 1910, 10:1.

18 *Deseret Evening News*, May 25, 1910, 1:1.

19 *Salt Lake Tribune*, September 14, 1911, 14:2; *Ogden Evening Standard*, September 19, 1911, 1:5 and September 28, 1911, 3:1.

20 *Ogden Evening Standard*, October 20, 1911, 6:1, November 1, 1911, 5:3, and February 8, 1912, 6:4; *Goodwin's Weekly*, October 28, 1911, 1:2.

21 *Salt Lake Tribune*, September 28, 1911, 3:1.

22 *Ogden Standard Examiner*, January 8, 1925, 12:1.

23 Ibid, December 18, 1924, 6:4 and January 8, 1925, 12:1.

CHAPTER 20: PARK CITY'S RACHEL URBAN

1 *Ogden Standard Examiner*, July 1, 1927, 3:3.

2 Cheryl Livingston, "Mother Rachel Urban, Park City's Leading Madam," *Worth Their Salt: Notable But Often Unnoted Women of Utah*, Whitley, Colleen, ed., (Logan: Utah State University Press, 1996), 126-127; Raye Carleson Ringholz, *Diggings & Doings in Park City*, (Park City, UT: Self Published, 5th Edition, 1983), 65.

3 Livingston, "Mother Rachel Urban," 128; Ringholz, *Diggings & Doings in Park City*, 65.

4 *Salt Lake Herald*, June 5, 1908, 3:2.

5 Utah State Historical Society, Historic Preservation Research Office, Information Form for 555 Deer Valley Road in Park City, https://npgallery.nps.gov/NRHP/GetAsset/ecfb05c5-3ed6-4435-a0ad-8458db9f6588/, accessed June 7, 2020.

6 Livingston, "Mother Rachel Urban," 128.

7 *Park Record*, January 3, 1914, 8:3

8 Ibid., October 24, 1914, https://newspapers.lib.utah.edu/details?id=7949203&q=%22Rachel+Urban%22, accessed June 22, 2020.

9 Ibid., June 22, 1917, 7:4

10 Courtney Titus, "Dead in her bed," Way We Were column, *Park Record*, October 22, 2014, https://newspapers.lib.utah.edu/details?id=22621993&page=2&q=%22Rachel+Urban%22, accessed June 7, 2020.

11 Ibid.

12 "George Charles Urban," Findagrave.com.

13 *San Pedro News Pilot*, March 24, 1927, 1:5.

14 *Park Record*, March 25, 1927, 2:1

15 Ibid., September 9, 1998, 9.

16 Anna Bloom, "Kimball finds more than 1,000 burials unrecorded," *Park Record*, November 15; 2005, https://www.parkrecord.com/news/kimball-finds-more-than-1000-burials-unrecorded/, accessed June 25, 2020.

CHAPTER 21: NO NOSE MAGGIE

1 Jody Tesch Sorenson, *Queen of the Desert* (Spokane, WA: Chickadee Publishing, 2007) 31, 33, 37.

2 Ibid., 49–50.

3 Ibid., 52–53.

4 Ibid., 60–63, 71.

5 Frank Beckwith, "Gone But Not Forgotten," *Salt Lake Tribune*, March 5, 1950, 66; Sorenson, *Queen of the Desert*, 71.

6 Sorenson, *Queen of the Desert*, 65.

7 Ibid, 72, 76–80.

8 Beckwith, "Gone But Not Forgotten."

9 Sorenson, *Queen of the Desert*, 81–82.

10 Ibid., 82–83.

11 "Mary Ann Devitt Laird," findagrave.com.

12 Expedition Utah, https://www.expeditionutah.com/forum/index.php?threads/ghost-town-joy-juab-county-ut.5412/, accessed May 5, 2020.

SELECTED BIBLIOGRAPHY

------•••------

BOOKS

Agnew, Jeremy, *Brides of the Multitude: Prostitution in the Old West* (Lake City, CO: Western Reflections Publishing Co., 2008).

Albert, Alexa, *Brothel: Mustang Ranch and Its Women* (New York and Canada: Random House, 2001).

Alexander, Thomas G., and Allen, James B., "Mormons and Gentiles: A History of Salt Lake City," Volume V, *The Western Urban History Series* (Boulder, Colorado: Pruett Publishing Company, 1984).

Allen, James B., and Leonard, Glen M., *The Story of the Latter-day Saints* (Salt Lake City, UT: Deseret Book Co., 1976).

Best, Hillyer, *Julia Bulette and Other Red Light Ladies: An Altogether Stimulating Treatise on the Madams of the Far West* (Sparks, NV: Western Printing & Publishing Co., 1959).

Brents, Barbara G., Jackson, Crystal A., and Hausback, Kathryn, *The State of Sex: Tourism, Sex, and Sin in the New American Heartland* (New York: Routledge, 2010).

Brown, Dee, *The Gentle Tamers: Women of the Old Wild West* (Lincoln, NE, and London: University of Nebraska Press, 1958).

Brown, Mrs. Hugh, *Lady in Boomtown: Miners and Manners on the Nevada Frontier* (Reno and Las Vegas: University of Nevada Press, 1968).

Brown, Robert L., *Colorado Ghost Towns—Past and Present* (Caldwell, ID: The Caxton Printers, Ltd., 1981).

Center of Military History, *United States Army in the World War 1917–1919: American Occupation of Germany, Volume II* (Washington D.C., United States Army, 1991).

Cerveri, Doris, *With Curry's Compliments: The Story of Abraham Curry* (Elko, NV: Nostalgia Press, 1990).

Collins, Jan MacKell, *Good Time Girls of California: A Red-Light History of the Golden State* (Guilford, CT: Globe Pequot, 2021).

———. *Good Time Girls of Colorado: A Red-Light History of the Centennial State* (Guilford, CT: Globe Pequot Press, 2019).

———. *Good Time Girls of the Rocky Mountains: A Red-Light History of Montana, Idaho and Wyoming* (Guilford, CT: Globe Pequot Publishing, 2020).

———. *Wild Women of Prescott, Arizona* (Charleston, SC: The History Press, 2015).

DeLong, Charles E., *Life and Confession of John Millian: (properly, Jean Marie A. Villain) Convicted as the Murderer of Julia Bulett, as Given by Him to His Attorney* (Virginia City, NV: Lammon, Gregory & Palmer, 1868).

Flinchum, Robin, *Red Light Women of Death Valley* (Charleston, SC: The History Press, 2015).

Florin, Lambert, *Colorado-Utah Ghost Towns* (Seattle: Superior Publishing Company, 1971).

———. *Ghost Towns of the West* (New York: Superior Publishing/Promontory Press, 1971).

Goldman, Marion S., *Gold Diggers & Silver Miners: Prostitution and Social Life on the Comstock Lode* (Ann Arbor: University of Michigan Press, 1981).

Harold B. Lee Library, Brigham Young University, *Encyclopedia of Mormonism* (New York: MacMillan Publishing Company, 1992).

Hulbert, Archer Butler, *Forty-Niners* (Boston: Little, Brown and Company, 1931).

Hulse, James W., *The Silver State: Nevada's Heritage Reinterpreted*, 3rd edition (Reno: University of Nevada Press, 2004).

MacKell, Jan, *Brothels, Bordellos & Bad Girls: Prostitution in Colorado 1860-1930* (Albuquerque: University of New Mexico Press, 2003).

———. *Cripple Creek District: Last of Colorado's Gold Booms* (Charleston, SC: Arcadia Publishing, 2003).

———. *Red Light Women of the Rocky Mountains* (Albuquerque: University of New Mexico Press, 2011).

Monahan, Sherry, *The Wicked West: Boozers, Cruisers, Gamblers and More* (Tucson, AZ: Rio Nuevo Publishers, 2005).

Moynahan, Jay, *The Prairie Pioneer Prostitutes' Own Cookbook* (Spokane, WA: Chickadee Publishing, 2000).

Nichols, Jeffrey, *Prostitution, Polygamy and Power: Salt Lake City, 1847–1918* (Urbana and Chicago: University of Illinois Press, 2002).

Oldham, Willa, *Carson City: Nevada's Capital City* (Carson City: Nevada State Museum, 1991).

Quinn, D. Michael, *Same-Sex Dynamics Among Nineteenth-Century Americans: A Mormon Example* (Champaign: University of Illinois Press, 2001).

Ringholz, Raye Carleson, *Diggings & Doings in Park City* (Park City, UT: self published, 5th edition, 1983).

Roberts, Richard C., and Sadler, Richard W., *A History of Weber County* (Salt Lake City: Utah State Historical Society, 1997).

Rutter, Michael, *Upstairs Girls: Prostitution in the American West* (Helena, MT: Farcountry Press, 2005).

Scott, Patricia Lyn, and Thatcher, Linda, eds., *Women in Utah History Paradigm or Paradox?* (Logan: Utah State University Press, 2005).

Seagraves, Anne, *Soiled Doves: Prostitution in the Old West* (Hayden, ID: Wesanne Publications, 1994).

Snyder, Charles McCoy, *Comic History of Greece: From the Earliest Times to the Death of Alexander the Great* (Philadelphia, PA: J. B. Lippincott Company, 1898).

Sorenson, Jody Tesch, *Queen of the Desert* (Spokane, WA: Chickadee Publishing, 2007).

Stevens, Joseph E., *Hoover Dam: An American Adventure* (Norman: University of Oklahoma Press, 1988).

Thompson, George A., *Treasure Mountain Home: Park City Revisited* (Salt Lake City, UT: Dream Garden Press, 1993).

Time-Life Books, *Gamblers of the Old West* (Alexandria VA: Time-Life Books, 1996).

Utah Gazetteer, 1892-1893 (Salt Lake City, UT: Stenhouse & Co., 1892).

Watt, Ronald G., *A History of Carbon County* (Salt Lake City: Utah State Historical Society, Carbon County Commission, 1997).

Whitley, Colleen, ed., *Worth Their Salt: Notable But Often Unnoted Women of Utah* (Logan: Utah State University Press, 1996).

Wedertz, Frank S., *Bodie 1859-1900* (Bishop, CA: Sierra Media Inc., 1969).

Williams III, George, *The Redlight Ladies of Virginia City Nevada* (Riverside, CA: Tree by the River Publishing, 1984).

———. *Rosa May: The Search for a Mining Camp Legend* (Riverside, CA: Tree by the River Publishing, 1982).

Wolle, Muriel Sibell, *The Bonanza Trail: Ghost Towns and Mining Camps of the West* (Chicago: Sage Books, a subsidiary of the Swallow Press for Indiana University Press, MCMLIII).

DOCUMENTS

Young, Walker R., "Complaint as to Conditions in Las Vegas, Nevada-Boulder Dam-Colorado River," August 25, 1930, Records of the Bureau of Reclamation, "General Administrative and Project Files, 1930-1945, Colorado River Project," National Archives and Records Administration, Rocky Mountain Region, Denver, Colorado.

INTERNET

"8 Famous Brothels That Have Closed Over the Years," October 2, 2018, RedLightVegas, https://redlightvegas.com/famous-closed-nevada-brothels/.

Abbott, Glen, "Baddest Town in the Old West—Pioche, Nevada,"
    December 20, 2011, The Travelingringo, http://travelingringo
    .com/2011/12/baddest-town-in-the-old-west-pioche-nevada/.

ANCESTRY.COM:
California, Death Index, 1905–1939
California, Prison and Correctional Records, 1851–1950
California, Voter Registrations, 1866–1898

CENSUS:
Seventh Census of the United States, 1850
Eighth Census of the United States, 1860
Ninth Census of the United States, 1870
Tenth Census of the United States, 1880
Twelfth Census of the United States, 1900
Thirteenth Census of the United States, 1910
Fourteenth Census of the United States, 1920
Fifteenth Census of the United States, 1930
Sixteenth Census of the United States, 1940
Colorado, County Marriage Records and State Index, 1862–2006
Colorado, Divorce Index, 1851–1985
Cuyahoga County, Ohio, Marriage Records and Indexes, 1810–1973
History of Utah, Volume 2
Montana, Birth Records, 1897–1988
Nebraska, Marriage Records, 1855–1908
Nevada, Death Certificates, 1911–1965
Nevada State Census, 1875
New York, State Census, 1905
Ohio, County Marriage Records, 1774–1993
Ohio, Wills and Probate Records, 1786–1998
Salt Lake County, Utah Civil and Criminal Case Files, 1852–1887
US City Directories, 1822–1995
US, School Catalogs, 1765–1935

US, Social Security Applications and Claims Index, 1936–2007
Utah, Cemetery Inventory, 1847–2000
Utah, Death and Military Death Certificates, 1904–1961
Utah Death Index, 1905–1951
Utah, Select County Marriages, 1887–1937
Utah, Select Marriages, 1887–1966
Utah, Wills and Probate Records, 1800–1985
Washington, Death Index, 1940–2017

Archives West, "Women in Utah Politics Oral History Project," http://
    archiveswest.orbiscascade.org/ark:/80444/xv37860, accessed
    November 12, 2019.
Balls, Jami, "History of the Stockade and Salt Lake's Red Light
    District," Utah History to Go, https://historytogo.utah.gov/red
    -light-district/.
Barber, Alicia, "Reno's Red Light District: The Colorful History of
    Brothels in Washoe County," KUNR, April 24, 2019, https://www
    .kunr.org/post/reno-s-red-light-district-colorful-history-brothels
    -washoe-county#stream/0.
"Big 4 Ranch and Brothel," https://big-4-ranch-brothel-and-vip-spa
    .business.site/.
"The Big Four," Ely, Nevada, http://www.bigfourranch.com/ABOUT/
    index.htm.
"Bobbie's Buckeye Bar," Raise the Stakes, http://raisethestakeseditions
    .com/bobbies-buckeye-bar/.
"Bronc Alley—Red Light District at the West End of High Street,
    Ely, Nevada," US Genweb, http://theusgenweb.org/nv/whitepine/
    Towns/Ely_walking_tour/westendhighst.htm.
"Brothel Owner's Interview Eludes Historians," *Business Insider*,
    https://www.businessinsider.com/notorious-utah-brothel-owners
    -interview-eludes-historians-2020-2.
Butz, Alison, "Park City's History," Historic Park City Utah, October
    13, 2010, https://historicparkcityutah.com/news/park-citys-history,
    accessed June 21, 2020.

"Corner of 13th & B Streets 1908, CRIB ROW," http://theusgenweb
.org/nv/whitepine/Towns/Ely_walking_tour/13thstcribrow.htm,
accessed June 7, 2020.

Comella, Lynn, "My Nevada 5: Prostitution in Las Vegas," University
of Nevada, Las Vegas, September 11, 2014, https://www.unlv.edu/
news/article/my-nevada-5-prostitution-las-vegas.

"The Crib," Airbnb, https://www.airbnb.ie/rooms/24593220?guests
=1&location=Goldfield%2C%20NV&source_impression_id=p3
_1587945663_0puyM4gu1KrjiwY8&adults=1.

Curmudgeon, "Big Doin's on Historic 25th Street," September 27,
2008, http://wcforum.blogspot.com/2008/09/big-doins-on-historic
-25th-street.html, accessed June 1, 2020.

"Desert Club," Wayback Machine, https://web.archive.org/web/2003
0210025936/http://www.nvbrothels.net:80/closed/desert.htm.

Devoto, Mark, "Ogden: The Underwriters of Salvation," January 1,
2016, http://mdevotomusic.org/?p=322, accessed May 7, 2020.

"Ely Nevada History and Photos," http://theusgenweb.org/nv/white
pine/Towns/ely.htm.

Findagrave.com

"Expedition Utah," https://www.expeditionutah.com/.

"Goldfield Cemetery Stories," Goldfield Historical Society, http://www
.goldfieldhistoricalsociety.com/featured-storyGoldfieldCemetery
Stories.html.

"Goldfield Historic District," National Register of History Places,
https://npgallery.nps.gov/GetAsset/3a85979f-2f68-47b4-a13c
-e32bce1c1c6f.

"Gold Hill History," Western Mining History, https://westernmining
history.com/towns/nevada/gold-hill1/.

"Goldfield, Nevada," Goldfield Fire Works, https://goldfieldfireworks
.com/index.php/esmeralda.

"Goldfield Nevada," walking tour booklet, Goldfield Historical
Society, 2013, http://goldfieldhistoricalsociety.com/Goldfield_2013
_Booklet_Web.pdf.

"Goldfield, Nevada," Western Mining History, https://westernmining history.com/towns/nevada/goldfield/.

Goldman, David, "You Can't Get Rid of It So You Might as Well Tax It: The Economic Impact of Nevada's Legalized Prostitution," Seton Hall University, Law School Student Scholarship, 2012, 7–8, https://scholarship.shu.edu/cgi/viewcontent.cgi?article=1009& context=student_scholarship.

Halleran, Kevin, "Wasatch Mountains," History To Go, https://history togo.utah.gov/wasatch-mountains/.

Hendrickson, Rachel, "The Virginia City Great Fire of 1875," Brigham Young University, Intermountain Histories, https://www .intermountainhistories.org/items/show/246.

Internet Movie Database, www.imdb.com.

Las Vegas Defense Group, https://www.houselaw.com/nv/defense/ laws/solicitation-of-prostitution/, accessed November 9, 2020.

Luce, Stewart, "Virgil Walter Earp in Goldfield," Goldfield Historical Society, http://www.goldfieldhistoricalsociety.com/featured-story VirgilWalterEarpGoldfield.html.

McCracken, Bob, "Brothels, Mines of Equal Value during Rhyolite boom," *Pahrump Valley Times*, October 24, 2014, https://pvtimes .com/news/brothels-mines-of-equal-value-during-rhyolite-boom/.

————, *A History of Tonopah, Nevada* (Tonopah, NV: Nye County Press, 1990), Nye County History, http://nyecountyhistory .com/tonopahbook2/tonopahhard.pdf.

"Micca House," National Register of Historic Places Inventory Nomination Form,https://npgallery.nps.gov/NRHP/GetAsset/ NRHP/75001112_text.

Mount, John, "The Lost and Forgotten History of Johnston's Army, the Utah War, and Camp Floyd 1857-1861," Utah Civil War Association, http://www.researchonline.net/pmwiki.php?n =Miscellaneous.Article48.

National Park Service, https://npgallery.nps.gov/.

Nevada Adventures, http://www.nevadadventures.com/ghost%20
    towns/whitepineco/elymurrycreek/elymurraycreek.html.
"Nevada Territory Census," Nevada State Library, Archives and Public
    Records, http://www.nsladigitalcollections.org/browse/censuses.
Nichols, Jeff. "A Grand Night Out," https://www.mappingslc.org/
    essay/item/40-grand-night-out, accessed May 7, 2020.
Norwood, Arlisha R., "Mary Baker Eddy," National Women's History
    Museum, https://www.womenshistory.org/education-resources/
    biographies/mary-eddy, accessed May 22, 2020.
Online Nevada Encyclopedia, http://www.onlinenevada.org/.
"Park City History Bits," KPCW, January 30, 2014, https://www
    .kpcw.org/post/park-city-history-bits-january-30-2014#stream/0,
    accessed May 15, 2020.
"The Pony Express Stations in Utah in Historical Perspective,"
    National Park Service, https://www.nps.gov/parkhistory/online
    _books/blm/ut/2/sec2.htm.
"Rosa May Oalaque," Bodie.com, https://www.bodie.com/history/
    cemetery/78-rosa-may-oalaque/.
"Salty Adventures into Cartooning History," https://gocomics.typepad
    .com/rcharvey/2013/09/salty-adventures-into-cartooning-history
    .html, accessed May 20, 2020.
Scharding, Laura Elizabeth, "Fat Ann, Baths and Brothels: Sexual
    Economies of the Wild West," UCD School of Archaeology, https://
    www.academia.edu/16996775/Fat_Ann_baths_and_brothels
    _sexual_economies_of_the_Wild_West.
Schindler, Hal, "The Oldest Profession's Sordid Past in Utah," http://
    www.policeprostitutionandpolitics.net/pdfs_all/Historical%20
    Prostitution%20Articles%20Info/Mormons%20run%20brothels
    %20Utah%20History%20to%20Go.pdf.
"'Speed Racer's' Driving Directions to Nevada's Legal Brothels,"
    http://www.sex-in-nevada.net/directions/ElkoCo.html.
Stringfellow, Kim, "Desert Gold: Part I," KCET, https://www.kcet.org/
    shows/artbound/desert-gold-part-i.

Swear Education, https://walnet.org/swear/SwearEducation.pdf.

Tonopah Nevada Cemetery Brochure, https://www.tonopahnevada
.com/CemeteryBrochureOnline.pdf.

"Tonopah Multiple Resource Area," National Register of Historic
Places nomination form, https://shpo.nv.gov/uploads/documents/
64000532_-_Tonopah_MRA.pdf.

"Tonopah Nevada history," https://www.tonopahnevada.com/history/.

US Department of the Interior, Bureau of Land Management, General
Land Office Records, https://glorecords.blm.gov.

"Utah Central Rail Road," UtahRails.net, https://utahrails.net/utah
rails/uc-rr-1869-1881.php.

Utah Department of Heritage & Arts, Classified Photographs, https://
collections.lib.utah.edu/.

UTAH HISTORY ENCYCLOPEDIA

Launius, D., "World War II in Utah," https://www.uen.org/utah
_history_encyclopedia/w/WWII.shtml, accessed June 11, 2020.

Powell, Allen Kent, "Prohibition," https://www.uen.org/utah_history
_encyclopedia/p/PROHIBITION.shtml#:~:text=Utah%20did%20
not%20enact%20prohibition,the%20manufacture%20and%20
consumption%20of, accessed May 25, 2020.

Utah State Historical Society, Historic Preservation Research Office,
Information Form for 555 Deer Valley Road in Park City, https://
npgallery.nps.gov/NRHP/GetAsset/ecfb05c5-3ed6-4435-a0ad
-8458db9f6588/, accessed June 7, 2020.

V&T Railway Commission, https://vtrailway.com/about/history/.

"Visit Ogden," https://www.visitogden.com/about-ogden/ogden
-history/, accessed May 20, 2020.

"Western Desert Ranges," https://www.summitpost.org/utah-western
-desert-ranges/190033#chapter_5.

Western States Marriage Index, Brigham Young University Idaho,
https://abish.byui.edu/specialCollections/westernStates/about
WesternStates.cfm.

"Winnemucca Brothels," Wayback Machine, https://web.archive.org/
web/20030207184813/http://www.nvbrothels.net:80/win.htm.

"You're darn tootin'!" Grammarphobia, December 2, 2019, https://
www.grammarphobia.com/blog/2019/12/darn-tootin.html,
accessed May 11, 2020.

MAPS

Sanborn Fire Insurance Map from Carson City, Carson City County,
Nevada. Sanborn Map Company, January, 1885. Library of
Congress Geography and Map Division, Washington, D.C. 20540-
4650 USA.

Sanborn Map Company, Sanborn Fire Insurance Map from Ely, White
Pine County, August 1907, Library of Congress Geography and
Map Division, Washington, D.C. 20540-4650 USA.

Sanborn Map Company, Sanborn Fire Insurance Map from Ely, White
Pine County, Nevada, April 1912, Library of Congress Geography
and Map Division, Washington, D.C. 20540-4650 USA.

Sanborn Fire Insurance Map from Goldfield, Esmerelda County,
Nevada. Sanborn Map Company, April, 1905. Library of Congress
Geography and Map Division, Washington, D.C. 20540-4650
USA.

Sanborn Fire Insurance Map from Goldfield, Esmerelda County,
Nevada. Sanborn Map Company, 1906. Library of Congress
Geography and Map Division, Washington, D.C. 20540-4650 USA.

Sanborn Fire Insurance Map from Goldfield, Esmerelda County,
Nevada. Sanborn Map Company, 1909. Library of Congress
Geography and Map Division, Washington, D.C. 20540-4650 USA.

Sanborn Fire Insurance Map from Las Vegas, Clark County, Nevada.
Sanborn Map Company, Feb, 1923. Library of Congress Geography
and Map Division, Washington, D.C. 20540-4650 USA.

Sanborn Fire Insurance Map from Ogden, Weber County, Utah.
Sanborn Map Company, 1890. Library of Congress Geography and
Map Division, Washington, D.C. 20540-4650 USA.

Sanborn Fire Insurance Map from Ogden, Weber County, Utah.
   Sanborn Map Company, 1906. Library of Congress Geography and
   Map Division, Washington, D.C. 20540-4650 USA.
Sanborn Fire Insurance Map from Salt Lake City, Salt Lake City
   County, Utah. Sanborn Map Company, 1911. Library of Congress
   Geography and Map Division, Washington, D.C. 20540-4650 USA.
Sanborn Fire Insurance Map from Tonopah, Nye County, Nevada.
   Sanborn Map Company, April, 1905. Library of Congress
   Geography and Map Division, Washington, D.C. 20540-4650 USA.
Sanborn Fire Insurance Map from Tonopah, Nye County, Nevada.
   Sanborn Map Company, July, 1909. Library of Congress Geography
   and Map Division, Washington, D.C. 20540-4650 USA.
Sanborn Fire Insurance Map from Tonopah, Nye County, Nevada.
   Sanborn Map Company, September, 1917. Library of Congress
   Geography and Map Division, Washington, D.C. 20540-4650 USA.

NEWSPAPERS

Arkansas:
Arkansas Democrat Gazette

Arizona:
Arizona Republican

California:
Daily Alta California
Los Angeles Herald
Los Angeles Times
Modesto News Herald
Oakland Tribune
Sacramento Daily Union
San Bernardino Sun
San Pedro News Pilot

Colorado:
Leadville *Carbonate Chronicle*

Idaho:
Elmore Bulletin

Illinois:
Chicago Daily Tribune
Chicago Tribune
Chicago Weekly Times

Kansas:
Olathe Mirror
Olathe Mirror-Gazette

Nevada:
Carson Daily Appeal
Carson City *Morning Appeal*
Carson City *Daily State Register*
Elko Daily Independent
Elko Independent
Eureka Sentinel
Gold Hill Daily News
Gold Hill Evening News
Goldfield News
Goldfield News and Weekly Tribune
Goodwin's Weekly
Las Vegas Age
Las Vegas Review-Journal
Las Vegas Sun
Nevada Appeal
Nevada State Journal
Pahrump Valley Times

Park Record
Pioche Weekly Record
Pioche Record
Reno Gazette Journal
Tonopah Bonanza
Tonopah Daily Bonanza
Virginia City *Daily Territorial Enterprise*
Virginia City *Evening Bulletin*
Virginia Evening Chronicle
Virginia City *Territorial Enterprise*

New Jersey:
Trenton Evening Times

New York:
New York Times
Syracuse Herald

Pennsylvania:
New Castle News

Ohio:
Lima News

South Dakota:
Turner City Herald

Utah:
Carbon County News
Daily Corinne Reporter
Deseret News
Deseret Evening News
Latter-day Saints' Millennial Star

Millard County ProgressMorgan County News
Ogden Evening Standard
Ogden Herald
Ogden Standard
Ogden Standard Examiner
Park Record
Salt Lake City *Mountaineer*
Salt Lake City Daily Tribune
Salt Lake Herald
Salt Lake Herald-Republican
Salt Lake Tribune
Truth: the Western Weekly
Vernal Express

Washington, D.C.:
Evening Star

PAPERS

Lyle J. Barnes, "Ogden's Notorious 'Two-Bit Street,' 1870–1954,"
Master thesis, Utah State University, Logan, Utah, 1969.
Alexandra L. Simmons-Rogers, "RED LIGHT LADIES: Settlement
Patterns and Material Culture on the Frontier," thesis submitted to
Oregon State University, October 28,1983.
Marie Katherine Rowley, "'So Much for Fond Five-Dollar Memories':
Prostitution in Las Vegas, 1905–1955," University of Las Vegas
Theses, Dissertations, Professional Papers, and Capstones, 2012.

PERIODICALS

Journal of Mormon History
Nevada Historical Society Quarterly
Pacific Historical Review
Utah Historical Quarterly

Youth and Mountains: Student Essays on Sustainable Mountain Development

PAMPHLETS

City of Ogden and National Register of Historic Places Walking Tour pamphlet, n.d.

INDEX

—●●—

ABOUT THE AUTHOR

Jan MacKell Collins has been a published author, speaker, and presenter since 2003. Her focus has always been on western history, with an emphasis on historical prostitution. Ms. Collins also has been featured on several radio programs in Arizona, California, and Colorado. She has appeared on television in Colorado and Arizona, as well as on an episode of TruTV's *Adam Ruins Everything*. Ms. Collins currently resides in Oregon, where she continues researching the history of prostitution.